WHAT DO I DO MONDAY?

BOOKS BY JOHN HOLT
How Children Learn
How Children Fail
The Underachieving School
What Do I Do Monday?

E. P. DUTTON & CO., INC.

John Holt

WHAT DO I DO MONDAY?

NEW YORK   1970

Published simultaneously in Canada by
Clarke, Irwin & Company Limited, Toronto and Vancouver

Library of Congress Catalog Card Number: 71-122782

"It came burning hot into my mind, whatever he said and however he flattered, when he got me into his house, he would sell me for a slave."

JOHN BUNYAN

*"So you're through with your learning
so go out and start earning."*

FROM A GRADUATION GIFT CARD

CONTENTS

8 | CONTENTS

WHAT DO I DO MONDAY?

1

WHAT DO I DO MONDAY?

This is a book for teachers, for parents, for children or friends of children, for anyone who cares about education. It is about learning and above all some of the ways in which, in school or out, we might help children learn better and perhaps learn better ourselves.

For years, like many people, I thought of learning as collecting facts or ideas. It was something like eating, or being given medicine, or getting an injection at the doctor's. But from my own experience, and that of children, and from books, I have come to see learning very differently, as a kind of growing, a moving and expanding of the person into the world around him.

In the first part of this book I will try to share my vision of learning. To many, these ideas will be very new, strange, puzzling, or even wrong.

The usual ways of ordering ideas in a book will not work very well here. These are what we might call logical orders, the way we arrange thoughts when we are classifying them or when we are trying to win an argument. We list ideas according to some scheme. Or we start with some premise, A, that we think the reader will agree with. Then we try to show that if A is true, B must be true; if B, then C, and so on until, like a lawyer, we have proved our case, won our argument with our readers. But I am not trying to win an argument. I don't feel that I am *in* an argument. I am seeing something in a new way and I want to help others see it, or at least look at it, in that way. For this, a step-by-step straight-line logical order will not help. This is not the way we look at a picture or a statue or a person or a landscape, and it is not the way we ask people to look at these things—when we really want them to see them, or see them anew. We look at the whole, and at the parts. We look at the parts in many different orders, trying to see the many ways in which they combine, or fit, or influence each other. We explore the picture or the landscape with our eyes. That is what I would like to ask you to do.

As I write, these ideas and quotes, these bits of the landscape of learning that I will ask you to look at and see with me, are written on many small pieces of paper which I have read many times, in many different orders, trying to find the best way to present them. There is no one best way. If I could, I would give you these papers and ask you to read them in whatever order you liked, shuffle them up, read them in another order, shuffle again, and so on. Because of the way books are put together, I can't do that. The most I can ask, and do ask, is that after you have read this first section of the book, you read it again, so that you will be able to see each part of it, each chapter, in the light of all the other chapters. Or you might skim through the chapters, reading some of one, some of another, or reading them first in one order, then another. The point is that all the parts of what I am trying to say are connected to and depend on all the other parts. There is no one that comes first. No one of them came first to me. They have grown in my mind, all together, each influencing the other, over the years. In this form I offer them.

2

THE MENTAL MODEL

We all know many things about the world. What form or shape does our knowledge take? We may be able to say some of what we know, though in many people there is a deep and dangerous confusion between what they say and think they believe and what they really believe. But all of us know much more than we can say, and many times we cannot really put it into words at all.

For example, if we have eaten them, we know what strawberries taste like. We have in us somewhere knowledge—a memory, many memories—of the taste of strawberries. Not just one berry either, but many, more or less ripe, or sweet, or tasty. But how can we really speak of the *taste* of a strawberry? When we bite into a berry, we are *ready* to taste a certain kind of taste; if we taste something very different, we are surprised. It is this—what we expect or what surprises us—that tells us best what we really know.

We know many other things that we cannot say. We know what a friend looks like, so well that we may say, seeing him after some time, that he looks older or no older; heavier or thinner; worried or at peace, or happy. But our answers are usually so general that we could not give a description from which someone who had never seen our friend could recognize him.

These are only a few very simple examples among many. In

Michael Polyani's excellent book *Personal Knowledge,* we can find more, particularly in the chapter about connoisseurship. The expert wine or tea taster can identify dozens or perhaps scores or hundreds of varieties, and can say whether a sample of a given variety is a good sample. The violinist can play a number of instruments and hear differences between them that most people, even those who like music, cannot hear. The expert mechanic, like some of the machinists who once served with me on a submarine, can often tell by listening to the sound of an engine whether it is running properly and, if not, what may be wrong with it.

There are examples for other senses. Some tennis players, I among them, always grip the racket so that the same part of the handle faces up. After a while this makes a very subtle change in the shape of the handle. This would be a hard difference to see or measure. But the player knows instantly whether he has his usual grip or whether he must give the racket a 180-degree turn to get it right. Certain warm-up or sweat shirts are made symmetrically; when they are new there is no difference between front and back. The first time I put one on it feels the same forward or backward. But after wearing one a time or two, I soon put enough of my own shape into the shirt so that I can tell right away whether I have it on "backwards"—it *feels* wrong.

We don't smell as well as dogs or many other creatures do, but we can still remember certain smells for a long time, or recall them after a long time. These smells may be very strongly connected with memories of other things. The smell of a certain kind of soap, or polish, or dust, or cooking, or perfume, or any combination of these can make us feel very powerfully the sense of a person or a place we once knew, or an event. The smell may even make us feel again much of what we felt many years before.

From the examples given one might assume that we still have our knowledge in the shape of a list, but that this list, instead of being of words or statements, is largely made up of other kinds of memories—pictures, sounds, smells, the feel of things. This is only a very small part of the truth. For these memories or impressions are linked together. They have a structure. Thus the sound of a certain song always brings back to me a Libertyphone record player covered in brown leather, my grandmother's house, even a certain room and the view from the window of that room, plus a host of other connected memories.

There is another kind of game I can play, and often do play when I am restless but want to sleep. I think of a place I know, and in my mind I walk about in that place, seeing what I could see if I were actually there. Having fond memories of the plaza in Santa Fe, I very often, in my imagination, stand there, turn in a complete circle, and as I turn see the trees in the middle of the plaza and the various buildings around it. I can take a mental walk through many other parts of Santa Fe, or my home town of Boston, or many other cities I know, or through many houses in which I have visited or lived. I can walk, as it were, from my room in the Faculty Club at Berkeley, where I lived for three months, down the stairs, out onto the campus, and from there down the hill to Telegraph Avenue, or other parts of the city. Or I can ride up the main ski lift at the Santa Fe Ski Basin, or in general go anywhere in my mind that I have been in real life. Many people have played such games, and many others will find it easy to do if they try.

The model exists in time as well as space. We all remember tunes; some of us remember whole songs, symphonies, operas. This is clearly not just a matter of remembering all the individual notes in a tune. We can whistle or sing a tune we know in any one of a great many different keys, beginning on any note given us. What we have in mind is the whole structure of the tune, which exists in time. This structure is in the nerves and muscles that make the notes we sing or whistle; we don't have to learn all over again to sing or whistle the tune every time we do it in a new key, and we do not consciously *think* about the intervals between one note and the next. Good musicians can even improvise this way on their instruments.

We remember many other events, things we have seen happen or that have happened to us. We play over in our mind these things that have happened, or that might happen, or that we would like to have happen. Our daydreams are events in time, in an imagined and hoped-for future. These daydreams may be very practical and useful. When I was teaching, I often used daydreams, so to speak, to decide what I would do in class and how I would do it. Wondering whether the children might like a project, I would run a scenario in my mind, imagine myself doing it, imagine them responding. Often I could not make the scenario play. As the saying goes, I could not "see" or "picture" myself doing it. Or I could not picture the students responding in any alive and interesting way. If so, I would usually give up the project. If I could not make it work in my mind, I could probably not make it work in the classroom. Sometimes a scenario would play very well in my mind, but not work at all in class. From this I learned that my mental model of these children and their responses was not accurate, not true to fact. Next time I thought about them, I could use that experience to help me think a little better.

Today, when I am going to speak at a meeting, and am thinking about what to say there, I give many imaginary speeches in my mind. Given what I know about the audience I will be speaking to, I try to find one that feels right, but it happens very often that I don't know the audience I will be speaking to, have no feel of them, don't know the room in which we will meet, don't know what they have been doing or in what mood or spirit they have come to hear me. Therefore I almost have to make changes at the last minute, sometimes quite large changes, depending on the feel of the room, or what a previous speaker has said, or even on how I am introduced. This can be nerve-racking, but it keeps me from boring myself, and therefore, I hope, my hearers.

When we say someone has good intuition, or has a way with people, or is very tactful, what we are saying is that he has a very good mental model of the way people feel and behave. It is a mistake to assume that intuition or judgment must always be unscientific, less reliable than some sort of test. The intuition of one who has had wide experience and really learned from it is more reliable and scientific than anything else we could find. It takes into account thousands of subtle factors we could never build into a controlled situation or a test.

Our mental model not only exists in, and has in it, all the dimensions of space. It also extends into the past and the future. We can use it to think about what happened and about what will or might happen. We do this much more than we suppose. For example, I am standing on a street corner, waiting to cross. Some cars are coming down the street toward me. Very quickly I decide whether to cross ahead of them or not. How do I decide? What I do is project in the future those cars coming down the street and myself crossing. I *see* myself crossing and the cars coming. If it looks as if it is going to be close, I "decide" not to try to cross. All this happens in a very small fraction of a second. What is important is that I don't make any symbolic calculations; I don't think, "That car is coming at forty miles per hour, I will walk at four miles per hour, etc." In computer terms, I use what they call an analog computer, a computer which is a model of the actual situation.

We make use of these projections into the future in sports, or in driving a car, or in doing anything where motion, time, and distance are involved. We do not make calculations. Take the example of baseball. A great many variables affect the flight of a batted baseball. Perhaps some outfielders could name them all; many certainly could not. What they have is a mental model that enables them to know, given a certain day, with certain conditions of wind and weather, given a certain pitch, given a certain swing and a certain sound of bat against ball, given the first flash of the ball leaving the bat, just how they have to move—in what direction, how fast, for how long—to be in position to catch that ball when it comes down. Sometimes, after that first quick look, they may not even see the ball again until just before it hits their glove. The reason that the coaches, before the game, bat out fly balls for the outfielders to catch is not just to warm them up, but to help them adjust their mental models for the conditions of that particular time and place, the light, the density of the air, the wind, and so forth.

Other examples are easy to find. I have never played basketball and have no skill at it. One day I was in a gym shooting baskets. After a short while a mental model of the proper flight of a basketball began to build itself in my mind. I had a sense of the path along which the ball should travel if it was to go in. Almost as soon as it left my hand, I could see whether it was on its proper path or not, and thus tell, and quite accurately, whether it was going in. It didn't go in very often, but that was because I didn't have the right mental model in my muscles to make the ball take the track I knew it ought to take.

In tennis, a good player learns to tell, almost faster than thought, whether his own serve, or his opponent's lob or passing shot, will be in or out. Or he knows, from the flight of the ball in the first few feet after it leaves his opponent's racket, where he will have to go to be in position to hit it. He does this by "seeing," in the future, in his mind and in his muscles, where that ball is going, and then going there. When we have played often, and our model is in good adjustment, we do this well. When we play after a long layoff, we are rusty, we are fooled, we don't get to the right place.

In the same way, the driver of a car, wanting to pass, seeing a car coming in the opposite lane, projects into the future in his mind the data he has about his car's motion and the other car's motion toward him. If it "looks" all right, he passes. If his model is a good one, he gets by with room to spare. If his model is a bad one, he may crash, or force the oncoming driver to slow down. Or he may be one of those drivers who misses a great many opportunities to pass because he does not realize that they are safe.

Once I stood in the middle of a very small town with a five-year-old, waiting to cross the street. In either direction the street went for several hundred yards before going up a hill and out of sight. There was very little traffic, and that slow moving. But we waited for a long time, because that child would not move as long as he could see a car coming either way. Being then only ten or eleven myself, I was not thinking about models, only about getting across that street—which I can see in my mind's eye right now. Did the child have such a bad mental model that he saw every car as rushing in and hitting him? Or was he following some kind of rule in his mind that said, "Don't cross if there's a car coming." I don't know. It did take us a long time to get across that street.

The point here is that that child did not just *think* differently from me about that street. He *saw* it differently. I want to stress this very strongly. What I have tried to show in these examples, and could show in thousands more—though you can supply your own—is that not just our actions and reactions but our very perceptions, what we think we see, hear, feel, smell, and so on, are deeply affected by our mental model, our assumptions and beliefs about the way things really are. In a great variety of experiments with perception, many people, many times over, have shown this to to be true. Therefore it is not just fancy and tricky talk to say that each of us *lives,* not so much in an objective out-there world that is the same for all of us, but in his mental model of that world. It is this model of the world that he *experiences.* We are not, then, stating an impossible contradiction, or using language carelessly, when we say that I live *in* my mental model of the world, and my mental model lives *in* me.

3

THE WORLDS I LIVE IN

We can say, then, that we live in a number of worlds. One is the world within our own skin. I live within my skin, inside my skin is me and nothing but me, I am everywhere inside my skin, everything inside my skin is me.

At the same time I (inside my skin) live in a world that is outside my skin and therefore not me. So does everybody else. If we look at things this way, we can say that we all live in two worlds.

But this now seems to me incomplete. As we have seen, there is an important sense in which each of us lives in a world that is outside our skin but that is *our own,* unique to us. We express this view of things in many ways in our common talk. We speak of someone "sharing his world," or of "living in a world of his own."

The idea of the mental model may make this more clear. Suppose I am sitting with a friend in a room. At one side of the room is a door, closed, leading to another room. I have been in this other room many times, have spent much time in it; my friend has never seen it. That room exists for me and for him, but in very different ways. In my mind's eye I can see it, the furniture and objects in it. I can remember other times I have been in it and the things I did there. I can "be" there in the past, or right now, and in the future. My friend can do none of these things. The room is not a part of his mental model, but beyond the edge of it, like the parts of old maps marked Terra Incognita—Unknown Lands. He can, of course, speculate about what *might* be in that room, what it *might* be like. But he does not know.

Let us think of ourselves, then, as living, not in two, but in three or even four different worlds. World One is the world inside my skin. World Two is what I might call "My World," the world I have been in and know, the world of my mental model. This world is made up of places, people, experiences, events, what I believe, what I expect. While I live, this world is a part of me, always with me. When I die, it will disappear, cease to exist. There will never be another one quite like it. I can try to talk or write about it, or express it or part of it in art or music or in other ways. But other people can get from me only what I can *express* about my world. I cannot share that world directly with anyone.

This idea, that each of us creates and has within him a world that is and will always be unique, may be part of what men once tried to express when they talked about the human soul. And (among other things) it is what makes our government's talk about "body counts" in Vietnam so obscene.

World Three is something different. It is, for my friend, the world on the other side of the door. It is the world I know *of*, or know something *about*, but do not know, have not seen or experienced. It has in it all the places I have heard about, but not been to; all the people I have heard about, but not known; all the things I know men have done, and that I might do, but have not done. It is the world of the possible.

World Four is made up of all those things or possibilities that I have not heard of or even imagined. It is hard to talk about, since to talk about something is to put it, to some extent, in World Three. An example may help. For me, Argentina, or flying an airplane, or playing the piano, are all in World Three. For a new baby, they are all in World Four. Almost everything in my World Two or Three is in his World Four. Not only is my known world bigger than his, but so is my world of possibilities. The world he knows is very small; the world he knows *about* is not much bigger.

Within each world I know some parts much better than others, some experiences are much closer to me than others, more vivid, more meaningful. In World Three, for example, the world I know something about, there are things about which I know a great deal, so much that they are almost part of my real experience, and others about which I know much less. Indeed, the boundary between Worlds Two and Three is not at all sharp or clear. One of the things that makes us human is that in learning about the world we are not limited wholly to our private and personal experiences. Through our words, and in other ways, we can come very close to sharing our private worlds. We can tell others a great deal about what it is like to be us, and know from others much of what it is like to be them. If not for this, we would all live, as too many do now, shut off and isolated from everyone else.

In the same way, the boundary between Worlds Three and Four is not clear either. There are possibilities that are so far from possible that it is hard to think about them at all. I know enough about Sweden to have at least some feeling about what it would be like to go there or live there. About Afghanistan or China I know much less. I can speculate a little about what it might be like to be on the surface of the planet Mercury. Beyond that there is the galaxy, and other galaxies, and possible other universes that I have no way to think about. I can have some feeling about what it might be like to do or be certain things. It is much harder for me to imagine what it might be like to have a baby, or be on the brink of death. As for being, say, an amoeba, or a star, I cannot consider the possibility at all. As some things in my real or known world are more real or more deeply known than others, so some things in my possible world are more possible than others.

4

LEARNING AS GROWTH

By now it may be somewhat easier to see and feel what I mean in saying that we can best understand learning as growth, an expanding of ourselves into the world around us. We can also see that there is no difference between living and learning, that living *is* learning, that it is impossible, and misleading, and harmful to think of them as being separate. We say to children, "You come to school to learn." We say to each other, "Our job in school is to teach children how to learn." But the children have been learning, all the time, for all of their lives before they meet us. What is more, they are very likely to be much better at learning than most of us who plan to teach them how to do it.

Every time I do something new, go somewhere new, meet someone new, have any kind of new experience, I am expanding the world I know, my World Two, taking more of the world out there into my own world. My World Two is growing out into my World Three. Very probably my World Three is also growing. As I go more places and do more things, I see and hear about still more places I might go, I meet more and more people doing things I might do.

One of the things that we do for children, just by being among them as ourselves, by our natural talk about our own lives, work, interests, is to widen their World Three, their sense of what is possible and available. But we only do this when we are truly ourselves. If children feel that we are pretending, or playing a role or putting on some kind of mask or acting as some kind of official spokesman for something or other, they learn nothing from us except, perhaps, and sadly enough, that since we cannot be believed and trusted there *is* nothing to be learned from us.

If we understand learning as growth, we must then think about conditions that make growth possible and the ways in which we can help create those conditions. That is the purpose of this book. Let me say here, in a very few words, some of the ideas I will be discussing at greater length in the next chapters.

The very young child senses the world all around him, both as a place and as the sum of human experience. It seems mysterious, perhaps a little dangerous, but also inviting, exciting, and everywhere open and accessible to him. This healthy and proper sense is part of what may cause some child psychologists to talk, unwisely I believe, about "infant omnipotence." Little children know very well that they are very limited, that compared to the people around them they are very small, weak, helpless, dependent, clumsy, and ignorant. They know that their world is small and ours large. But this won't always be true. They feel, at least until we infect them with our fears, that the great world of possibilities outside their known world is open to them, that they are not shut off from any of it, that in the long run nothing is impossible.

My grandfather used to say of certain people, "Know nothing, fear nothing." We tend to think of this of little children. We see their long-run fearlessness, their hopefulness, as nothing but ignorance, a disease of which experience will cure them. With what cynicism, bitterness, and even malice we say, "They'll learn, they'll find out what life is soon enough." And many of us try to help that process along. But the small child's sense of the wholeness and openness of life is not a disease but his most human trait. It is above all else what makes it possible for him—or anyone else—to grow and learn. Without it, our ancestors would never have come down out of the trees.

The young child knows that bigger people know more about the world than he does. How they feel about it affects, and in time may determine, how he feels about it. If it looks good to them, it will to him. The young child counts on the bigger people to tell him what the world is like. He needs to feel that they are honest with him, and that, because they will protect him from real dangers that he does not know or cannot imagine, he can explore safely.

We can only grow from where we are, and when we know where we are, and when we feel that we are in a safe place, on solid ground.

We cannot be made to grow in someone else's way, or even made to grow at all. We can only grow when and because we want to, for our own reasons, in whatever ways seem most interesting, exciting, and helpful to us. We have not just thoughts but feelings about ourselves, our world, and the world outside our world. These feelings strongly affect and build on each other. They determine how we grow into the world, and whether we can grow into it.

To throw more light on these ideas, to help us see them more clearly, let me quote, the first of many times, from George Dennison's *The Lives of Children,* the wisest and most beautiful book about children and their learning that I know.

> There is no such thing as learning except (as Dewey tells us) in the continuum of experience. But this continuum cannot survive in the classroom unless there is reality of encounter between the adults and the children. The teachers must be themselves, and not play roles. They must teach the children, and not teach "subjects."
>
> The experience of learning is an experience of wholeness. The child feels the unity of his own powers and the continuum of persons. His parents, his friends, his teachers, and the vague human shapes of his future form one world for him, and he feels the adequacy of his powers within this world. Anything short of this wholeness is not true learning.

"Continuum of experience" is a phrase I will use many times in this book. It means both the fact, and our sense of the fact, that life and human experience, past, present, and future, are one whole, every part connected to and dependent on every other part. "Continuum of persons" means that people are a vital part of the whole of experience. In speaking of "the natural authority of adults," Dennison says that children know, among other things, that adults "have prior agreements among themselves." This is a good way of saying in simple words what is meant by a culture. The child feels that culture, that web of understandings and agreements, all around him, and knows that it is through the adults—if they will be honest —that he can learn how to take part in it.

Of children learning to speak, which, as I keep reminding teachers, we must by any standards see as being vastly harder than the learning to read we do so much worrying about, Dennison says:

> Crying is the earliest "speech." Though it is wordless, it is both expressive and practical, it effects immediately environmental change, and it is accompanied by facial expressions and "gestures." All these will be regularized, mastered by the infant long before the advent of words.
>
> Two features of the growth of this mastery are striking:
>
> 1. The infant's use of gestures, facial expression, and sounds is at every stage of his progress the true medium of his being-with-others. There is no point at which the parents or other children fail to respond because the infant's mastery is incomplete. Nor do they respond as if it were complete. The infant quite simply, is one of us, is of the world precisely as the person he already is. His ability to change and structure his own environment is minimal, but it is real: we take his needs and wishes seriously, and we take seriously his effect upon us. This is not a process of intuition, but transpires in the medium he is learning and in which we have already learned, the medium of sounds, facial expressions, and gestures.
>
> 2. His experimental and self-delighting play with sounds—as when he is sitting alone on the floor, handling toys and babbling to himself—is never supervised and is rarely interfered with. Parents who have listened to this babbling never fail to notice the gradual advent of new families of sounds, but though this pleases them, they do not on this account reward the infant. The play goes on as before, absolutely freely.
>
> The infant, in short, is born into an already existing continuum of experience. . . . He is surrounded by the life of the home, not

by instructors or persons posing as models. Everything that he observes, every gesture, every word, is observed not only as action but as a truly instrumental form. [In short, as one of a great series and complex of actions, all tied together, with real purposes and consequences, one undivided whole of life and experience around him.] It is what he learns. No parent has ever heard an infant abstracting the separate parts of speech and practising them. . . . A true description of an infant "talking" with its parents, then, must make clear that he is actually taking part. It is not make-believe or imitation, but true social sharing in the degree to which he is capable.

Albert North Whitehead wrote, in *The Aims of Education:*

The first intellectual task which confronts an infant is the acquirement of spoken language. What an appalling task, the correlation of meanings with sounds. It requires an analysis of ideas and an analysis of sounds. We all know that an infant does it, and that the miracle of his achievement is explicable. But so are all miracles, and yet to the wise they remain miracles.

In the same book he wrote that we could not and should not try to separate the skills of an activity from the activity itself. This seems to me his way of talking about the continuum of experience. We have not learned this lesson at all. We talk about school as a place where people teach (or try to) and others learn (or try to, or try not to) the "skills" of reading, or arithmetic, or this, that, or the other. This is not how a child (or anyone else) learns to do things. He learns to do them by doing them. He does not learn the "skills" of speech and then go somewhere and use these skills to speak with. He learns to speak by speaking.

When we try to teach a child a disembodied skill, we say in effect, "You must learn to do this thing in here, so that later on you can go and do something quite different out there." This destroys the continuum of experience within which true learning can only take place. We should try to do instead in school as much as possible of what people are doing in the world.

5

THE WORLD BELONGS
TO US ALL

Another idea I want to stress, that is closely and deeply connected with everything else I will say in this book, is the idea of *belonging*. This is a way of saying what I have in other words said about the young child—that he feels the world is *open* to him. But another quote from *The Lives of Children* will show more clearly what this feeling can mean to the learner, or what the lack of it may mean.

Let us imagine a mother reading a bedtime story to a child of five. . . . We can judge *the expansion of self and world* [italics mine] by the rapt expression of the face of the child, the partly open mouth and the eyes which seem to be dreaming, but which dart upward at any error or omission, for the story has been read before a dozen times. Where does the story take place? Where does it happen in the present? Obviously in the mind of the child, characterized at this moment by imagination, feeling, discernment, wonderment, and delight. And in the voice of the mother, for all the unfolding events are events of her voice, characteristic inflections of description and surprise. And in the literary form itself, which might be described with some justice as the voice of the author.

The continuum of persons is obvious and close. The child is expanding into the world quite literally through the mother . . .

here the increment of *world*, so to speak, is another voice, that of the author. . . . Because of the form itself, there hover in the distance, as it were, still other forms and paradigms of life, intuitions of persons and events, of places in the world, of estrangement and companionship. The whole is supported by security and love.

There is no need to stress the fact that from the point of view of learning, these are optimum conditions. I would like to dwell on just two aspects of these conditions, and they might be described, not too fancifully, as *possession* and *freedom of passage*.

Both the mother, in reading the story, and the author, in achieving it, are *giving* without any proprietary consciousness. The child has an unquestioned right to all that transpires; it is of his world in the way that all apprehendable forms are of it. We can hardly distinguish between his delight in the new forms and his appropriation of them. Nothing interferes with his taking them into himself, and vice versa, expanding into them. His apprehension of new forms, their consolidation in his thoughts and feelings, is his growth . . . and these movements of his whole being are unimpeded by the actions of the adults.

Compare this experience with a description of José, an illiterate twelve-year-old boy with whom Dennison worked at the First Street School in New York.

[José] could not believe, for instance, that anything contained in books, or mentioned in classrooms, belonged by rights to himself, or even belonged to the world at large, as trees and lampposts belong quite simply to the world we all live in. He believed, on the contrary, that things dealt with in school belonged somehow to school. . . . There had been no indication that he could share in in them, but rather that he would be measured against them and found wanting. . . . Nor could he see any connection between school and his life at home and in the streets.

Found wanting! Not long ago a college professor, in a letter in response to an article of mine, said in defense of college entrance examinations that many students were *"not equal* to the college experience." (Italics mine.) But here, in a very specific example, is what the feeling of being shut out, and later allowed in, meant to José:

> . . . one day we were looking at a picturebook of the Pilgrims. José understood that they had crossed the Atlantic, but something in the way he said it made me doubt his understanding. I asked him where the Atlantic was. I thought he might point out the window, since it lay not very far away. But his face took on an abject look, and he asked me weakly, "Where?" I asked him if he had ever gone swimming at Coney Island. He said, "Sure, man!" I told him that he had been swimming in the Atlantic, the same ocean the Pilgrims had crossed. His face lit up with pleasure and he threw back his head and laughed. There was a note of release in his laughter. It was clear that he had gained something more than information. He had discovered something. He and the Atlantic belonged to the same world! The Pilgrims were a fact of life.

Every so often, at a meeting, or to a group of people, I try to read that story. I can get as far as José's laugh, but there I choke up and have to stop. Perhaps without meaning to, perhaps without knowing that we are doing it, we have done a terrible thing in our schools, And not just in the slums of our big cities. Reviewing Dennison's book in *The New York Review of Books,* I wrote:

> Our educational system, at least at its middle- and upper middle-class layers, likes to say and indeed believes that an important part of its task is transmitting to the young the heritage of the past, the great traditions of history and culture. The effort is an unqualified failure. The proof we see all around us. A few of the students in our schools, who get good marks and go to prestige colleges, exploit the high culture, which many of them do not really understand or love, by pursuing comfortable and well-paid careers as university Professors of English, History, Philosophy, etc. Almost all the rest reject that culture wholly and utterly.
>
> The reason is simple, and the one Dennison has pointed out— their schools and teachers have never told them, never encouraged or even allowed them to think, that high culture, all those poems, novels, Shakespeare plays, etc., belonged or might belong to them,

that they might claim it for their own, use it solely for their own purposes, for whatever joys and benefits they might get from it. Let us not mislead ourselves about this. The average Ivy League graduate is as estranged from the cultural tradition, certainly those parts of it that were shoved down his throat in school, as poor José was from his Dick and Jane.

It is our learned men and their institutions of learning, and not our advertising men or hucksters of mass entertainment, who have taken for their own—and by so doing, largely destroyed for everyone else—the culture and tradition that ought to have belonged to and enriched the lives of all of us.

6

THE LEARNER IN
HIS MODEL

Each of us has a mental model of the world as we know it. That model *includes ourselves*. We are in our own model. We remember what we have done, how we felt about it as we did it, how we felt about it afterward. We have a sense of who we are and what we can do. Most of us do not like to be surprised about the world, to find that it is very different from what we had supposed. We like even less to be surprised about ourselves. Years ago the psychologist Prescott Lecky wrote a very important book—long neglected, since the fashion was to think that we could best understand men by looking at rats—called *Self-Consistency*. In it he showed some of the many ways in which people act to protect their ideas about themselves, even when these ideas were not good.

We have feelings about ourselves, the world we know, and the world we know about. These feelings depend on and very powerfully affect each other. If we think of ourselves as bad, stupid, incompetent, not worthy of love or respect, we will not be likely to think that the worlds we live in are good. Even if we have fairly good feelings about ourselves, a sudden change in those feelings will affect our feelings about everything else. On those days when life seems without hope and I feel that man and his works are doomed, I try to remind myself that this doom is in me, not out there. This does not make the gloom go away, or even stop the world from looking hopeless. But I do not get trapped in a cycle of despair—I feel bad, so the world looks bad, so I feel worse, so it looks worse, and so on.

This is not to say that when I feel fine everything looks fine. The world is full of things that look bad no matter how I feel. Our war in Asia, to name only one. Poverty, injustice, cruelty, corruption, the destruction of the living earth of which we are a part. A list would be too long. What is changed by my feelings is not what is out there but what I think I and others may be able to do about them.

Several things help me ride out spells of gloom and depression, keep me from getting trapped in a cycle of despair. One is that since I have been through that tunnel before, I know there is an end to it and that I can go through it. Also, since I more often feel good than bad, I can assume that bad feelings will in time give way to good ones. When a person who is used to being healthy gets sick, he thinks, This won't last; I'll soon be up and about. A person who is used to being ill, exhausted, and in pain, if he does have a spell of feeling well, thinks, This can't last.

This is in part why children who are used to failing are so little cheered up when now and then they succeed.

Another thing that helps me get over feeling badly is that my life is full of things that boost my morale and give me pleasure. To name only a few of these, I love music, I love the beauty of the world, I love my home town, or at least the very pleasant parts of it that I live and work in, I love the feeling of having a home town. I know many people that just seeing cheers me up. I am also cheered by what I know of other people, friends, colleagues, allies, comrades-in-arms as it were, struggling to make a decent society and world. I am cheered by my feeling that I have done good work myself, and when that will not boost my morale, I can boost it by thinking about what others are saying and doing. And I am good at clutching at straws in the news, an unexpected reason for hope, for feeling that we aren't licked yet, we may still make it.

The point of all this is that it is impossible to draw a line between what I know about the world and how I feel about it. My feelings about the world are part of my knowledge about it, my knowledge part of my feelings. All the time, they act on each other.

How I feel about myself and the world I know affects in turn how I feel about the world outside my mental model, the world I will grow into if I grow at all. A person, like José, who feels badly about himself and as much of the world as he does know is not likely to feel that the part of the world he does not know is going to be any better than the rest. It will not look inviting, but full of possibilities of danger, humiliation, and defeat. He will feel it, not as luring him out, but as thrusting in, invading those few fairly safe places where he has even a small sense of who and where he is. He will think the world he does not know must be even worse than the world he does. So he shrinks back from it, and it crowds in on him. This is what Dennison means when he speaks of a child as being "invaded" by his environment or by an experience, or when he says of José that he "again and again *had drawn back from experience in fright and resentment.*"

The fearful person, child or adult, is in retreat. The world he knows, and the unknown world outside that, threaten him, drive him back. What is the way of this going back? He forgets, represses, casts out those bad experiences. I used to spend hours trying to "teach" certain parts of arithmetic to certain fifth graders. They often learned, or seemed to learn, what I had been trying to teach them. In only a day or two they had forgotten. The total experience of sitting across a table from me, worrying about what I wanted, worrying about whether they would be able to give it to me, worrying about disappointing me again, feeling for the thousandth time stupid and inadequate, knowing that the fact that they were working alone with me was a kind of proof that they were stupid, if any more proof were needed—all of this bad experience they cast out of their minds, including the things that they had supposedly succeeded in learning.

Part of the shrinking back, then, is forgetting. Another part is quite different. The person who is not afraid of the world wants understanding, competence, mastery. He wants to make his mental model better, both more complete, in the sense of having more in it, and more accurate, in being more like the world out there, a better guide to what is happening and may happen. He wants to know the score. Like the thinker in Nietzsche's quote, he wants answers. Even if they are not the answers he expected, or hoped for, even if they are answers he dislikes, they advance him into the world. He can use any experience, however surprising or unpleasant, to adjust his mental model of the world. And so he is willing, and eager, to expose himself to the reality of things as they are. The more he tries, the more he learns, however his trials come out.

This is the spirit of the very young child, and the reason he learns so well.

The fearful person, on the other hand, does not care whether his model is accurate. What he wants is to feel safe. He wants a model that is reassuring, simple, unchanging. Many people spend their lives building such a model, rejecting all experiences, ideas, and information that do not fit. The trouble with such models is that they don't do what a good model should do—tell us what to expect. The people who live in a dream world are always being rudely awakened. They cannot see life's surprises as sources of useful information. They must see them as attacks.

Such people, and they are everywhere, of all ages and in all walks of life, fall back in many ways on the protective strategy of deliberate failure. How can failure be protective? On the principle that you can't fall out of bed if you're sleeping on the floor; you can't lose any money if you don't place any bets. But there is more to the strategy than the idea that you can't fail if you don't try. If you can think of yourself as a complete and incurable failure, you won't even be tempted to try. If you can feel that fate, or bad luck, or other people made you a failure, then you won't feel so badly about being one. If you can think that the people who are trying to wean you from failure are only trying to use you, you can resist them with a clear conscience.

A man who feels this way slips easily into fatalism and even paranoia. If he assumes that everything is bad, he can't be disappointed if a particular thing turns out to be bad. If he says that all men are bad, and that when they seem to be something else they are just trying to trick him, that everyone is against him, that life on earth is hell and our duty only to endure it and not to try to change it or make it better, he will at least have the cold comfort of being able to say all the time, I told you so. Such people slip easily into one of the popular religions of our time, various ways of worshiping power and violence and suffering. Some of these may even go under the name of Christianity. Just as a man may feel his love of God as an expression of his feeling that the world is full of people and places and experiences to be loved and trusted, he may equally well turn to a love of God out of a feeling that *nothing* else can be loved or trusted. "God is good" can mean that many things are good, or on the other hand that nothing else is any good. A man may cling desperately to the belief that Jesus loves him because he is certain that nobody else does. Thus Christianity can all too easily, as I fear it has for many people in our country, turn into a religion of hate and despair.

7

PLACE AND IDENTITY

Learning is a growing out into the world or worlds around us. We can only grow from where we are. If we don't know where we are, or if we feel that we are not any place, we can hardly move at all, not with any sense of direction and purpose.

When we look at a map to find out how to get somewhere, we look first for something that says, "You are here." Or we say to someone, "Where are we on this map?" If we cannot find ourselves on the map, we cannot use it to move, it is no good to us.

Dennison says of José:

> It would have been pointless to simply undo the errors in José's view of the world and supply him with information. It was essential to *stand beside him on whatever solid ground he might possess.* [Italics mine.]

The learner, child or adult, his experience, his interests, his concerns, his wonders, his hopes and fears, his likes and dislikes, the things he is good at, must always be at the center of his learning. He can move out into the world only from where he already is in it. The old joke says, "If I were going to the post office, I wouldn't start from here." But we have to start from here, the particular, individual *here* of each child and every child we work with.

37

In *How Children Fail* I described some of the incredible confusions about numbers in the minds of my fifth graders. For years
their teachers had tried to teach them arithmetic from where they
thought they ought to be, instead of finding where they were and
beginning from there. The children had learned nothing. If we
don't let a child move from where he is, he can't move at all. All
he can do is try to fool us into thinking he is moving. Indeed, he
cannot even hold the ground he has. José was far less able to learn
at twelve than he had been at six, and so were many of the supposedly bright suburban children I taught. We cannot stand still in the
world. Only by moving out into the world do we keep it real. If we
do not grow into it, it closes in on us, and turns, as it does for so
many, into a haze of fantasies, delusions, nightmares.

Of José, Dennison writes again:

> His passage among persons—among teachers and schoolmates
> both, and among the human voices of books, films, etc.—is
> blocked and made painful by his sense of his "place", that is, by
> the measurements through which he must identify himself: that
> he has failed all subjects, is last in the class, is older than his
> classmates, and has a reading problem.

Let me repeat, "by the measurements through which he must
identify himself." I have said many times to school people that, for
just the reason Dennison gives, we cannot be in the business of
education and at the same time in the business of testing, grading,
labeling, sorting, deciding who goes where and who gets what. It is
not just that when we are being judged we think only of the judge
and how to give him what he wants. It is not just that when we
have been made enough afraid of failure we may think that the
surest way to avoid failing is never to try. To do this much damage
to children would be bad enough. But a child who has been made
to think of himself as no good soon becomes unable to meet the
world on any terms. His fear makes everything look fearful.

The Scottish psychiatrist Ronald Laing, whose books seem to
me of enormous importance, says in his latest book, *Self and
Others:*

... The person in a false position has lost a starting-point of his own from which to throw or thrust himself, that is, to project himself, forward. He has lost the place. He does not know where he is or where he is going. He cannot get anywhere however hard he tries.

To understand the "position" from which a person lives, it is necessary to know the original sense of his place in the world he grew up with. His own sense of his place will have been developed partly in terms of what place he will have been *given* . . .

The importance of Laing's work is this. He does most of his work with what are called schizophrenics—the seriously mentally ill. He has not, as far as I know, concerned himself much with schools or school experiences. What he says about the mentally ill is that what we call their illness—a way of behaving that, whether destructive or not, is odd and embarrassing to others—is not a "disease" that has crept into their minds from outside, but a way of dealing with an intolerable situation into which other people, usually close relatives, have put them. Barbara O'Brien, in her extraordinary book *Operators and Things,* her account of her own experience of schizophrenia, shows that it was the people she worked with and among that put her in a conflict she could not stand.

Laing has tried to find what kinds of experiences these mentally ill people had before they "became ill." What he found, to put the matter very bluntly, is that people go crazy because other people drive them crazy. His findings are horrifying because the things that people—without meaning to—make other people crazy by doing are very much like a great many things we do to children in schools.

In *The Politics of Experience* he pointed out that most conventional treatment of the people we call "mentally ill" is based on what he calls "the invalidation of their experience." This is a phrase he uses many times. By it he means that in effect we say to the mentally ill that their ways of perceiving and experiencing the world, their ways of reacting to it and communicating about it, are crazy and have to be canceled, wiped out, done away with. Instead, they have to perceive, experience, respond, and communicate more or less as we do. Until then, they stay locked up. In one place he says that many people leave institutions only because "they have decided once again to play at being sane."

It is not only that during their treatment other people invalidate the experience of the mentally ill. It was this invalidation of their experience, the terrible uncertainty and confusion into which other people put them, that helped to drive them crazy.

In *Self and Others* Laing writes:

> There are many ways of invalidating and undermining the acts of the other. . . . They may be treated as mere reaction in the other to the person who is their "true" or "real" agent, as somehow a link in a cause-effect chain whose origin is not in the individual . . . Jack may expect credit or gratitude from Jill by making out that *her very capacity to act is due to him.* [Italics mine.]

We cannot miss the parallel with what we do in school. Schools, teachers, parents all believe that their job is to make learning happen in children, and that if it happens it is only because they made it happen. I have known parents who became anxious and angry whenever I told them about something that their children had done on their own initiative and for their own reasons. These people, like many teachers, had to believe that anything good the child did or that was in him came and *could* come only from them. It is as if we all dream of seeing in print, someday, a statement by some famous person that all he is he owes to us. Perhaps, having despaired of putting much meaning into our own lives, having given up on ourselves as worthless material, we have to work our miracles and justify our lives through someone else. I cannot make anything of myself, but I can and will (if it kills you) make something of you.

Such feelings may have much to do with why so many older people, teachers or otherwise, are so threatened by the demand of young people for independence, for the right to run their own lives and learning, for their refusal to be only what someone else wants them to be. Those feelings may even have a good deal to do with the pleasure that some people seem to get out of reading about the shooting of students, or even dreaming about shooting all of them.

More times than I can remember, teachers or parents have said to me, of some child, "He didn't want to do something, but I made him do it, and he is glad, and if I hadn't made him he would never have done anything." The other day a pleasant and probably kindly coach and swimming instructor told me about some child who hadn't wanted to swim, but he had made him, and the child had learned and now liked it, so why shouldn't he have the right to compel everyone to swim? There are many answers. The child might have in time learned to swim on his own, and not only had the pleasure of swimming, but the far more important pleasure of having found that pleasure for himself. Or he might have used that time to find some other skills and pleasures, just as good. The real trouble, as I said to the coach, is this: I love swimming, and in a school where nothing else was compulsory I might see a case for making swimming so. But for every child in that school there are dozens of adults, each convinced that he has something of vital importance to "give" the child that he would never get for himself, all saying to the child, "I know better than you do what is good for you." By the time all those people get through making the child do what they know is good for him, he has no time or energy left. What is worse, he has no sense of being in charge of his life and learning or that he could be in charge, or that he deserves to be in charge, or that if he were in charge it would turn out any way other than badly. In short, he has no sense of his identity or place. He is only where and what others tell him he is.

This has the effect on learning that we might expect, and that Dennison has so vividly described. But it has far worse effects than that. Laing writes:

> Every human being, whether child or adult, seems to require significance, that is, *place in another's world*. . . . The slightest sign of recognition from another at least confirms one's presence in *his* world. "No more fiendish punishment could be devised," William James once wrote, "even were such a thing physically

possible, than that one should be turned loose in society and remain absolutely unnoticed by all the members thereof."

But of course as Dennison and many others have pointed out, this is exactly what happens in so many schools. For most if not all of the day, the child is not allowed to respond to the other children, but is required to act as if they were not there. The teacher, in turn, responds to the child, not as he is, but only in terms of the tasks he has been given to do and the way he wants him to behave. If he does what is wanted, he is "good"; if not, or if he does something else, he is bad, a problem, and has to be dealt with as such. He has no "place," no identity.

Laing writes:

> What constantly preoccupies and torments the paranoid is usually the precise opposite of what [we might expect]. He is persecuted by being the centre of everyone else's world, yet he is preoccupied with the thought that he never occupies first place in anyone's affection. . . . Unable to experience himself as significant for another, he develops a delusionally significant place for himself *in the world of others.*

In short, he is driven toward paranoia, not only by his need to make a mental model that will justify his failures and protect him against disappointment, but also by his feeling that he does not really make a difference to anyone.

It is not hard to see how the widespread (in this country at least) belief that every man is the natural enemy and rightful prey of every other man must affect those many people who take it seriously.

Laing quotes Gerard Manley Hopkins:

> ". . . my self-being, my consciousness and feeling of myself, that taste of myself, of *I* and *me* above and in all things, which is more distinctive than the taste of ale or alum, more distinctive than the smell of walnut leaf or camphor, and is incommunicable by any means to another man."

Laing then writes:

> The loss of the experience of an area of *unqualified privacy,* by its transformation into a quasi-public realm, is often one of the decisive changes associated with the process of going mad.

This is blood chilling. One of the things adults do, and above all in schools, is invade, in every possible way, the lives and privacy of their students. There are master keys to the students' "lockers" in schools, so that administrators may search them any time they feel like it. There are almost no places in most schools where students may talk together. The whole hair battle, which some schools, thank goodness, have given up, was only a way of saying, "Nothing about you is yours, everything about you is ours, you belong wholly to us, you can withhold nothing." And I think with deep regret and shame of the times when I, like millions of other adults, scolding a child or ordering him about, have said, "Take that expression off your face!" It seems now an extraordinary and unforgivable crime against the human person, the human spirit.

8

THE GROWTH OF
THE SELF

Many books have been written about what is called the problem of identity in our times. Erich Fromm has pointed out, in *Escape from Freedom* and in many of his other books, that the ties that in earlier times told people who they were, ties of family, place, clan, craft, caste, religion, do not exist and that people must therefore, as most are not able to do, create an identity out of their own lives, or else try to get an identity by submerging themselves in some collective identity—club, party, nation—and in identifying themselves with some source of power.

Too many of the American flags we see on cars and other places are not a symbol of patriotism, of love for a place or many places, for people, for life. They are only a symbol of distrust, hatred, and power. The people who display these flags feel them as a fist at the end of their arm, big enough to smash anyone they dislike, and even the whole world. A truer symbol might be the hydrogen bomb.

One night I was watching TV when a station went off the air. The last thing we heard was "The Star-Spangled Banner." As it played, we saw on the screen, as double exposure, the flag waving in the breeze, and behind it—what? Mountains? Deserts? Historic buildings? Figures of great men? No—none of these. Only weapons of war—battleships, guns firing, bombers.

Today's young people are very much and rightly concerned with identity. They refuse to believe that they are only whatever the schools and adults say they are or want them to be. But if they are not that, what are they? They do not know and do not know how to find out. One of the reasons many of them use various kinds of psychedelic drugs is that they hope the drugs will help them find out.

I do not think the young, or anyone else, will find their identity by hunting for it. Certainly not if they do all their hunting inside their skins, or heads. What makes me *me*, and not somebody else, is my mental model, the world as I know it, the sum of my experiences and of my feelings about them. We find our identity by choosing, by trying things out, by finding out through experience what we like and what we can do. Not only do we discover our identity, find out who we are, by choosing, we also make our identity, for each new choice adds something to our experience and hence to our world and to ourselves. Dennison wrote of "the expansion of self and world." We expand ourselves as we expand our world.

Laing writes in *Self and Others:*

> Everyday speech gives us clues we would be wise to follow. It hints that there may be a general law or principle that a person will feel himself going forward when he puts himself into his actions . . . but that if this is not so, he will be liable to feel that he is "going back" or is stationary, or "going around in circles" or "getting nowhere." In "putting myself into" what I do, I lose myself, and in so doing I seem to become myself. The act I do is felt to be me, and I become "me" in and through much action. Also, there is a sense in which a person "keeps himself alive" by his acts; each act can be a new beginning, a new birth, a re-creation of oneself, a self-fulfilling.
>
> To be "authentic" is to be true to oneself, to be what one is, to be "genuine" . . .
>
> The act that is genuine, revealing, and potentiating is felt by

me as fulfilling. This is the only *actual* fulfilment of which I can properly speak. It is an act that is me; in this action I am myself; I put myself "in" it. In so far as I put myself "into" what I do, I become myself through this doing.

In this understanding Dennison writes, very early in *The Lives of Children:*

> . . . the proper concern of a primary school is not education in a narrow sense, and still less preparation for later life, but the present lives of the children—a point made repeatedly by John Dewey, and very poorly understood by his followers.

"Poorly understood" is certainly an understatement here. What this means to those who do understand it we can see in Dennison's description of a little girl, Maxine, whose life in the public school had been a disaster, an endless round of failures and crises.

> Maxine was no easier to deal with at First Street than she had been at the public school. She was difficult. The difference was this: by accepting her needs precisely as needs, we diminished them; in supporting her powers, in all their uniqueness, we allowed them to grow.

Supporting powers is, of course, exactly what we do not do in most schooling. We do not give children extra time to work at what they like and are good at, but only on what they do worst and most dislike. The idea behind this, I suppose, is something nutty like a chain being no stronger than its weakest link. But of course children are living creatures, not chains or machines.

> Let us imagine Maxine in a regular classroom. (And let me say here that *every* child is plagued by apparently special problems and unmet needs.) She is quite capable of concentrating for short periods of time. She learns rapidly and well. But the lesson goes on and on. . . . She feels herself vanishing in this swarm of children, who are not only *constrained to ignore her* [italics mine] but constitute a very regiment of rivals interposed between herself and the teacher, her one source of security. The deep confusions

of her life are knocking at her forehead—and who better to turn to than a teacher? She does it indirectly. She runs across the room and hugs her favorite boy, and then punches her favorite boy, and then yells at the teacher, who is now yelling at her, "Do you have a boyfriend? Does he lay on top of you?" . . . pleasure, fertility, and violence are all mixed up here and she wants desperately to sort them out. And there is her new daddy, and something he has done to her mother. And there is the forthcoming rival (baby).

All these are the facts of her life. If we say that they do not belong in a classroom, we are saying that Maxine does not belong in a classroom. If we say that she must wait, then we must say how long, for the next classroom will be just like this one, and so will the one after that. . . . She was too vigorous, and too desperate, to suppress all this.

And here is José, trying to read, or perhaps trying to try to read:

When I used to sit beside José and watch him struggling with printed words, I was always struck by the fact that he had such difficulty even *seeing* them. I knew from medical reports that his eyes were all right. It was clear that his physical difficulties were the sign of a terrible conflict. On the one hand he did not *want* to see the words, did not want to focus his eyes on them, bend his head to them, and hold his head in place. On the other hand he wanted to learn to read again, and so he forced himself to perform these actions. But the conflict was visible. It was as if a barrier of smoked glass had been interposed between himself and the words: he moved his head here and there, squinted, widened his eyes, passed his hand across his forehead. The barrier, of course, consisted of the chronic emotions I have already mentioned: resentment, shame, self-contempt, etc. But how does one remove such a barrier? Obviously it cannot be done just in one little corner of a boy's life at school. Nor can these chronic emotions be removed as if they were cysts, tumors, or splinters. Resentment can only be made to yield by supporting the growth of trust and by multiplying incidents of satisfaction; shame, similarly, will not vanish except as self-respect takes its place. Nor will embarrassment go away simply by proving to the child that there is no need for embarrassment; it must be replaced by confidence and by a more generous regard for other persons. . . . But what conditions in the life at school will support these so desirable changes? Obviously they cannot be taught. Nor will better methods of instruction lead to them, or better textbooks.

I think with sorrow, because I did not then understand well enough what he needed and was asking of me, of a fifth grader I taught, a constant irritation and troublemaker, though in many ways lively and bright. One day he was annoying me and everyone else in the class. In exasperation I suddenly asked him, "Are you *trying* to make me sore?" Perhaps surprised into honesty, perhaps hoping I might hear, as I did not, the plea in his answer, he said, "Yes." But I only said something like, "Well, don't." This is not to say I did nothing for him; we spent a good deal of time together after school, and I think he got something from me. But not enough, not what he needed.

Laing writes:

> Some people are more sensitive than others to not being recognized as human beings. If someone is *very* sensitive in this respect, they stand a good chance of being diagnosed as schizophrenic.
>
> If you need to give and receive *too much* "love," you will be a high risk for the diagnosis of schizophrenia. This diagnosis attributes to you the incapacity, by and large, to give or receive love in an adult manner.

People like this, if children, are almost certain to do badly in school, and may well be "diagnosed" as being "hyperactive," "emotionally disturbed," and the like. In the book by Frances Hawkins from which I will quote later in this book, a teacher says of a deaf four-year-old, "That one will have to learn to obey." *That one!*

Over and over school people ask me about "control," about "discipline," about "chaos." They talk as if a classroom of young children were a cage of ferocious wild beasts who, once aroused, would destroy and kill everything in sight. What in fact they do, and what the limits truly are, we can see from Dennison's description:

> The word "limits", then, does not mean rules and regulations and figures of authority. It refers to the border line at which individual and social necessities meet and merge, the true edge of necessity. This is as much as to say that the question Who am I? belongs to the question, Who are you? They are not two questions at all, but one single, indissoluble fact.
>
> How did Maxine ask this dualistic question? She asked it by stealing Dodie's soda pop, and by shouting some loud irrelevancy when Rudella was trying to question her teacher, and by taking all the magnets from the other children and kicking her teacher in the shins, and by grabbing Elena's cookies at lunchtime. And what answers did she receive? But let me describe the public school answers first, for she had done the very same things in the public school. She had stolen someone's cookies, but it was the teacher who responded, not the victim, and so Maxine could not find out the meaning of her action among her peers. Nor could that long and subtle chain of childrens' reactions—with all their surprising turns of patience and generosity—even begin to take shape. And when Maxine confronted the teacher directly, shouting in class and drowning her out, she was punished in some routine way and was again deprived of the individual response which would have meant much to her . . .

This last sentence is worth thinking about. What are these routine punishments? In some schools a teacher might only say something like, "We don't do that kind of thing here." More likely there would be demerits, or stayings after school, or trips to the principal's office. If the child is a boy, there might be physical violence from the teacher. In all of these the point is that the child is made to feel, not that he has annoyed real people by breaking into a real conversation, but only that he has broken some rule, interrupted the working of the organization. What comes from the teacher is not a protest, not a personal cry of outrage—"For God's sake, Maxine, why do you have to interrupt all the time when I'm talking to so-and-so!", but only orders, threats, punishments. From a personal response Maxine might learn many things: that people can and do talk seriously to each other, that their talk means something and is important to them, that they can feel it as an attack—as indeed it is—if someone tries to stop them from talking. But in a regular school there is no such real talk. The teacher talks about what is in the curriculum or lesson plan or Teacher's Manual; the children play—or perhaps refuse to play—whatever parts are set out for them.

> At First Street Maxine tested the limits and arrived—lo and behold!—at limits. She snatched up Dodie's soda pop and proceeded to drink it: one swallow, two—Dodie gapes at her wide-eyed—three swallows—"Hey!" Dodie lunges for the bottle. Maxine skips away, but Dodie catches her, and though she does not strike her, she makes drinking soda pop quite impossible. Maxine has much to think about. Apparently the crime is not so enormous. Dodie allowed her two swallows, but was obviously offended. More than that Dodie will not allow. An hour later they are playing together. Dodie did not reject her. You can play with Dodie, but you can't drink up all her soda pop. She runs fast too, and I bet she'll hit me some day. (Dodie did finally hit Maxine one day—and they still remained playmates—and the days of stealing soda pop were long gone.)
>
> Maxine takes Elena's cookies. That's over in a minute. Elena throws her to the floor and kicks her in the rear, cursing at her in Spanish. The kicks don't hurt, but they're kicks all the same. This is no source of cookies! But Elena is impressive in her ardor, and perhaps she is a source of security, a really *valuable* friend. An hour later they are playing in their "castle." Elena is the queen, and Maxine, for several reasons, chooses to be her baby.
>
> . . . As for the kids, when they are all yelling at her together, they are too much even for her own formidable powers of resistance. While she can absorb endless numbers of demerits, endless hours of detention, endless homilies and rebukes, she must pay attention to this massed voice of her own group. She needs them. They are her playmates. . . . She knows now where the power lies. It's right there under her nose. The kids have some of it and the teachers have the rest. And they really have it, because there's no principal, no schedule, no boss. Why even the teachers blow their lids!

There were times at the First Street School during which Dennison and other teachers had to protect some of these terribly anxious and hysterical children—usually the boys—from each other. But most of the time, as he points out over and over again, the children in their dealings with each other were wiser, fairer, kinder, and more sensible than adult judges and rulers would have been likely to be. I have never seen more true mean spiritedness among children than when they were in a school and a class in which adults tried to prevent or, if they could not prevent, to settle all their quarrels. Nothing was ever truly worked out, settled, finished.

In the second and main part of this book I talk about some of the materials and projects that teachers can bring into a free learning and exploring environment. But we must understand from the start, as Dennison shows over and over in his book, that the most rich, varied, and useful things in the environment, when they are allowed to make full use of each other, are the children themselves, for reasons that he makes very clear:

> Children relate to one another by means of enterprise—play, games, projects. Which is to say that they are never bogged down in what are called "interpersonal relations." [They] get on with some shared activity that is exciting . . .
> . . . [they] relate to one another's strengths and abilities, since only these make enterprise possible. . . . Nor do they sacrifice activity for comfort. Nor is their hopefulness, like the hopefulness of many adults, compromised by aborted judgment, a barrier against disillusionment . . .

In many schools people are beginning to try to help children develop and better understand their feelings. Good idea—but how? By letting the children discover and express and work out their feelings in action and interaction? No; that is as forbidden as ever. Instead, the children and their teacher, every so often, sit in a circle and *talk about their feelings*. To help the good work, solemn textbooks are printed and, I suppose, read and "discussed," which tell the children that other people, too, have "bad feelings" about their baby brother, their parents.

To allow children to grow up whole will take much greater change than this.

9

THE KILLING OF
THE SELF

It seems to me a fact that the schooling of most children destroys their curiosity, confidence, trust, and therefore their intelligence. More and more people are coming to understand this. Dennison says *"all the parents I know* of school age children . . . express the fear that the schools will brutalize their children."* In the last year or two, many people have spoken or written about their small child, bright, curious, fearless, lively, only to say, I don't know what will happen to him in school, I'm afraid of what will happen, I wish I could keep him out. I have not kept an accurate count, but I would say that at least half of the people who have said this are themselves teachers or administrators. The man who said it to me most recently was a school principal.

There is really no use in looking for people to blame. The first causes go too far back. Too many people are involved. And of them, most if not all thought they were acting for the best, doing what was right. I myself, for many or most of the years I was a teacher, did almost all of the bad things I have talked about. Indeed, I think I never did more harm than when my intentions were the best. Later, when I stopped trying to play God in the classroom and became more modest, I became less harmful, perhaps even useful.

53

People used to ask me why I didn't write a book called *How Teachers Fail*. I told them that I had written it. *How Children Fail* is in fact about the continuous failure of a teacher—me.

But this is no excuse for closing our eyes to the meaning of what we are doing. In *The Underachieving School* I said, as I have here to some extent, that schooling destroys the identity of children, their sense of their own being, of their dignity, competence, and worth. I now feel the damage goes still deeper, and that the schooling of most children destroys a large part, not just of their intelligence, character, and identity, but of their health of mind and spirit, their very sanity. It is not the only source, but it seems to me a major source, perhaps the most important, of the schizoid and paranoid character and behavior that are a mark of our times, and the root cause of our deadly human predicament.

Let me return again to Ronald Laing, who seems to me to understand more about madness as a *process* than anyone else I know of. In *The Divided Self* and in other works he writes about the schizoid personality—splitting in half—and the schizophrenic—wholly split. What he says, in a word, is that such people do not fall in half, but are *torn* in half, pulled apart by their experiences, the people around them, and the demands they make on them. An important part of this process is what Gregory Bateson has called "a double-bind situation." Laing writes of it as follows:

> [In a double-bind situation] one person conveys to the other that he should do something, and at the same time conveys on another level that he should not, or that he should do something else incompatible with it. The situation is sealed off for the "victim" by a further injunction forbidding him or her to get out of the situation, or to dissolve it by commenting on it . . . the secondary injunction may, therefore, include a wide variety of forms: for example, "Do not see this as punishment"; "Do not see me as the punishing agent"; . . . "Do not think of what you must not do" . . .

Let me point out again that Laing is not writing about schools. But how terribly his words fit. Most adults would feel that they were being severely punished if they had to endure for long the conditions under which many children live in school. I am often told by program chairmen at meetings of teachers that "you can't keep teachers sitting for more than an hour and a half." And during this time, as I can see—the people in back think I can't—they don't hesitate to talk, read, write notes, doze a bit, or whatever. But these same people require children to sit absolutely still for hours at a time. Indeed, the limits we put in many schools on freedom of speech, movement, and even facial expression are far more stringent than anything we would find even in a maximum security prison. In many classrooms children are not only required for most of the day to sit at desks, without any chance to move or stretch, but they are not even allowed to change their position, to move in their chairs. If they do, they are quickly chastised or ridiculed by the teacher. This would be very effective punishment if meant as such. But the child is forbidden to think of it as punishment, or to ask why he should submit to this inhuman treatment. He is forbidden to think that these people who are doing these things to him are in any way his enemies or that they dislike or fear him. He is told to believe that they care about him, that what they do, they do for his sake, his good. He is made to feel that if he resists these orders not to speak or move, or even to change the expression on his face, or turn his head away from the teacher for even a few seconds, that if he even resents or questions these things, he is somehow bad, wicked, and really deserves harsher punishment, such as a physical beating, which many teachers and schools are still only too ready to give him.

Laing continues:

> . . . many things [said by Paul about Peter] cannot be tested by Peter, particularly when Peter is a child. Such are *global* attributions of the form "You are worthless" "You are good." . . . What others attribute to Peter implicitly or explicitly plays a decisive part in forming Peter's own sense of his own agency, perceptions, motives, intentions: his identity.

Most of our schools convey to children a very powerful message, that they are stupid, worthless, untrustworthy, unfit to make even the smallest decisions about their own lives or learning. The message is all the more powerful and effective because it is *not* said in words. Indeed—and here is the double-bind again—the schools may well be *saying* all the time how much they like and respect children, how much they value their individual differences, how committed they are to democratic and human values, and so on. If I tell you that you are wise, but treat you like a fool; tell you that you are good, but treat you like a dangerous criminal, you will feel what I feel much more strongly than if I said it directly. Furthermore, if I deny that there is any contradiction between what I say and what I do, and forbid you to talk or even think about such a contradiction, and say further that if you even think there may be such a contradiction it proves that you are not worthy of my loving attention, my message about your badness becomes all the stronger, and I am probably pushing you well along the road to craziness as well.

Many feel that the Army is destructive psychologically as well as physically, but it is probably far less so than most schools. The Army wants to destroy the unique human identity of its soldiers, so that they will be nothing but soldiers, will have no identity, life, or purpose except the Army and its mission. But the Army at least does not *pretend* to do something else. It does not pretend to value its soldiers as unique human beings, to value their differences, to seek their growth, to have their best interests at heart. It has only its own interests at heart. Soldiers are only means to its end. The message is loud and clear; there is no confusion at all. It does not ask the soldier to like the Army, or believe the Army likes him. It says only, "Do what we tell you, quickly and skillfully. The rest of your feelings are up to you." But schools demand the wholehearted support of those they oppress. It says, "We don't trust you, but you have to trust us."

I am often asked if I don't think that schools are better than they once were, and looking at pictures of some grim old schools, and reading of the schoolmaster and his switch—no different for that matter from the rattan still used, to my shame, in my home town of Boston—I think perhaps in some ways many of them are. Why are they then, as I deeply believe, so much more harmful? The reason is simple. In earlier days no one believed that a person was only what the school said he was. To be not good in school was to be—not good in school, bad at book learning, not a scholar. It meant that there were a few things you could not do or be— notably a clergyman or a professor. But the difference between book learning and other kinds of learning was clear. Most of life was still open, and the growing child had a hundred other ways, in his many contacts with adult life, to show his true intelligence and competence. As Paul Goodman has said, and it cannot be said too often, at the turn of the century, when only 6 percent of our young even finished high school, and half or less of 1 percent went to college, the whole country was run by dropouts. But now all roads lead through school. To fail there is to fail everywhere. What they write down about you there, often in secret, follows you for life. There is no escape from it and virtually no appeal.

One might expect or hope that in this very difficult situation children might be able to count on some help from their parents. For the most part, it has not been so. Laing—still not writing about schools—points up the terror of this situation.

> A child runs away from danger. In flight from danger it runs to mother. . . . Let us suppose a situation wherein the mother herself is the object that generates danger, for whatever reason. If this happens when the pre-potent reaction to danger is "flight" *from* danger *to* mother, will the infant run *from* danger or run *to* mother? Is there a "right" thing to do? Suppose it clings to mother. The more it clings, the more tense mother becomes; the more tense, the tigher she holds the baby; the tighter she holds the baby, the more frightened it gets; the more frightened, the more it clings.

Many black writers have spoken eloquently about the effect on black parents of knowing that they cannot do even the first thing that parents ought to do and want to do for the child, namely, protect him against danger. Black parents, particularly in places where neither they nor their children had even the legal right to life, let alone anything else, have for years been in the terrible position of having to tell their child to do things that he knew, and they knew, and he knew they knew, were in the deepest sense wrong, because to do anything else was impossibly dangerous. Worse, they had to punish their child for doing what they and the child knew was really the right thing to do. Thus, they had to tell their children to be submissive, to be cowardly, to fawn, to lie, to pretend to degrade themselves.

What kept this dreadful situation from driving people crazy was that, in their hearts, they knew that the white man who held their lives in the hollow of his hand *was* their enemy, that he meant them nothing but ill, that they owed him nothing at all, that they were morally justified in deceiving him as much as they could. They might tell a child that they would punish him if he did not call a white man Sir or Boss or Cap'n, but there was never even a second's confusion about whether the white man *deserved* to be so deferred to, whether he had any *right* to these titles. He was *not* better than they, but much worse, only dreadfully dangerous, more treacherous and cruel than any wild beast. Knowing this, they could preserve some shreds of pride, dignity, and sanity.

With respect to the schools their children go to, the position of blacks, other racial minorities, and indeed all poor or lower-income people, is much more difficult. Most of these schools obviously dislike, despise, fear, and even hate their children, discriminate against them in many ways, humiliate them, physically abuse them, and kill their intelligence, curiosity, hope, and self-respect. Yet poor people, except for a few blacks and Mexicans, and they only recently, have on the whole not been able to see that for the most part the schools are their enemy and the enemy of their children.

There is a terrible difference between the position of the poor with respect to the schools and that of oppressed minorities with respect to their oppressors. The black man once had to tell his children to submit to the white, to degrade themselves before him, to do whatever he said and even what he might want without saying, to run no risk of countering even his unspoken wishes. So the poor parent must tell his children to do everything that school and teacher says or wants or even seems to want. As the black parent used to have to punish his children for not doing what the white man said, so must the poor parent when his children get into "trouble" at school. But the oppressed black knew, and could tell his children, and make sure they knew, that because they had to act like slaves, less than men, did not mean that they were less than men. They were not the moral inferiors of the white man, but his superiors, and it was above all his treatment of them that made that clear.

Poor parents do not know this about the schools. As Ivan Illich, one of the founders of the Center for Intercultural Documentation (CIDOC), says, the schools are the only organization of our times that can make people accept and blame themselves for their own oppression and degradation. The parents cannot and do not say to their children, "I can't prevent your teacher from despising and humiliating and mistreating you, because the schools have more political power than I have, and they know it. But you are not what they think and say you are, and want to make *you* think you are. You are right to want to resist them, and even if you can resist them only in your heart, resist them there." On the contrary, and against their wishes and instincts, they believe and must try to make their children believe that the schools are always right and the children wrong, that if the teacher says you are bad, for any reason or none at all, you *are* bad. So, among most of the poor, and even much of the middle class, when the schools say something bad about a child, the parents accept it, and use all their considerable power to make the child accept it. Seeing his parents accept it, he usually does. So far—I hope not much longer—few parents have had the insight of a friend of mine who in his mid-thirties said one day in wonderment, and for the first time, "I'm just beginning to realize that it was the schools that made me stupid," or the parent who not long ago said to James Herndon, author of *The Way It Spozed to Be,* "For years the schools have been making me hate my kid." Even the most cruel and oppressive racists have hardly ever been able to make parents do that.

10

THE TACTICS OF CHANGE

This may be the place to think about what I call "goals" and "tactics," or about "near tactics" and "far tactics." By "goals" I mean simply what we would do, or the way things would be, if we could do them or have them just the way we wanted. By "tactics" or "tactical steps" I mean the things we do or could do, starting from where we are right now, to move in what looks like the right direction, to get a little closer to where we would like to be. Obviously none of us can do things or have things just the way we want. This is particularly and painfully true for teachers.

Many people feel so hemmed in by circumstances, and by people who hold power over them, that they feel it is a waste of time to think about goals. Other people call goal-thinkers "idealists," some wistfully, most contemptuously or angrily. A realist, according to them, and most Americans hate to think of themselves as being anything but realists, doesn't waste time thinking about what might be or ought to be. He looks at his immediate situation, decides what choices he has, and takes the one that seems the least troublesome.

This is not realism at all. Of course we are all walled in by circumstances, in one way or another. But only by trying to push out against the walls can we be sure where they are. Most people, and again teachers in particular, have less freedom of choice and action than they would like. But they almost certainly have more freedom than they *think*. For every teacher, and there have been and will be plenty, who has been fired for innovating, or threatening or defying the system, there are thousands who with no risk at all could do much more innovating or freeing up in their classrooms than they have ever tried to do. If many teachers have told me of their rigid and timid administrators, just as many principals and superintendents have said to me, "What do we do about teachers who won't get their noses out of the textbook and the Teacher's Manual, whose idea of teaching is to do exactly the same thing in the class that they have been doing for twenty years?" And I have too often seen really imaginative materials, which could and should have opened up many possibilities, used by teachers in the most narrow, humdrum, plodding, rote-memorizing kind of way.

If we don't push the walls out they will push us in. Nothing in life stands still. If tomorrow we do not try to get at least a little more life space, more freedom of choice and action than we had today, we are almost sure to wind up with less. G. B. Shaw put it well: "Be sure to get what you like, or else you will have to like what you get."

Some may say here that the freedom one person gains another must lose. Not so. There is no one lump of freedom, just so much and no more, from which everyone must try to claw the biggest share he can get. The greater freedom I have and feel—and in large part I have it because I feel it—has not been won at someone else's expense. To some extent, and I hope more all the time, more freedom for me means more freedom for others—administrators, teachers, parents, and above all students and children. The less we are bound in by some tight and rigid notion of the way things have to be, the more free we all are to move and grow.

There is still another reason why we must continually think about our goals. Without some sense of a goal, and hence a direction, we cannot even make sensible short-run "realistic" decisions. At meetings of educators I have often said, "If I were to ask you what was the best way out of this town, you would ask me where I wanted to go. If I then said that I didn't care where I went, all I wanted was the best route out, you would not think I was realistic, but crazy." Only if we know where we want to go can we decide which of the short-run steps, the near tactical decisions open to us, is the best one. Otherwise we do just what so many "realistic" administrators and policy-makers do—and not just in education—take the path of least resistance. The reason, for example, that our foreign policy-makers are so extraordinarly unsuccessful at defending or even knowing the short-run interests of the country is precisely that they never think about anything *but* the short-run interests of the country. They have no vision of a world they would *like* to live in.

From this private definition of goals and tactics, it is easy to see what I mean by near and far tactical steps. For a school to say that a student need study history only if he wanted to, or as much as he wanted to, would be a far tactical step. A somewhat nearer tactical step would be to say that while students had to study some history, they could study whatever history they wanted, independently, working with an advisor or tutor. A still nearer step would be to have students studying definite history periods—Ancient, Middle European, American, etc.—and in regular classes, but with each student free to decide how he would manage his own studying. A still nearer step would be to use textbooks, but instead of one, a variety. And a very near step can be found in answer to the question I am often asked by teachers: "I have to teach such and such a course, and I am told what textbook I must use; what can I do?" In such a case, we might say something like this: "Here is the textbook we have to use in this course. At the end of the year you're supposed to have a rough idea of what is in it. But how you go into this book is up to you to decide. You can start at the beginning and read to the end, or start at the end and work back to the beginning, or begin in the middle and work both ways, or in any way and whatever way seems most interesting to you and makes most sense."

Most of the suggestions I will make in this book, though not all of them, are fairly near tactical steps. They assume the kinds of schools most children go to and most teachers teach in—fixed curriculums, regularly scheduled classes, and the like. I will not try to say for every step how near or far it is. Each teacher can decide this for himself. Not all will decide the same way. A near step for one may look impossibly far for another.

My aim in this book is not to give all the answers to the question, "What can I do?" There is no end to these answers. I hope, by giving a few answers, to get people to start finding and making their own answers. Before long, perhaps helped or inspired by this book and others, teachers and parents and children themselves will think of countless things to do that neither I nor any other curriculum innovator has yet thought of. For that is where innovation should begin, and true innovation can only begin—at the learning place, home or school or playground or world, in the imaginations and interests and activities of the adults and children themselves.

11

THE TEACHER AS COP

When there is much freedom of choice, we teachers are driven or pulled toward some kind of realism and sanity. When there is none, we are driven toward absurdity, impotence, and rage.

Not long ago, after five months teaching in a ghetto junior high school, a young teacher wrote a letter to her school of education saying, in part:

> It might be that your program is all right and that the inner city school is the unavoidable cause of my dismay (my next subject). But, whatever the classroom situation, it does seem that there should be more extremely closely supervised practice teaching experience in the MAT program.

To which we might ask, supervised by whom? If, as seems to be the case, the people who have been teaching for years in ghetto schools don't know how to do it, how are they going to tell young teachers how to do it?

> How to tell you about [my school]?
> At 8:40 I am meant to be standing in the hall outside my classroom, welcoming in my children, preventing them from running down the halls, killing each other, passing cigarettes, etc. . . .

She seems to suggest that running down the halls, passing cigarettes, and killing each other are all crimes, that one is as likely to happen as another, and that all are equally serious. This alone says a great deal, more than she may be aware of, about this teacher's attitudes toward the students. Perhaps she doesn't mean "killing each other" literally. What then *does* she mean? Do many students kill each other in this school? *Do* many of the students in the school kill each other when out of school? Does this teacher know anything about the lives of the children she is teaching?

> . . . however, I can't make it to the hall because I haven't mastered the taking of the attendance yet. Each day I have four separate attendance sheets to fill out (twice, needs to be done after lunch). A criss and then a cross in blue or black ink. Red pen for mistakes. About eight different kinds of notations for different sorts of lateness . . . postcards home, right then, for those who are absent. "T-slips" for probation for those who are absent five days. At the end of the week there's the fifth attendance form, which involves averages.

What teachers ought to do, all over the country, and what schools of education ought to be encouraging them to do, is quite simply to refuse to fill out these forms. If the schools want to run a jail business, let them find their own jailers, let them devise methods of punching in, as at a factory, let them handle their self-made problem any way they want. But it is not the proper business of teachers, and we ought not to have anything to do with it. Meanwhile, mark everyone present. Or if this arouses too much suspicion, mark only one or two people absent each day. We can hardly suppose that it is good for children to be in this kind of school or classroom, or that in setting the law on them we are doing them a favor.

> Gerald Glass comes bopping in, no longer screaming obscenities with each breath (the threat of a 600 school worked); he leans over my desk and for the third time this week there's liquor on his early morning breath. "Why, Gerald, you know school isn't the place to come in drunk to." "———, I ain't drunk. I know how to hold my liquor." What to say?

What not to say. If I had been in Gerald's shoes, I would have felt insulted by that "drunk," as in fact he was. It is, after all, possible to drink without being "drunk." Furthermore, to suggest to any American, of whatever age, that he can't handle his liquor is a deadly insult—and probably more so in Gerald's culture than in most. He is clearly drinking as a way of proving something about his manhood or fitness for manhood—something precious to him and attacked by everything in the school. Doesn't the teacher know this? She would if she took half a minute to think about it. She would not think of calling a friend or a contemporary "drunk" because she smelled liquor on his breath. But Gerald, being black, young, and a student, is triply sheltered from such courtesies. Would it not have done just as well to say, "Gerald, please don't drink before coming to school"? Looking through his eyes, a very good reason for taking a few nips before school every day would be to annoy a teacher who had no use for him anyway.

> Three minutes to get Juan to sit down; two minutes to get Raul to take off his jacket. Christine refuses to be seated because on her chair is a large obscene drawing. Everywhere there is obscene poetry; a festival of bubble gum, candy wrappers, spitballs, stolen pens, inveterate boredom, carelessness, profound illiteracy.

Three minutes to get Juan to sit down! Why is this worth three minutes? Why half a minute? If there is something worthwhile for Juan to do, he can do it either sitting down or standing; if he can't do it standing, he will sit to do it. If he doesn't think it worth doing, he won't do it *either* standing or sitting. So why three minutes of class time to get him to sit? What is important here?

Why is Raul's coat not Raul's business? Are we to believe that no one can learn anything with one's coat on?

All this worry about obscenity! Who are we kidding here? These once-forbidden words are widely used at every level of our culture and can be found in profusion in books sold widely in the most respectable stores and bought and read by the most respectable people. Why does this crusade seem so important to the schools? The U.S. Navy, in World War II, was much smarter. We, the college-educated officers, did not feel we had to cure the enlisted men of using the obscenities that made up about every fourth word in their language (and quite a few in our own). Nor did we assume that the war against Japan could not begin until obscenity had been driven out of the U.S. Navy. Whose idea is it that obscenity, part of the everyday language of the culture of most poor children, must somehow be driven from the classroom before learning can come in? And why does it not occur to us that this obscenity has a good deal to do with the way they feel about the schools and what we do in them?

Bubble gum, candy wrappers. Does paper on the floor make learning impossible? Stolen pens. Students in one upper middle-class private school where I taught could not keep notebooks, textbooks, pens, often even clothing, in their lockers. All teen-agers, even suburban, have a weak notion of private property. When they need something badly, they take the nearest that comes to hand. Perhaps they mean at the time to give it back; sometimes they do.

Boredom. Almost all children are bored in school. Why shouldn't they be? We would be. The children in the high status and "creative" private elementary schools I taught in were bored stiff most of the day—and with good reason. Very little in school is exciting or meaningful even to an upper middle-class child; why should it be so for slum children? Why, that is, unless we begin where schools hardly ever do begin, by recognizing that the daily lives of these children are the most real and meaningful, and indeed the only real and meaningful things they know. Why not begin their education there? It can be done. People have done it, and are doing it. There are many good books about the way to do it: *The Lives of Children, The Way It Spozed to Be, Thirty-six Children,* (Herbert Kohl), and others. (See my reading list at the end of this book.)

> The whole place is mad and absurd; going to school is going to war. My classes are devoted to trying to get the kids to open their notebooks, stay seated, stop talking, stop writing obscenities in the text, stop asking to go to the bathroom, stop blowing bubbles, stop, stop, stop. We have not started to *learn* yet, I am afraid . . .

The place is mad and absurd, all right; but I am afraid nothing in it is as mad and absurd as this poor young teacher who after all is only trying to do the absurd things her absurd bosses have told her to do. Going to school, as *she* goes, is indeed going to war. But we, the adults, started the war, not the children. They are only fighting back as best they can. We promise poor kids that if they will do what we want, there are goodies waiting for them out there. They know that these promises are false. All this stop, stop, stop. Why is it so necessary? A child will open a notebook when he has something he wants to write in it. If he doesn't want to write anything, what difference whether the notebook is open or not? "We have not started to learn yet . . ." The teacher certainly hasn't, though the children have probably learned a good deal about the teacher, at least how to bug her. Why must all these other things be done *before* the learning starts? Let some worthwhile activity start, and is it not possible that many of these other things will gradually stop, just because they are less interesting? Is it not at least worth a try? Worth some thought?

> For my supervisor I spend at least 15 hours over the weekend making exquisite lesson plans. The effort I put out for them so fatigues, angers, and uses me that Monday morning I'm only ready to tell the whole job to "forget it."

Fifteen hours! Talk about absurd. And all the more so when it was clear that not a tenth of them would ever be put into effect. Was this the least effort that would get by? Did this teacher try, just to see what might happen, to get by on twelve hours? Ten? Six? Did the experienced teachers *all* spend fifteen hours on *their* lesson plans? Of course not. And does this poor teacher believe that her Monday morning feelings were lost on the children, that they did not know what she thought about her "whole job," which was, after all, helping them? We can be sure that they knew, and this knowing did as much as anything else to block their learning.

12

THE TEACHER AS GUIDE

We talk a lot about teachers "guiding" in schools. Most of the time we just mean doing what teachers have done all along—telling children what to do and trying to make them do it. There is, I suppose, a sense in which the word "guide" can mean that. If I guide a blind man down a rough path, I lead him, I decide where he is to go, give him no choice. But "guide" can mean something else. When friends and I go on a wilderness canoe trip in Canada, we plan our trip with a guide who knows the region. We know what we are looking for—fishing good enough to give us a chance to catch our food, a chance of good campsites, trails not too rough to portage and not too obscure to follow, not too many people, no airplanes dropping in, no loggers. We discuss this or that lake, this or that alternative route, how long it would take to get from this place to that. Eventually, using the guide's answers to our questions, we plan our trip. He, knowing the landings, the places— often hard to spot—where the trails meet the lake's edge, comes with us, to help us get where *we* have decided we want to go.

Or, as a friend of mine put it, we teachers can see ourselves as travel agents. When we go to a travel agent, he does not tell us where to go. He finds out first what we are looking for. Do we care most about climate or scenery, or about seeing new cultures, or about museums and entertainment? Do we want to travel alone or with others? Do we like crowds or want to stay away from them? How much time and money do we want to spend? And so on. Given some idea of what we are looking for, he makes some suggestions. Here is this trip, which will take so long and cost so much; here is this one, here is that. Eventually, *we* choose, not he. Then, he helps us with our travel and hotel arrangements, gets us what tickets and information we need, and we are ready to start. His job is done. He does not have to take the trip with us. Least of all does he have to give us a little quiz when we get back to make sure we went where we said we would go or got out of the trip what we hoped to get. If anything went wrong he will want to hear about it, to help us and other clients plan better in the future. Otherwise, what we got out of the trip and how much we enjoyed it is our business.

How do we teachers become good travel agents? Specifically, how do we work with the children? How, and when, and how much, and why do we intervene in their work and learning, start this, stop that, change from one thing to another? How do we get things going? How can we and the children use materials? How does this fit into "regular schoolwork"? This is an important tactical matter. Most of the people teachers have to deal with, some might say contend with, think that Work is what an adult tells a child to do and that schoolwork is done with books, pencil, and paper. Using materials, and exploring them freely, these people call Play. They see it, almost by definition, as useless, if not positively harmful. It may be something that children have to do a certain amount of, like eat, sleep, or go to the toilet, but it is of no real *use,* it doesn't add anything to their schoolwork or learning, or help them get ahead in the world. The less of it we can have, the better. So we need to understand, to reassure ourselves and to convince others, some of what is happening when children "play" with materials, and how this fits into their conventional schoolwork, and how we can help it fit better. Very specifically, how does the play of young children, who need play most and get the most from it—it *is* their work, their way of exploring the world and the nature of things—how does this play fit in with our rather panicky need to get them started on reading and writing? "Panicky" fairly describes how most of us feel about this—and this panic is the source of most of what we call "reading problems." There has just appeared an extraordinarily interesting and important book, by Frances Hawkins, called *The Logic of Action—From a Teacher's Notebook*. It is published by the Elementary Science Advisory Service of the University of Colorado, in Boulder, Colorado, and costs $1.95. Order it from them. It is a most useful companion to this book. Mrs. Hawkins begins:

> There are six stories recorded in these pages, but they rely on translation from the originals—which were told in the language of action. To the infant of our species this is a universal language. But for these particular four-year-olds it was still their only means of communicating; they are deaf.
>
> I speak of the language of action in this study for another reason: because it is also . . . the language of choice. We choose as we act, we act as we choose. The account of these six children is one of manifold encounters with a *planned but unprogrammed environment* [italics mine], and of their choices within it. . . . it is a teacher who must provide the material from which choices are to be made in a classroom.
>
> More than twenty-five years ago my own apprenticeship began in San Francisco, first in a middle class district but then for four years in the slums. . . . And there, with depression children and dustbowl refugees, I lost one blind spot—my middle class "inner-eye," as Ralph Ellison calls that mechanism which interferes with seeing reality. I began to see these children as strong and hungry to learn. *The school administration tried in more than one way to convince me that such children could not really learn very much* [italics mine]. But I was too naïve and stubborn to be persuaded . . . and the children and their parents supported me with much contrary evidence.

More of this evidence can be found in many other places, notably Herbert Kohl's *Thirty-six Children,* Rober Coles's *The*

Children of Crisis, Julia Gordon's *My Country School Diary,* my own *The Underachieving School,* and, from a group of poor village boys in Italy, a book called *Letter to a Teacher.* You can find it in many collections of the writing of poor children: *Mother, These Are My Friends,* or *Talking about Us,* or *The Me Nobody Knows,* or the periodical *What's Happening,* written and published by children in New York City, and perhaps many others.

Mrs. Hawkins continues:

> The group of four-year-olds we came to work with had a special standing in this public school. Their teacher, Miss M., was working under a university-sponsored program called Language Arts, and was not employed by the school. . . . I had been asked by the professor in charge of the Language Arts program to participate in it, to bring variety and enrichment from my experience with children of this age using materials of early science. [I had] one morning a week . . . a fifth of the children's time in school, for some fifteen weeks. Our early visits with Miss M. were pleasant and, in terms of my personal relationship with her, continued to be easy. But I soon realized that in welcoming our efforts she [believed] that *what we brought* had no connection with her Language Arts. If Miss M. sensed any relationship between our visits and her own work, she kept it to herself.

We cannot blame Miss M. for this, or any other schoolteachers. The idea that the wholeness of life and experience could and must be learned by breaking it down into a whole lot of fields, disciplines, bodies of knowledge, skills, each separate and whole, none connected with any other, was not invented by teachers of children, but by our specialists and experts in higher learning. Teachers have been told this for so long that by now most of them, like poor Miss M., believe it.

> . . . [the children] made out of [this situation] the best of two worlds, and took grist for their mills from each. They folded away their once-a-week behavior and interests with us on their days with Miss M., and to some extent they held in reserve their attitudes toward Miss M.'s work while with us. . . . In the beginning we left some of our materials at the school between visits, but

Miss M. indicated to us that this complicated her language work with the children. Until the end of the term, therefore, when Miss M. requested some of the equipment, nothing remained between visits. However . . . our visits were not without effect on Miss M. . . . Because she genuinely liked the children Miss M. enjoyed the evidence of their development and hence generously acknowledged it when she saw that it was furthered by our visits. . . . In return we encouraged her, I believe, to rely on her better inclinations, which the school establishment did not do.

So much for the popular notion that all the adults in school, in their dealings with children, must be consistent. Children learn while still babies that Mommy is not like Daddy, and that neither one of them is the same from one day to the next, or even from one part of a day to the next. They learn—it is one of the most important things they learn—how to sense at any moment what is possible, expected, forbidden, dangerous. It is not children who need and want the rigid order and sameness we find in most schools, but the schools themselves.

In his excellent book *The Open Classroom,* Herbert Kohl points out that in many schools a teacher who is not doing exactly what all the other teachers are doing, and particularly if he is making his classroom more free and interesting and active and joyous, even if he keeps quiet about what he is doing, will probably be seen by many other teachers as a threat. This is not a reason for not going ahead, but we must not be surprised by it.

Now a short quote which shows why I find Mrs. Hawkins' book so valuable. To teachers, who are eager to work with children in new ways, I always say, "I know time is short, and that at the end of a day of teaching you are tired, but try to keep some kind of a journal in which you write down the things you think of doing, and why, and how you do it, and how it all works out. It may some-day help others, and it will certainly help you." My own books, *How Children Fail* and *How Children Learn,* are largely made up of such journals, often written as letters to my friend and colleague Bill Hull, and later to a few others.

Mrs. Hawkins writes:

. . . teachers, some in the field and most entering, have asked me in one way or another that these notes include my own understanding, beliefs, and mode of operating. "Please don't put it down as if it just magically happens," they say. I have tried . . . to take off from a particular incident where the children spell out *for me* the reality of my theoretical understanding of how learning occurs, how they contradict it, or, what is even more to the point, how they add to and change that understanding.

Another important point:

Just how much and what a teacher should know in advance about the children in her class is a matter of disagreement in the field. I prefer to be told little, *to be forced to observe much* [italics mine]. Far from implying that I do not value a child's out-of-school life, this preference means that I do not trust the effect of an information filter . . . created by others' observations and evaluations on my own early analysis.

In other words, we are all too likely to see, and only to see, what we look for, or what we expect to see. If teachers feel they have to read what other teachers have said about the children in their class, they should wait until they have had at least a couple of months to get to know them and to make their own impressions. Every child should have every year—better, every day—a chance to make a fresh start. Gross physical defects, of course, are things we should know about. More often than not we know very little about them. As George von Hilsheimer, head of the Green Valley School in Orange City, Florida, points out in his very important new book *How to Live with Your Special Child,* (Acropolis Press), among troubled and difficult children, even the children of rich parents, there is far more and far more serious ill health than most schools or other helpers of children ever know about. About other kinds of defects I am much more skeptical. Of one fifth grader I was told, on the evidence of the most respectable specialists and experts, that because of severe brain damage there were all kinds of things that he could not do and should not be asked to do or even allowed to try to do—presumably, since his failure to do them would discourage or panic him. Before the year was out the child had done most of these things and many other things far more difficult and complicated, not because I asked him to, but because he wanted to, because this is what his friends were freely doing.

Mrs. Hawkins goes on:

> What concerns me as a teacher is the child's behavior as it reflects his anxieties and joys; his physical posture, energy, and health; his choices and refusals [my note: Dennison is important on the right of refusal]; his habits and humor. To get so wide a picture of a child outside his home requires a classroom rich in challenge and variety with a climate of probing, trying, weighing. If this cumulative information proves inadequate for me to provide well for a child, *then* I must seek help from a parent, a social worker, or a therapist.

Until then, it seems to me, we should let the child decide how much of his life outside the school he wants to share with us. The same at home, too. Many parents are always pumping their children to find out what they did in school and are distressed when, as often happens, the child says, "Nothing much." What the child may be saying is, "Never mind; it's not your business; you don't have to know everything about me."

To young people who ask how they may best prepare themselves to teach, I say, "See as much as you can of children in places other than schools. Spend as much time as you can in situations where you are not a wielder of authority. If you don't quite know a lot about children before you meet them in the classroom, you won't learn much about them there. In most classrooms as they are, and even if the children are being relatively honest with you and not playing con games, what you see will only be a very narrow part of their whole range of behavior." I had the good luck to begin my teaching in a brand-new and very small school, with children new to all of us. Also, since I had no "training," I had never read anything about education. Moreover, in my previous work with the World Federalists, in which I traveled a great deal and stayed with many families with children, I came to know, quite well, and over a number of years, many children—more, perhaps, than most people know in all their lives. It was also my good luck to be not just teaching, but working and living with my students, seeing the whole of their lives, I could not help but know that the stupid and defensive and self-defeating behavior I saw so often in my classes must somehow be caused by me and the class, since outside the classroom none of these children was in any way stupid.

Here Mrs. Hawkins describes what is so very important, the very beginnings of her work with these children.

In the cafeteria that first morning we all sat at the adult-sized table, smallest chins at table level. Miss M. brought a tray . . . with individual milk cartons, straws, and graham crackers for the children. The tray was pushed by the children, in a perfunctory manner, from one to another. There was some silent signaling among them. For example, one would break crackers in a way-to-be-copied, as do hearing threes and fours. The others would copy and then, looking at each other, would eat the crackers to the last crumb. The tray was again pushed from child to child and empty cartons put on it. The routine had been maintained. The adults had coffee and cookies, and *this* adult was not learning enough about the children.

To stimulate some spontaneous (and hence more significant) behavior, I broke routine and put my coffee cup on the children's tray. (Miss M. had politely indicated that our cups should be carried to the kitchen.) Astonishment was the immediate reaction on the children's faces as they looked from each other to my out-of-place cup. Then they expressed their astonishment to one another by pointing as if to say, "Look what that grown-up did." Their change of facial expression encouraged me. I joined their reaction in mock censure of myself and the joke was shared by some. Two or three children cautioned me that I was *not* to do that by shaking heads and fingers at me—with humor.

Feeling that I had succeeded in some sort of exchange with the children I continued. To an accompaniment of louder, stranger throat-laughter (the first I'd heard), I next turned the coffee cup upside down on the tray. Now the laughter turned to apprehensive glances at Miss M.—I had gone too far! Miss M. laughed with relief, I thought, at the way I was failing to fit the school patterns. In turn the children took their cue from her and apprehension became curiosity, a more useful by-product for school. We had established our first channel of rapport, shared over forbidden fruit.

A lovely description of a lovely beginning. It says so much. Play—it cannot be said too often—is children's work, and we cannot learn anything important from them, or help them learn anything important, unless we can play, and play with them. Because we do not understand that children's play is serious, we think the only way to play with children is to do something silly. We make two little equations: serious = solemn and gay = silly. As a result, if we do try to play with children—think what it means that most of us call this "getting down to their level"—we are likely to feel foolish and self-conscious. This is neither any help nor any fun for the children.

We are often told that we must not surprise children, that they must have rigid and unchanging order, set routines everywhere. This is simply pasting our needs onto them. Also, it contradicts what we know about living things at the most fundamental biological level. I forget whose principle it is—name begins with a W, I think—established by thousands of experiments, that as we repeat the same stimulus over and over it loses more and more of its effect. We learn *only* through surprises, through what is new, which is what a surprise is. What we call sensory deprivation is not really the absence of sensation so much as the absence of change. Much of it brings on hallucinations; enough may very well bring on madness.

There is something about Mrs. Hawkins' first play with these children that is very important to understand. She did not, like many adults trying to play with children, force herself on them, violate their privacy and dignity, chuck them under the chin or whirl them about or say silly things to them. Her putting her cup on the tray did not require, or demand, or even ask a response from the children. It was like the courtesy of a person who asks you a favor in such a way that it will be very easy for you to say No. The children were able to refuse without even having to seem to refuse. It is most important, when meeting children of any age for the first time, to approach with this kind of tentativeness, gravity, and courtesy. And it is astonishing how quick most children are to make friends with people who do not ask them, but simply indicate that they are ready.

Back in the classroom, Mrs. Hawkins intervened again. The children were having a free play period. About this a word must be said. Miss M. allowed it without believing in it. I suspect this is the way most nursery schools feel about as much free play as they allow. Mrs. Hawkins says, "My implied belief that the children and I could learn from free play was a welcome but improbable idea for Miss M. 'Most people think nothing of importance goes on in free play,' she said." The decision to give the children this free play period was Miss M.'s, but *she had kept it a secret.* This says a great deal. Then, after the children had played for some time:

> . . . [I introduced] into the arena of three children who were building with blocks a large cardboard box which was used to store the blocks. I tipped it on its side and moved a small truck into it, thinking of a garage. The children's reaction . . . *was indicative of their response to any novelty or variation suggested by an adult. They were amazed at my entrance.* [Italics mine.]

Those seem to me some of the saddest words ever written. They remind me that somewhere a child defined an adult as someone who has forgotten how to play.

There was, I should underline, a totally passive attitude on the part of Miss M. toward the play period. This was in direct contrast to her kindly-authoritarian, sometimes annoyed attitude during Language Arts. In their programming for young children neophytes see their role as either:or—either completely in control, or completely withdrawn. It takes time and experience [my note: and a good deal more than that] to find a more natural way of stepping in and out. That kind of detail cannot be laid out in advance.

This is, of course, what is fundamentally and incurably wrong with the whole idea of lesson plans. It took me years to learn that when I went to a class with every step and every detail of the period thoroughly planned and ready in my mind, it would be a terrible class, the children anxious, timid, trying to con me, saying, "I don't get it," wildly grabbing for answers. If, on the other hand, I went to a class with no more than the faint beginning of an idea, a tentative first step, and often not even that, ready to see what the children had to offer and to work from that, things usually went well.

Visiting a non-coercive school on the West Coast not long ago, and talking with some of the teachers, I said something about adults in such a school sharing some of their interests and skills and enthusiasms with the children. One of the young teachers said scornfully, "Yeah, we'll all be magicians and do our little tricks." I said that I knew what he meant and wanted to avoid, but that for people to tell other people, especially those they like, about the things that interest them and please them is a completely natural and human thing to do. It has nothing to do with some people being older and some younger, or some teachers and some students. If we rule this out in our school or class because of some kind of theory, we make that school or class just that much less natural and human, we are playing a role instead of being what we are. To use a good word of Paul Goodman's, it is inauthentic.

Everyone talks today about the "role" of the teacher. It is a bad way of talking. In the first place it implies that we are pretending to be what we are not, or that in doing what we do we are only playing a part, acting *as if* we were what we appear to be, not truly committing ourselves to the work. In the second place the word "role" is vague. It lumps together many ideas, words, which are different, and ought to be separately understood and used. To teachers who talk about their "role," I say, "What do you mean? Do you mean your task, what someone else tells you to do? Do you mean what you tell yourself you ought to do, what you would do if you could do what you wanted? Do you mean what you actually do, the way in fact you occupy your time in the class? Do you mean someone else's understanding of your function and purposes, that is, *their* reasons for putting you in that classroom, or do you mean your own understanding of that function and purpose, your own reasons for being in the class?" These ideas ought to be kept straight.

Back to Mrs. Hawkins and her interventions:

> But watch the children. When I tipped the large cardboard box on its side, the three builders looked at me with surprised scrutiny. . . . It seemed to question: my role? [my note: What is that lady here for, and what is her relationship to us, how can we safely treat her and respond to her?] whether the box was a plaything? what their response should be? Then with a consensus of action they turned the box back on its bottom and showed me a thing or two.
>
> For many minutes they played: Three could fit inside the box scrunched together. . . . They climbed in and out, one, two or three. . . . They closed the flaps. . . . One sat on top. . . . They knocked on the closed box, with one inside and two out. [Dots are Mrs. H.'s.] On and on and on, oblivious of observers, they invented as they played. The unspoken excitement and exploitation of the box showed me these children internalizing bits and pieces of relational ideas: *inside, outside, closed, open, empty, full.* I mused on how one would use such involvement to build these words into reading and speaking at an appropriate later time.

The word "concept" is also fashionable these days, and there is much talk about "the role of the school in concept formation," etc. Does "concept" mean anything very different from "idea"? Children are good at figuring out ideas. Even these little children, without hearing and without speech, had grasped the meaning of the ideas *inside, outside,* etc. What we can do, and it is often useful, is to help them find our labels *for the ideas they have already grasped.* This is what I have said, in all my books, about children and symbols. Most of the time, we keep giving children new symbols—usually words—and then using other symbols—more words—to tell them what the first words mean. It is a mistake. We must begin by moving from the real, the concrete, the known, to the abstract or symbolic, by talking and writing with them about what they know and see and do. Only after they have many times turned known meanings, their meanings, into symbols will they begin to be able to get some meaning from new symbols. For example, to help a child understand maps, we should not explain them, but let him, help him, *make a map.*

> After school Miss M. and I discussed the episode: how it was obvious that their implicit information around *empty, full, three,* etc. was being put into place *for* these children *by* them, and that appropriate explicit words could follow in reading and speaking, the more easily if one remembered and used such rootlets. [My note: i.e. such experiences with materials.] From this and later conversations with Miss M. I assumed more than I should have about her understanding of the close coupling between the thing and the naming of it. I realized how much a concurrent seminar was needed but circumstances on both sides seemed to make this impossible.

The more things we can give children to *do,* to handle, work with, the greater the chance that from these materials *they* will get ideas that we may then be able to help them turn into symbols or words. Thus in some of my later chapters about measuring I suggest that children do things that students don't ordinarily do until they get to college and take a course called Statistics—and even then they may not *do* them, only read about other people doing them. But children who have done such measuring and comparing can often then be introduced to the names and formulas that a statistician would use to describe what they have been doing. After they get to know a certain number of these formulas, they may be ready and even eager to think about the formulas in general, and about algebra, which can be seen, among other ways, as the language of formulas, a very compressed way of making certain kinds of statements about reality.

Mrs. Hawkins' point about the seminar is also important. Teachers who are beginning to work in new ways with children need a great many opportunities to talk about their work, both with each other and with people with more experience. We may understand an idea, in the sense of knowing in general what it means, and believe in it, and still be a long way from understanding all or even many of its possibilities, applications, consequences, and difficulties. When I first said that children should freely direct and control their own learning, without concern or manipulation or fear, I *thought* I understood the meaning of what I was saying. I know now that I was only just beginning to learn what that meant and implied.

People who work with children in new ways need to be helped to find the meaning of much that is happening in their classes. They are swamped with new experiences, which they have to get into some kind of order. Also, they are anxious about whether they are doing the right thing, or indeed doing anything at all. They need to be reassured. One of the main reasons for the healthy growth of this kind of schooling and learning in Leicestershire County in Great Britain is that the County educational authority, under its director Stewart Mason, and through its advisors, made it possible in many ways for teachers to have these kinds of discussions and to get this kind of support. Any school administrators trying to effect some of these changes must, I think, have some such seminars as a continuing and permanent part of their in-service program. I know it is hard to find time for such things, but time must be found.

One day Mrs. Hawkins brought into the class, among other things, a plastic wading pool (3 feet in diameter), and jars, coffee pots, and syringes.

Everyone tried his hand at the water pool this morning. . . . Phillip, unaware of anyone's scrutiny, would fill his large plastic syringe with water by pulling out the plunger while the tip was submerged, and then shoot the water to the opposite side of the pool. . . . Janie kept watching Phillip's actions. Quite obviously she wanted to do the same thing with her syringe, but she was unable to fill it with water, the first step in this desirable sequence. (Her trouble here is not unique to four-year-olds. We have watched adults . . . pull out the plunger in the air, put the tip of the syringe-tube into the water, then push the plunger down . . . . . nice bubbles rise to the surface, but the syringe does not fill with water.)

. . . After some interest in the unplanned bubbles, Janie turned again to watch how Phillip got water into the stubborn syringe. Then, say Claire's notes, "She *thought* about it." With syringe out of the pool she pushed down the plunger, then put the tip in the pool and slowly pulled up the water into the transparent syringe. . . . To write about it is to some degree to share her pleasure.

. . . Both children are nibbling at some very nice pieces of the real world—a liquid state of matter, volume, space, the reality of air, force, time. We can say that in some sense children do this all the time. But whether our schools appreciate and encourage this kind of engagement by providing time and equipment for children *and* their teachers is a question. We have watched teachers in our laboratory, with no children present, letting themselves explore with color, water, mirrors, mobiles, balances, and pendulums. They are amazed and delighted at the pleasure which accompanies their learning. Others, of course, stand by writing notes in their notebooks, looking for lesson plans or magic formulas, unable to touch and try. Though they have college degrees they are deprived. It is not easy [my note: it is impossible] for a teacher to provide for a kind of learning she does not know and appreciate herself from experience. I digress here to make a plea not only for children, who suffer when a teacher does, but for the many teachers I meet who are unhappy, bored, and lost.

For some years now in Leicestershire County they have held every year a five- or six-day residential workshop for teachers, in which for many hours or days at a time they could do just this kind of experimenting and working with materials and activities in art, science, math, music, movement and dance, and other things. Some of the best moments in these workshops are spent talking with other teachers over coffee or beer. Such workshops are an essential part of the kind of administrative support that teachers get in the county, and that has made such growth possible. Some Leicestershire teachers have given such workshops in different parts of this country—in Boston and Cambridge, in Vermont, where the State Department of Education is doing all it can to further this kind of learning (as is the State Department in North Dakota), and in other places. All the people I know who have taken part in such workshops say, like Mrs. Hawkins, that some teachers plunge right in, using the materials with increasing pleasure and skill, but that many others stand back afraid, like my friend in *How Children Learn,* who would not even touch a pendulum because she did not know what it was "supposed to do." We need to start this kind of training sooner. People often ask me what are the implications for teacher training in the kind of learning I favor. One answer is that we must in as many ways as possible give our student teachers the kinds of choice and control in learning that we hope they will someday give to their own students. We must teach them once again what many of them will long have forgotten—how to play, how to confront the new and strange with curiosity, imagination, enthusiasm, energy, confidence, hope, and joy.

Mrs. Hawkins then makes a point that cannot be too strongly stressed:

. . . [the deaf children], I observed, used too little initiative with *materials provided by the teacher* in lessons or directions; they too closely watched for a routine to follow. [My note: like the supposedly gifted fifth graders I described in *How Children Fail.*] In this again they are not unlike older school children in a bleak setting and more dictatorial atmosphere, who rely less and less on the inner and often competent direction they bring from home. In such atmospheres it is as if the open or disguised denigration of who they are and what they bring from poor homes finally destroys or transforms to violence what it has failed to honor. . . . We see it happen to our children in class after class, with monotonous certainty.

This is, of course, what the drive for community control of schools is about, and why it is so essential.

In the rest of the book Mrs. Hawkins describes the wide variety of materials she brought to the class and the things she and the children did with them. She does so in detail and with great perception, vividness, and life. By the time we finish we feel we know these little children—and we worry about what is going to happen to them, and become of them. I hope what I have said will persuade you to read this indispensable book.

13

THE THEFT OF LEARNING

Many feel, as I used to, that our institutions of higher learning, colleges and universities, are among the more or less helpless and innocent victims of the troubles and divisions of our society. I now suspect they are among the chief causes of them. My reason for thinking this is suggested in the title of this chapter, and more fully in the following quote from Dennison. Late in *The Lives of Children,* after saying why in his opinion even our more enlightened and human educational experts have done so little good, he says:

> What is the social action of jargon? I have said that true communication is communion and change. Jargon is not innocent. The man who speaks it, who prates in front of us of roles and reciprocally operative groups, and evaluative maps, and the aims of the curriculum, and better fits, and superordinate and subordinate persons means to hold us at a distance; he means to preserve his specialty—his little piece of an essentially indivisible whole—precisely as a specialty. He does not mean to draw near to us, or to empower us, but to stand over us and manipulate us. He wishes, in short, to remain an Expert. The philosopher, by contrast, wishes all men to be philosophers. His speech creates equality. He means to draw near to us and empower us to think and do for ourselves.

The fault of our universities, of our intellectuals and academics, is that they have made themselves into Experts instead of Philosophers. They have largely destroyed, for most of us, our so vital sense that the world, human life, human experience, is a whole, and everywhere open to us. They have taken the great common property of human knowledge and experience, which ought to belong to us all, and made it into private property. Like the men who long ago enclosed the common land in rural England, or those who later fenced in much of the open range in our own West, they have cut up our common property into little pieces, fenced them in, put up signs saying No Trespassing and Entrance by Permission Only. About this, I feel much like the unknown people's poet who wrote, about the enclosure of the common lands in England:

> *The law condemns both man and woman*
> *Who steals the goose from off the common*
> *But lets the greater felon loose*
> *Who steals the common from the goose.*

Human experience, knowledge, culture is everyone's. No one ought to have to prove that he deserves it or has a right to it. It ought to have been used for a great upward leveling, to make a universal aristocracy of wisdom and learning. It was and is used instead to make a hierarchy, a pyramid of men, with the learned men self-placed at the top. Let me repeat again, they do *"not mean to draw near to us, or to empower us, but to stand over us and manipulate us."*

I have called this a fault, but it seems to me a moral error so serious that it might better be called a sin or a crime. The learned say to the less learned, "We know more than you, therefore we are better than you, we have the right to tell you what to do, you have no right to question us or argue with us, in fact, you have no right to any serious opinions at all." Examples of this can be found everywhere, not least of all in much fashionable writing about the future, which assumes that our experts will control the lives of most men far more completely than they do today. Not long ago a historian, reviewing a book by a colleague, said of him that he had earned the right to make generalizations, to think about the meaning of history in our lives, by twenty-three years of research. I wondered where that left me, and the rest of us. Was history then none of our business? Were we forbidden to think about it? Were we expected to take on faith whatever any licensed expert might tell us about it? Most people learned in school, like José, that history, and almost everything else that might empower them to think and do for themselves, was not open to them, and was only something against which experts would judge them and find them wanting. So with culture, the arts, everything that might have added to the quality of their lives. James Conant said not very long ago that liberal education should be for only about 15 percent of the people; for the rest, vocational training would be enough. Few learned men protested. Nor does the so-called average man, well trained in his schooling. He thinks, Art, music, dance, theater, books, writing, learning, ideas, words themselves—all that fancy stuff is not for me. Give me something that will help me make more money. When he complains about what he calls "student riots," it is because he thinks they are costing him money. A student gave me not long ago a paper assignment that one of his English professors had given him. It read, in part, as follows:

> Write a paper upon some aspect of Shakespeare's dramatic technique utilizing two or three plays. The paper should be 5–8 pages, typed on bond paper. It must use correct footnote and bibliography forms. (Buy an *MLA Style Sheet* from any bookstore for 50¢ if you are not sure about correct forms.) . . .
>
> For this paper you will study the plays as compositions, analyzing any one of the ways Shakespeare uses to make each aspect of his composition successful. Some of the elements of dramatic composition you could consider (with a few of the possible perspectives from which you could consider them) would be: [My note: I have listed this professor's elements, but left out his perspectives, of which there were several for each element.] verse; characterization; kinds of action; uses of theme; uses of the stage and/or stage effects; decorum; kinds of dramatic structures; ways of revealing the central values of the ultimate force in the play's

universe; the kinds of values the plays present, or the kinds of force they assert to be real; the parts of the composition which function as antagonists; kinds of speech; ways in which the plays are unified—or not successfully unified; act and scene divisions; kinds of acting techniques required; uses of comic elements in serious plays.

In each case the point of your discussion will be why these elements are made as they are. Your intention will be to analyze the element you discuss and provide a basis for analyzing its effectiveness in the plays you discuss. You should show why it works or fails to work, why its use is more successful than its use in another. . . .

The objective of the assignment is to give you a chance to examine the plays as artistically composed structures. The great plays are not great because of their stories, people, or ideas. They are great because their elements are brilliantly chosen and shaped as well as efficiently utilized. Their greatness is clear *only when* [italics mine] one sees how these less extensive patterns work, and then sees how they work together in a play to create a single all-inclusive pattern.

This is not an easy assignment. But when you complete it you can be *fully aware* [all italics mine], in *at least one specific and concrete way,* why some of these plays are *as awesome* as they are.

How well we know the voice of this teacher. He seems to be praising Shakespeare; in fact he is praising himself. Shakespeare does not belong to people like you and me, but to people like him. "The great plays are not great because of their stories, people, or ideas." In short, not for any of the reasons that clods like you and me might have expected. "Their greatness is clear only . . ." Shakespeare is a mystery, a labyrinth. The experts like him have the key, and you and I cannot come in unless he lets us in. "You can be fully aware, in at least one specific and concrete way . . ." Note the tone of that *at least.* Even after writing this paper we will only be aware of one way, one little way, in which these plays are "awesome." Our expert has many other secrets and mysteries. The heart of the temple is still closed to such as you and me. One wonders how the plays survived, in what strange ways people came to know and love them, before these experts came along to show the way.

We can find more examples of this kind of arrogance, and contempt, in a splendid new book about the teaching of English and particularly writing, *Up Taught,* by Ken Macrorie, Professor of English at Western Michigan University, and published by the Hayden Press in New York City. It has some superb writing by students. It also has some superb examples of the way many university people talk to students. Here are three samples:

> You will consult at least fifteen separate sources, half of which are books, and half periodicals. Take notes on 4 x 6 cards, not 3 x 5, and be prepared to present them upon demand. Bibliography and footnotes will follow the MLA style sheet. At least one thousand words, with a cover sheet that includes a statement of purpose. The paper should have a clearly indicated introduction, body, and conclusion. Do not use the word "I" except in the conclusion of the paper.

Found in the hall near a classroom for the Humanities course:

Letters to students

Nr. 8

I would like to make one thing absolutely clear:

Shoddy essays mirroring shoddy thought will not obtain a passing degree.

Shoddy thought indicated that the student concerned did not cooperate to reach a reasonable degree of EFFICIENCY LEVEL, and that his INFORMATION LEVEL is completely unsatisfactory.

Dean and Area Chairman rightly insist on essays being properly planned, well arranged and written in fluent good English that a university student of medium ability should master without difficulty.

Essays should not be written in a way that avoids all study and effort, and, superficially, gives the impression of personal conclusions as arrived "after careful consideration of underlying facts."

Essays have to account for facts. Essays have to state generally accepted ideas about facts. Essays can state personal opinions or personal conclusions which do not conform with generally held views as long as some logically ordered reasoning has been added that warrants deviation in opinion or judgment of the writer of the essay concerned.

Macrorie points out, as he hardly needs to, that even by the standards English teachers think are important this is a dreadful piece of writing. Here is one more sample:

> Part of a dittoed memorandum for students.
> ASSIGNMENTS: For each assigned book you must turn in a statement of thesis for each chapter or section of each book. All thesis statements should begin, "The thesis of chapter—is. . . ."
> ATTENDANCE: I expect you to be in attendance at all class meetings. It is my choice as to how to handle absences. Since absences can affect the grade a person receives, I am sure you will want to take this into consideration before being absent.
> PARTICIPATION: As I expect you to be in class, I also expect you to participate in class discussion. My teaching method is to get at important aspects of the subject matter through discussion. The dialogue is really the heart of the class. I expect you to contribute; if you don't there are penalties involved. If you are the intelligent, but "strong and silent type," I suggest that you find a class or an instructor that better suits your silence and recalcitrance . . .

There is no need, and no way, to comment on this. Imagine having to spend a year in the company of such a man. Imagine having to know books through him. Imagine having your future career depend on him. May we hope he is an exception? No help for us there; as Macrorie and many others have shown, he is all too typical. Where then does all his arrogance and contempt come from? Macrorie answers:

> Looking back to my graduate school days, I realize where the notion that American students are dull and inept human beings comes from. At the highest reaches of teaching, where adults are studying for the Ph.D. and M.A. degrees, students are demeaned, and there they learn the arts of demeaning others.
> Every six months or so the head of my department in that graduate school would hold receptions at his apartment and I would tell my wife I wouldn't go, but I always went. There one evening I remember one of my fellow students was asked to slice the ham. I think it was the head's wife who asked him, ever so gaily, so that everyone could hear. He trembled, a young man with few social graces and reason to believe he was on the edge

of flunking out of graduate school. He said he'd rather not, and was led to the table and given the knife. One of my friends leaned over to me and whispered that this was the symbolic carving. Each year, he said, a questionable man is treated in this manner.

This is a terrible story. And it should be noted that the graduate school was a famous one at one of our "best" universities. How has it happened that these institutions of higher learning, supposedly devoted to truth and all the highest human values, should have produced so many people of such extraordinary meanness of spirit? Macrorie speaks eloquently to this point:

At moments I look at all professors, including myself, with understanding. We are no less victims of the system than our students. In the schools we were brought up as slaves. Someone or something opened to us the possibility of becoming overseers. We submitted to the required trials, said, "Yes sir," to the professors in graduate school and moved out of slavehood. But we did not escape the system. That was not presented as a possibility. So we stayed with slavery, as overseers. Some of us acted more decently and liberally toward the slaves than others, but like the best slaveowners—Thomas Jefferson, for example—we perpetuated a system *which robs young people of their selfhood.* [Italics mine.]

Now I realize why the tone of this book oscillates between bitterness and charity. Writing it, I felt like the person who confronts the reality of the extermination of Jews under Hitler's regime. In Germany and elsewhere, all men who allowed that to happen, including German Jews, were responsible, but not responding. We permitted the most massive attempt at genocide ever undertaken. Where were we? What were we?

We say we didn't know. The systems, old and new, had taught us not to notice what happened to Jews. Or if we noticed, not to talk, not to stir up trouble. So there's the reasonable explanation. It must be given weight.

Yet the criminality of our neglect should be shouted to the hills.

I don't think the comparison is much overdrawn. I suspect the German universities, with their arrogant and vain and status-proud learned men, had much to do with the alienation of the German people that paved the way for Fascism. I use the word "alienation" very carefully, not just to mean the sense of being vaguely discontented, but in the precise sense of feeling out of place, or having no place. In that same sense our universities have done much to alienate people here, and to a most dangerous degree prepared the ground for some native American brand of Fascism, which now seems uncomfortably close. I am not interested in blaming them any more than any other people in the schools. But let us not pretend that the pure and lofty message of the universities somehow gets lost or adulterated on its way down through the lowly secondary and primary schools. The message is the same all the way. There is a clear, straight, and unbroken line from the child sitting bored and terrified at his desk to the Ph.D.

What we don't have, and must have, is freedom—to choose or to reject, to use as we please. We speak of great literature, great art, great music, great ideas. What makes them great is not that they are so complicated or difficult that only a few can make use of them, but precisely the opposite, that they have more possibilities of pleasure and growth, because there are more ways of using them and getting something out of them. The people who first saw Shakespeare's plays, or heard the music of Bach, were not most of them learned men.

But a man cannot say Yes to something with all his heart unless he has an equal right to say No. Only those who have said Yes to it can and do keep a cultural or human tradition alive.

14

THE WHOLENESS OF
LEARNING

Let me sum up what I have been saying about learning. I believe that we learn best when we, not others, are deciding what we are going to try to learn, and when, and how, and for what reasons or purposes; when we, not others, are in the end choosing the people, materials, and experiences from which and with which we will be learning; when we, not others, are judging how easily or quickly or well we are learning, and when we have learned enough; and above all when we feel the wholeness and openness of the world around us, and our own freedom and power and competence in it. What then do we do about it? How can we create or help create these conditions for learning?

Perhaps I can make more clear what I mean by the wholeness of learning or experience by talking about my own discovery of mathematics. At school, I was always a fairly good math student. It bored me, but it didn't scare me. With any work at all, I could get my B. But after many years I knew that although I could do most of the problems and proofs and remember the theorems and formulas, I really didn't have the slightest idea what it was all about. That is, I didn't see how it related to anything—where it had come from, what it was for, what one might ever do with it.

Some years after I left the Navy I came across a series of

books, written to help people with little or no math training understand some of the new and large ideas in mathematics. They were written by a Mr. and Mrs. Lieber. The first of them was *The Education of T. C. Mits.* There was a character called SAM, whose initials stood for Science, Art, and Mathematics. The point of the books was that people should not be afraid of new ideas in these fields, and that if they took the plunge, exposed themselves to them, they would find them not so terrifying or difficult.

The books themselves were very well done. Mr. and Mrs. Lieber, in one sense at least, were excellent teachers. They would have been very good at writing out programs. They understood how easily and quickly a learner, moving into new territory, is frightened by uncertainty, contradiction, or logical steps that cover too much ground. So they were very careful to define their terms in words the learner would understand, to move ahead slowly and patiently, taking time to illustrate their points and to reassure the reader. Anyone who didn't panic could follow them through their argument.

But at the end of each of their books, though I had enjoyed being able to follow them on their journey, and liked the feeling of knowing something I hadn't known before, I was still uneasy, dissatisfied. I was not sure why. It seemed that there must be more to this new idea than I had been told. I was not able to bring my unease into focus, to get hold of it, find words for it, until I had finished their book on *Galois and the Theory of Groups.* I had been able to follow them, step by step, to the end of the book. But at the end I felt as if I had been blindfolded and then led along a carefully prepared path. "Now put your foot here, easy now, that foot there . . ." I didn't stumble, but I wanted to take the blindfold off and say, "Where are we, anyway? How did we get here? Where are we going?" What had led Galois to invent this theory? What had made it seem worth inventing? Had he been working on a problem that he and others had not been able to solve? What was the problem, what had he and the others been doing to try to solve it, what had started him in this direction? As it was presented to me, the Theory of Groups seemed disconnected from everything, or at least anything I could imagine. And once Galois had started to work on it, had he made any false starts, gone down any dead ends? Or did he go straight along, like the Liebers? And then, when he got the theory worked out, came to where I was at the end of the book, what did he do with it, how did he use it, where did he go next? Did it help him with the problem he had been trying to solve, and how?

In short, I felt like saying to my patient and hard-working guides, the Liebers, "Thanks for your help, but you haven't told me anything important, you've left out the best part."

Some years later, a former pupil and good friend of mine, then at college, was meeting calculus for the first time. Like many people, he was having trouble. He had the feeling I had had years before of being able to go through the motions, writing formulas and doing problems, but without any idea of what they were all about, seeing them only as a kind of mumbo-jumbo, meaningless recipes for getting meaningless answers to meaningless questions. He asked me one day if I would try to make some sense of it for him. I said I would. I began by trying to give him a very rough idea of the problem, philosophical as much as mathematical, that had started man on his search for the calculus. (What little I knew about all this I had picked up after I left school.) So I talked about the Greeks trying to think about instantaneous motion, described some of the Paradoxes of Zeno—the arrow, Achilles and the tortoise, etc. At any instant the arrow is not moving, since motion is distance covered in time; but then, since time is made up of a sum of instants, how can motion be possible? It is easy to say, if a car traveled five miles in ten minutes, its average speed in that time was thirty miles per hour. But what does it mean to ask how fast it is going at any instant, and how can we find out?

My friend saw the sharpness of the dilemma. I then showed how Cartesian or coordinate geometry made it easier to think about the problem, and thus prepared the way for men to solve it, by giving us a way to make a picture or map of something moving at various rates in space and time. We simply plot a graph of distance traveled against time. It could then be seen that the average speed between two points could be seen as the slope of the line joining them on the graph. From there we could see that the question: How fast is this object going at a particular instant?, could be asked as: What is the slope of the curve, or the tangent to the curve, at that particular point? We had then to find out what happened to that slope as the interval of time became smaller and smaller, and indeed what it meant to have something approach zero as a limit. My friend and I did some arithmetic, some algebra, derived the general formula for the differential at a point—all stuff he had had in the course. But now he said, "So that's it. Why didn't anybody tell me that? It's so simple when you see what it's about."

Exactly. What I had done, clumsily enough, was not to try to hand him a lump of knowledge, which people had already handed him and which he could not take hold of, but to take him on a kind of human journey with the people who had first thought about and discovered these things.

MEASURING AND COMPARING I

In these next few chapters I will be trying to suggest some answers to the question of the wholeness of learning or experience in the particular field of numbers, arithmetic, and mathematics. More specifically, I will be trying to suggest ways to bring to children both in home and school some of the continuum of man's experience with numbers. Instead of wasting endless time trying to get children to memorize meaningless and disconnected "facts" and recipes, we should use numbers inside the classroom to do what people use numbers to do outside the classroom—to measure, compare, analyze, predict.

Let's imagine ourselves working with an elementary school child or children, perhaps at home, perhaps in some kind of learning center, or in a regular schoolroom. We are going to be doing some experiments, measuring as accurately as we can, and over a period of time, the height of a number of children in the group. There are many ways to do this, and one experiment, sometime during the year, might be to have the children see how many such ways they could find. For the method I have in mind, we will need some materials:

1. A plumb bob. This is a weight, shaped rather like an old-fashioned top, that can be hung on the end of a string to give an accurate vertical. Surveyors use them; they can probably be found in stores that sell draftsmen's equipment, or perhaps a good hardware store.

2. A short carpenter's level.

3. An architect's scale. This is a ruler, triangular in cross section, so that there are six different measuring edges. Each of these has a different scale on them.

Note: A long carpenter's level might do the work of numbers two and three here.

4. A steel measuring tape, found in any hardware store.

5. A roll of narrow-width adding machine tape.

We could find or make substitutes for all of these except the measuring tape and the level. Knowing what a plumb bob looks like, we might find or make a weight of similar shape. The architect's scale is only being used as a flat piece of wood in this experiment—any very flat piece would do. And we could cut strips of paper instead of using the adding machine tape. But the adding machine tape is useful for many other things—I suggest some in *How Children Learn*. The plumb bob will be invaluable if the children do any surveying or mapping, excellent ways into both geography and mathematics. And the architect's scale can be very useful in mathematics; indeed, children will be nibbling at numbers and proportions in many ways if they just look and play with it. So these are probably good things to have around. They are inexpensive and durable, and the fact that adults use them in their work will make them interesting to many children.

One way of starting the experiment, if the children are old

enough to go to stores alone and buy things, might be to give the children the task of finding out where to get these materials, and then, with money supplied by the teacher, to go get them.

Many schools will not buy these materials for a teacher or class, for a number of reasons, none of them any good. If that is the case, we must try to beg, borrow, or buy them ourselves. A book could be written, and I hope will soon be written, about materials for classrooms, and how and where to get them for little or nothing. Resourceful teachers already know or can soon find out much about this. All I will say here is that it is our responsibility as teachers to have in our classrooms what the children need, to make a rich and varied environment for them to live, learn, and grow in. "The school won't let me get anything" is not an acceptable alibi for barren and dreary classrooms.

Most of the children will not have seen the plumb bob before. We might well have some conversation like this: "What is it used for?" It is used in surveying, and in building, to get a vertical line. "What does vertical mean?" It means what you get when you hang a weight, like a plumb bob, on a string—a line, going straight up and straight down. Pointing toward the center of the earth, or actually the center of gravity of the earth. "What does center of gravity mean?" "Is there some other kind of center?" "Is the center of gravity always at the other center?" "Suppose it isn't—then what?" To answer that last question we might get some kind of plastic ball that can be taken apart, if such can be found, and tape a weight to a spot on the inside of the ball. Then put the ball together and roll it. Most of the children will not have seen a ball roll that way, or imagined it possible. The eccentric ball will be popular. Little children may want to think up names for it, or for what it does, the way it moves. Someone might want to imitate it, do a dance like it.

"Why is it called a *plumb* bob?" Someone else may say that it doesn't look like a plum, it looks more like a pear. Kids of a certain age will find this very funny. Someone may suggest that it be called a pear bob. Good idea—inside the class, where everyone knows what you mean. Outside, where everyone else calls this thing a plumb bob, it will make more sense to call it that.

It is called a *plumb* bob because these bobs were once made of lead, which is *"plomb"* in French. Hence our word "plumber"— a man who works with lead. "What does a plumber do with lead?" He uses melted lead, or used to, to seal up the joints in pipes, so that they wouldn't leak under water pressure. Now plumbers may use other metals or alloys. "Why did they use lead?" Because it melts easily, at a much lower temperature than the metal the pipe is made of. The children will see, or they may ask, why that is important. Something to think about. "What other things do they use?" I don't know; you may have to ask a plumber. "What are alloys?" Mixtures of metals; you may be able to name some common ones. "Why do they mix metals?" Because sometimes a mixture of metals has properties, does things, that none of the pure metals does. Brass and bronze are tougher, harder (they don't mean the same thing, by the way), and stiffer than the copper or tin or zinc that go into them. Just as important, they resist corrosion. "What is corrosion? What causes it?" More things to think about. "What are pipes made of?" Sometimes cast iron, sometimes clay or copper, sometimes even plastic though plumbers don't like to have plastic pipes used in building, and get building codes passed to prevent it. Why? Because a man who has spent years becoming an expert in using hot metals to seal up metal pipes doesn't want to see plastic pipes used, because then he won't have anything to do, no job, no way to make money. And so forth.

It is vital that we *not* imagine ourselves standing up in front of the class with these objects, asking them what they are, and trying to pull these questions out of the children in a "discussion." The time for these questions to come out will be when we are using the materials. Nothing will turn the children off faster than the usual scene—children at their desks, teacher in front. "Now children, does anyone know what this is called?" Silence. "It is called a plumb bob. Isn't that a funny name? I wonder if anyone of you knows why it is called that?" . . . "Well, it is because . . ."

The carpenter's level is another interesting gadget. Some of the children may have seen one, know what it is used for, perhaps even used it. Many will not. "What is this for?" Carpenters use it, when they are building a house, or putting in shelves or cabinets, to make sure that floors, table tops, shelves, and so on, are level. "Why do they do that?" Something else to think about and discuss.

The children may ask how the level works. We can invite them to figure it out. They will put it on various things—books, tables, etc.—tipping them to a slope and seeing what happens to the bubble. "Why does the bubble do that?" We do not need to hurry to answer the question. Something more to think about and work on. If after a while no one has made any progress, we might get a bottle, preferably with clear and straight sides, fill it almost full with water, stopper it (with your thumb if nothing else is handy), and then tilt it back and forth. The children may ask, "What are you doing?" We say "Watch," and just go on doing it—always the best answer to that question. If there is some clear plastic tubing in the class—another good thing to have—you or the children can fill a tube almost full of water, stopper it, and then tilt it one way, then another. The air bubble will rise in the bottle or tube. In time, the children will see.

One point of this is that the real world out there is not divided up by dotted lines into a lot of little areas marked Physics, Chemistry, History, Language, Mathematics, etc. In the real world, one thing leads to another, each thing is connected to every other thing. The whole world can be explored starting from any place, wherever a child happens to be at the moment. We don't have to be afraid that a child's natural curiosity will make him a narrow specialist. Quite the opposite; it will lead him more and more out into the great oneness of the world and human experience.

A memory about bubbles. When I was little—ten, maybe younger—I used to like to play a game with the washcloth in the bathtub. I would lift up the wet washcloth into a kind of parachute shape, trapping some air under it. Then I would carefully gather in all the edges of the washcloth into my fist, making a kind of washcloth balloon. Then I would slowly draw this trapped bubble of air under water. I could feel it pulling up on my hand. If I squeezed the washcloth a little, a few tiny bubbles of air would leak through and come to the top of the water. The same would happen if I poked it. I could speed up or slow down the flow of bubbles, and if I squeezed hard all the air would come out at once. I played that game thousands of times. I loved feeling how hard the washcloth pulled up, and the nice firm-squishy feeling of the trapped air, and the fact that I could make just a few teeny bubbles come out if I wanted. Do all children play this game? We could ask them, or someday give a demonstration in class. Do some kinds of cloth hold air better than others? What happens with plastic, or Saran Wrap?

How are we going to use our materials? The plumb bob is so that we will be measuring up on an accurate vertical from the floor. The level is to make sure that the thing (in this case the architect's scale) that we put on top of the child's head, and over to the wall against which we are measuring, is level, since if it tipped it would throw the measurement off. Why go to this much trouble? One point is to show the children the kind of trouble people have to go to when they want accurate measurements. Seeing them, some children may think about other possible sources of inaccuracy—different thicknesses of socks, people not standing up equally straight or holding their heads the same way each time, or perhaps changes in the way we read the level or in the thickness of the pencil point with which we mark. One of the things we could do, to find out how important these are, would be to take a number of different measurements of the same child, having him step away from the wall each time and then go back, to see how much variation there was in our measurements. The children might find, like people in the larger world, that to get a really accurate measurement you must take several, and then use the average. This might in turn lead into the question of what is meant by the average of a number of measurements, and what are some ways (there are more than one, some easier than others) to find it.

Another reason for accurate measurement is that we are going to be measuring perhaps every week or so, and want to be able to detect very slight changes in the children's heights. This raises another question. How often is it sensible to measure? How often is too often? These are things that older children, at least, might think about and discuss. If a child grows, say, an inch and a half in the school year of nine months, then he is growing at about a sixth of an inch per month. Is this a noticeable, measurable difference? This is about a twenty-fourth of an inch per week. Can we measure that? What is the limit of accuracy of our measurement? Can we measure accurately the amount each child grows in a day? Does the rate of growth change much from one day to the next? What happens when someone gets sick? Stays up late? Does this make a difference we can measure?

Then what about different thicknesses of socks? How much variation does this make in our measurements? To find out, we could on a given day measure a particular child wearing thin socks, medium heavy socks, and thick socks. If the difference is noticeable, we could figure out how much to correct for it, and apply that to all measurements taken in the rest of the year.

If the children were poor, they might be embarrassed by the possibility of having others see holes in their socks, etc. It might then be better to start measuring everyone with shoes on, and wait for a child to suggest that the thickness of the shoe could affect the measurement. Or we might get a supply of the kind of hygienic paper slippers used around some public swimming pools, or in locker rooms, and measure everyone wearing them, over socks or perhaps over bare feet. Or we could suggest the alternatives to the children, and let them discuss and decide what would be the best way to do it.

Now for the measuring itself. If there is a closet inside the room, and if our plumb bob or long level shows us that the edge of the door jamb is vertical, we can use that to measure against. If there is no inside door, we must pick a space somewhere against the wall. We use our plumb bob to make a vertical line up the wall.

Then we use our steel measuring tape to measure up one of those lines just a little *less* than the height of our shortest child. If the shortest child is, for example, 43½ inches tall, we would measure up 43 inches. There we would mark, very carefully, right beside the vertical line, using the point of a pin or compass, a tiny hole, with a lightly penciled arrow to help us find it each time. This is our base mark. When we are ready to start measuring, we cut or tear off a length of adding machine tape, just a little *longer* than the difference between the heights of the shortest and tallest children. We tape this to the wall, so that its edge is right along our vertical line. We mark very carefully on the edge of this tape the point directly beside our base mark on the wall. Up comes the first child, and stands, back against the wall, his centerline, so to speak, in line with the edge of the tape. We put the architect's scale, or a very straight and flat piece of wood, if we don't have the scale, on the highest part of his head. On top of the wood we put the carpenter's level. (It will be handier to stick it on with masking tape or something like that, so that the wood and the level may be held with one hand.) We make the wood as level as we can, and then we mark with a very sharp pencil, or perhaps a pointed pin, compass, or scribe, the place where the underside of the wood touches the edge of our tape. The child steps away, we label that dot with his name, and we are ready for the next child. When all the children have been measured, we take down our tape, and measure the distance between the base mark and the dot for each child. Thus, if the base mark was 43 inches from the floor, and the individual mark for a child was 2½ inches up from the base mark, he is 45½ inches high.

There are several advantages of using tape and measuring from a base mark. The children may ask why we do it this way, instead of just putting a mark for each child and measuring up each time from the floor. The children might ask why we do it that way. You can tell them, or leave it as something to think and talk about. Either way is fine. Some of the reasons are these. If we mark on the wall instead of the tape, we not only run the risk (very serious in most schools) of getting in trouble with the custodian, but we also have to erase or clean off the wall every time so that we can see the new marks. Also, each time, we lose our original data, whereas if this is marked on a tape, we can date and save the tape. By measuring up from a base mark each time, we avoid whatever errors we might have in measuring up from the floor. Any error that we had in our first base-mark measurement remains constant throughout the year, which is fine, since what we are interested in is the *change* in children's heights. Also, it is less trouble to take down the tape and do our fine measurements on the top of a table or desk than to do all our measuring against the wall.

Assume now we have our measurements. If the class is very large, and many children are near the same height, we may have to use more than one adding machine tape in each day's measuring. We then take the tapes down and mark them; they are our original data. Then we measure the distances on the tape, as I have described, and from this get the height of each child. We can record this—at many places along here the children, or some of them, may want to help, which is fine—in a notebook, marked in columns—a height book, instead of a grade book.

What are some other things we can do with these heights? There are many. We can figure the median height for the class, and also the average. Children may ask what these words mean. They are not the same. The average is the sum of the heights divided by the number of children. The median is that height such that half the children in the class are taller than it, and half are shorter. We can figure the height-to-age ratio for each child in the class, and then the average of the height-to-age ratios for the whole class. The older children might ask whether we can do this by dividing up the sum of all the heights by the sum of all the ages. Will that come out the same as the average of the individual height-age ratios? The answer is No, though some children may insist that it ought to be Yes. How can we show, and prove, that they are different? Can some of the students find a way to do it? Such questions as this lead us to the question of what algebra is all about, what it is used for, what it was invented to do.

Having an average height-to-age ratio for the class, we can compare it with the ratio for other classes in the same school. If we have done this in previous years, we can compare the ratio of this class with the ratio for previous classes. We can look at the height-age ratio for all classes in the school (if we can get such figures) and see whether the ratio itself remains more or less constant as children grow older (until they stop growing), or whether and when it changes.

We can also do some of these things for a height-weight ratio. Does this tend to remain constant from class to class? Does it tend to remain constant for a particular child as he grows older? Have people in the larger world studied these figures for large numbers of people and if so, who and why? (Doctors or physiologists would probably know something about this.) What is the average height-weight ratio of the school's football team? Basketball team? How does it compare between girls and boys?

One of the most interesting things we can do with our heights is to plot them on a graph against time. We can do this for the children at the start; soon, depending a little on age and skill, many or most of them will want to do this for themselves. We should get 10 squares/inch graph paper or finer, so that we can get the whole year's growth on one graph. Along the bottom, or horizontal axis of the graph, we can plot the dates. The heights we can plot vertically. Here we run into the question of scale. Do we want to make 1 inch on the vertical axis of the graph equal 1 inch change in height? This will enable us to see on the paper how much the child has actually grown. On the other hand, if we enlarge the scale, if we let 4 inches on the graph equal 1 inch change in height, we can see more easily the changes in the rate of growth, and possibly the effect of such things as being sick, or going on a very pleasant vacation. Perhaps we can put both lines on the same graph, a blue line in one-to-one scale, a red line in the four-to-one scale. On a big graph on the wall of the class we could plot the average class height against time. Or, on one graph, using lines of many different colors, some broken, some dotted, some solid, etc., we might plot the heights of everyone in the class. (This would be more exciting to look at on an enlarged scale.)

I have described this measuring in some detail to give some sense of the feel, the style, of the kind of open and active classroom we are trying to bring about. Also, I want to suggest some of the ways in which one thing can and will lead to another, if we let it— the great number of possibilities for thought, discussion, work, and learning that lie in the simplest objects or ideas.

On the other hand, this book is not meant to be a Teacher's Manual, telling exactly what must be done and exactly how to do it. Nor am I saying that anyone ought to or must do in his own class the kind of measuring operation I have described. It would probably be interesting, and I would certainly try it out in any class of my own. But if, as you think about it, it seems boring, or artificial, or silly, if you can't imagine yourself doing it without self-consciousness, don't try it. Try something else. You must not role-play in class—except in special situations in which everyone knows that is what you are doing. The rest of the time, be yourself.

This measuring might not work equally well with all children. Very young children might not understand or be interested in the need for such accurate measurements. They might not be interested, either, in the slow day-to-day progress of their growth. If we tell a six-year-old that he has grown a thirty-second of an inch since we last measured him, he may just look blank. Perhaps this careful measuring might interest some children and not others. Then we can measure the interested ones and skip the others. If they say, "How come not me?" Invite them in. A good way to check interest is to "forget" and see if any of the children remind us. "Aren't we going to do any measuring today?" From the way they say it, we can sense whether they are hoping for a No answer, or a Yes. Perhaps the whole class will forget for a week, or several weeks. Then someone may say, "Hey, how come you don't measure us any more?" We must not reply by saying we thought they were not interested. There is a kind of blame implied in this—here I think of all these lovely things for you to do and you don't even care—that the children won't miss. We don't want them to spend a lot of their time in class wondering if by saying No to something we suggest they will be hurting our feelings. So we just say, Shall I measure you today? and if they answer Yes, start the project again. The point is not to let this become another dead class routine, but to be ready to move with the interests of the children.

Perhaps seventh- or eighth-grade children will find the whole business of measuring heights a bit babyish. They know they are growing. Indeed, some of the girls may be growing much more than they want to. Just the mention of height may be embarrassing to them. If some of the more scientifically or mathematically inclined students are interested in the project as an experiment, we can let them take it over, and work out with their classmates the question of who gets measured and who doesn't. Also the time of measurement; there is no reason why all the measuring has to be done at one time in the day. Let the children do the measuring at times convenient to them.

The chances are that this measuring, as a whole-class and all-at-once activity, will be most interesting to third, fourth, and fifth graders. Children at this age are enthusiastic and sociable, and would enjoy the group measuring both as an experiment and as a get-together and ritual. The thing to do, with all such projects, is to try them out, and take our cues from the children. Let them show us, by their honest reactions, the best times and ways to do this work, or whether to do it at all.

We must always be ready to give up pet projects when they do not catch the interest and enthusiasm of the children, and to let them take the projects off in directions that we perhaps had not expected. More important, we must do this without disappointment or rancor, or feeling that we have failed or been rejected. This is not easy. For years I worked hard trying to think of interesting things to do with my students in class, and for years, though I covered up as well as I could, I felt a little badly if these projects failed. In time I got over this. We have been too long under the spell of the idea of the Gifted Teacher, whose every word or move works miracles in the classroom, for whom everything goes right and nothing goes wrong. This Gifted Teacher is a myth. The hard fact is that we teachers have low batting averages. A baseball player is doing well if he gets three hits in ten tries. A teacher does well to get one hit in ten tries, or even twenty. Teaching is human communication, and like all communication, elusive and difficult. We must learn from the children. And learn afresh every year: children and classes are different; what went wonderfully one year may not go well the next. In fact, we must be wary of the feeling that we know exactly what we are doing in class. When we are most sure of what we are doing, we may be closest to being a bore.

15

MEASURING AND
COMPARING II

What are some other things, interesting and important to at least many children, that we and they can measure and think?

One thing is time. Let us begin with a stopwatch. For a class, several are better. Wolverine Sports Supply, 745 State Circle, Ann Arbor, Michigan 48104, sells good ones for eleven dollars or so. (Order their catalog—much interesting stuff in it at good prices.) What are some things we can do with them?

A good way to begin is to show children how to use the stop-watch, and then let them use it for a while, without suggesting any-thing. On their own they will probably find interesting things to do with it. When they do, their ideas will give you a good place to start.

One project is to estimate the duration of time. Thus we might ask different members of the class to let us know how long they think a minute is. We can say, "Tell me when to start the watch, and then tell me when you think a minute is up." From this begin-ning we can duplicate a very interesting perceptual experiment. In one part of the experiment we ask different children, or the same child a number of successive times, to estimate the length of a min-ute—but we do *not* tell him after each estimate whether or by how much his estimate was too long or too short. Keep a record of a number of trials—the children will probably be glad to help with this—and then plot them on a graph. We will probably see that the successive estimates do not get better, and indeed do not even converge, but remain about as scattered as they were at the beginning. What is their average? How scattered are they? That is, if we calculate for each estimate the difference between it and the average of all the estimates, what is the average of these differences? How erratic are our judgments of time?

We can then run a number of successive trials, only this time after each estimate say how good that estimate was—45 seconds, 71 seconds, or whatever. If we graph these new estimates, we will probably see that successive estimates do get better, and tend to converge on something close to 60 seconds.

When we plot on a graph this second group of estimates—we can show how to do this as we go along—we will find some things that may be interesting to look at and think about. Do the estimates keep getting closer and closer the longer they go on, or do we reach a point where the amount of scatter remains about the same? If so, about how much? Do successive estimates tend to approach 60 seconds from the same side or both sides? By this I mean, if a child's first estimate is low, will all his following estimates be low, but getting closer and closer to 60 seconds? Thus, for example, 40 seconds, 48 seconds, 52 seconds, 56 seconds. Or will he make one low estimate, then one high one, then a low one, and so close in from both sides? Thus, 40 seconds, 75 seconds, 52 seconds, 64 seconds, etc. In this regard, will all the children in the class be alike, all coming in on the target from the low or the high side, or will some come in straddling the target? Does this tactic, this pattern of closing in on the target, differ for children of differing ages? If so, how? For a child, does it differ from one day to another?

Another thing—how do children's estimates of the length of a minute vary with their age? I would guess, without ever having tried it, that little children would tend to err on the low side, and that as they got older children would have a closer idea of the length of a minute. At some point children meet such folklore rules for counting seconds as saying, "A thousand and one, a thousand and two, a thousand and three, etc.," or the one I still use, "One hippopotamus, two hippopotamus (or -potami, if you prefer), three hippopotamus, etc." Are there other such folklore rules, and if so, what are some? Will children in a class, after doing some of this estimating, invent some rules of their own, and if so, what? Will any children, without this being suggested, think to use their own heartbeat or pulse? If a child has been estimating minutes without any such rule, will telling him a rule improve his estimating, and if so, how much? Among the children of a particular age, how much variation is there in their estimates? In any one child, is this consistent from day to day, or week to week? That is, will the child who today guesses 36 seconds guess in that range a week later? Does there seem to be any connection between temperament and time estimates—that is, does time seem to go faster for nervous or energetic children than for calmer or slower-moving children? Can we find a connection for any given child between his emotional state and his time-estimating ability? And if we later measure children's quickness in various ways, is there a connection between quickness and time estimates?

Still more possibilities. We might expect that a child's guess of the length of two minutes would be about twice as long as his guess for a minute, for three minutes about three times as long, and so on. Is this true? Is it more true at some ages than others? My own guess would be that little children's estimates of, say, three minutes, would be less than three times their estimate of one minute, that their guess of ten minutes might not be much longer than their guess of five. But is this so? And if so, does this change with age, and how?

A child could do part of this test for himself, by himself. Thus, he could hold the watch face down, start it, stop it when he thought a minute was up, turn the watch over and see how much time did elapse, and then try again. Or a partner could record his estimates, but without telling him.

With children testing themselves, we could do another experiment. Let's suppose that a child, after a series of estimates *with* feedback (i.e. hearing each time how good his estimate was), has become able to guess a minute within 5 seconds either way. How much of his time-estimating ability will he lose in a day, or two days, or a week? That is, if he waits a day without doing any estimating, and then makes some estimates without feedback, how close will their average be? Clearly his time-estimating ability will drop off somewhat without practice. But will he eventually get to a point such that, no matter how many days he waits, his estimating ability will not worsen? How long does it take a child to reach this point? Is the time the same for all children—that is, do some hold their estimating skills more tenaciously than others? What is the average scatter at this skill-loss leveling-off point? Are these two figures—the time to reach the skill-loss leveling point, and the scatter to that point—the same from child to child? From one age to another? I would guess that little children would lose the skill somewhat more quickly, and that their scatter would be greater. Is this so?

What we are investigating, measuring, testing here is not just the ability to measure time, but some more fundamental ideas—the effect of no feedback and feedback in the gaining of a skill, the time to gain a skill, the limits of a skill, the time to lose a skill, and the limits of losing a skill. We could have children estimating weights, lengths, quantities. We could have them pace off what they thought was, say, 50 feet out in the schoolyard. Or we could have them estimate the distance between themselves, at various points in the schoolyard, and various objects.

We can see what an extraordinary amount of work with numbers—observing, recording, adding, subtracting, plotting—would be involved in all this. I hope that teachers will not think that the *point* of all this activity, all this investigating of skill growth and skill loss, is just to do some disguised arithmetic. Whoever thinks this way will completely miss the point, and will, in addition, spoil all this activity for the children. The *point* of all this investigating is to find an answer to a question; the only use of the arithmetic is to help us find it. Man did not think of measuring things so that he would get good at arithmetic; he measured things because he wanted or needed to find out or remember certain things about them, and he got better at arithmetic because he used it to do his measuring, and found that it helped. But it was the measuring, not the arithmetic, that was of chief importance. The need, the act that requires the skills, creates the skills.

Another related experiment would be to have children guess which of two objects or containers was heavier. Here we, and the child, would be testing one of his powers of discrimination. He will probably be able to tell which weight is heavier when the difference is as much as half a pound. But will he be able to tell if the difference is only an ounce or two? At what point will he be right only half the time; that is, at what point will the difference no longer seem to him to make any difference? Here again is a graph that we can plot for each child, or that each child can plot for himself. On one axis we plot the number of correct guesses out of, say, twenty tries; on the other axis, the difference between the two weights. What will the curve look like? For a fairly large difference, the child will probably guess right all the time. For a small enough difference, his performance will be no better than chance—that is, he will be right about half the time. But how steep will be the curve between these two points? Will this vary from child to child? Try the experiment yourself. What do you find?

From here we can begin to generate whole families of experiments. Some can arise out of our doing the discrimination test in two ways. One way would be always to have the two weights different, and always *to say* to the child that they are different, so that he did not have the choice of saying, even when he could not tell the difference, that they were the same. The other way would be to include from time to time the condition that the weights were the same, and to give the child the choice of saying that they were the same. This difference in the way of doing the test might produce many and interesting differences in the performance of the children. (By the way, it would be good, in all of these kinds of tests and experiments, if the parent or teacher also took part. If we prove to be less good than the children at making certain kinds of estimates, it will be all the more encouraging for them.) Thus I suspect that many children, when the differences in weight grow very slight and hard to detect, would try to avoid a hard choice by saying that the two weights were the same. In other words, the possibility of saying the two weights are the same may, for many children anyway, *decrease* their percentage of correct answers. Will this be equally true for all children? Will some children be more ready than others to make choices when making them is tough? Will this correlate with anything else we can observe about those children?

Obviously we can do our feedback experiments with this discrimination test. Do people get better at discriminating if, after each try, they are told which was the right choice? I would guess that it would make less difference in this kind of experiment than in those mentioned earlier, but I don't know this.

Another experiment. Here is our child trying to tell which of two weights is heavier. The difference is slight, so the test of discrimination is a fine one. If we keep a record, not just of the total number of correct tries, but of whether each try was correct or not, we can consider something else. Does his power of discrimination improve with more tries, or get worse? It seems very likely that it would get worse, for two reasons I can think of, and perhaps others. The first is a subtle one, a bit hard to describe. When we try to make this kind of discrimination, we have to rely on our impressions. But the longer we think about the matter, the harder we struggle to be right, the more we are liable to lose the freshness of that first impression. Our thoughts get in the way of our senses. And of course the other reason is that many children, particularly very young ones, would probably get bored after a fairly small number of tries.

We could perhaps test the first of these two ideas, that too much thinking and pondering destroys the freshness of impressions, by running the experiment in two ways. In one part, we would give children as much time as they wanted to decide which of the objects was heavier. In the other, we would give them a time limit in which to decide, after which we would take the weights away. Would putting a time limit on choice improve children's ability to discriminate? If so, here is another experiment—what time limit brings the best results? Too short a time would probably produce anxiety which itself gets in the way of discrimination. Which in turn suggests another experiment—can we and the children work out an experiment to see how anxiety affects discrimination? If we decided to do this, how would we go about producing more, or less, anxiety? How would it affect everyone's performance if we gave a reward for the best performance? Or if we gave some kind of penalty—which the students would have to agree on in advance—for the poorest performance? The threat of the penalty might have little effect on the confident child who did not expect to do badly. In the same way, the possibility of reward might do nothing for the child who thought he had no chance of winning it.

At least with somewhat older children, these subjects in themselves would make for some interesting discussions. What kinds of things make different people anxious, and why?

More experiments. Does our ability to guess the heavier of two objects depend on the absolute difference in weight, or the relative difference? It seems likely that the relative difference is what counts. A child could easily tell the difference between a one-ounce and a two-ounce weight, but could probably not tell the difference between a five-pound weight and a weight of five pounds one ounce. But what kind of relative difference do we have to have to make a difference? Five percent? Ten percent? Is this critical relative difference the same for light weights and heavy ones? Take for an example one I have made up. Let us suppose that a child, choosing between a one-pound weight and one slightly heavier, can guess the heavier weight at least three fourths of the time when the relative difference is 10 percent. Would this relationship—three-quarters correct choices for a 10 percent relative difference—be true for all weights? My guess would be that for very light weights a larger relative difference would be needed for the child to be able to tell the difference, and, oddly enough, that this would also be true for very heavy weights, since the child would be struggling too hard to hold the weight to be able to be very sensitive to differences. What is this relationship between relative difference and weight, and how does it vary from child to child, or from one age to another?

These are all research projects in the truest sense of the word —not like most so-called scientific experiments in school. Any one of them might engage the attention and activity of a number of children for quite a long time. In all of this, they will be working with numbers, calculating relative differences, expressing them as percentages, figuring out what 10 percent of, say, two pounds will come to in ounces.

Another variation. I have assumed that the two objects whose weights the children were comparing were of the same size and shape—weighted cans, jars, boxes, bags. How do our results change if the objects are of very different shape and size? My guess would be that, of two objects of the same weight, we would tend to feel that the smaller was heavier. Is this true? True for everyone? How does change in size and shape affect our ability to discriminate? Given two objects of the same weight, how much smaller does one have to be for us to sense it as being heavier?

We can do these discrimination experiments in many ways. We might use lines of different lengths—perhaps placed high enough on the wall so that the children couldn't measure them. Again, how much difference do we have to have in order for this to make a difference, to be noticeable? How does this vary with the length of the lines? With the distance separating the two lines? Clearly, the farther they are apart the harder it will be to discriminate. Will changing the thickness of the lines change the problem? The color of the background? Will a white line on a black background look longer than a black line of the same length on a black background?

This could in turn lead us into the whole field of optical (and indeed other sensory) illusions, which have always been fascinating to children—and to everyone. (A splendid book on this subject, for teachers or older children—though it would be interesting to have around in any class or home—is *Art and Illusion*, by E. H. Gombrich, published by Princeton University Press.)

We could test discrimination with areas of similar shape but different size—rectangles, triangles, circles, etc. The children, with the help of the teacher, would have to make up the materials for such experiments. This would in itself call for accurate measuring, drawing of exact right angles, use of compass to make geometrical constructions, etc. All of this would be interesting in itself. Doing it, the children would learn things about plane geometry. Then, for a given shape, we could find how much of a difference is needed to make a difference. Can we detect a 5 percent difference in area? Ten percent? Is it easier to detect these differences for some shapes than others—does the shape make a difference, and if so, what difference? What happens when we try to tell which of two different shapes has the larger area? Given a group of different shapes, all of the same area, will some look bigger than others, and if so, which? What shapes are "big" shapes and what "small" shapes? Suppose we make a shape like an amoeba, curvy, irregular. Will we see this as "big"—bigger than a circle or square of the same area—or "small"? And, by the way, how can we tell the area of a shape like this? How many ways could we find to do this? How do we go about making a circle with almost exactly the same area as a given square? Some older children may be interested in knowing that it is impossible to do this exactly, and that for centuries mathematicians struggled to find a way to "square the circle," that is, construct with ruler and compass a circle with an area equal to that of a given square. Still more advanced students may be interested in knowing (as I do not know) the proof that this cannot be done.

Still more variations are possible—though we seem to have strayed far from our stopwatch. Suppose the areas we are comparing are of different colors, and against different backgrounds. How will this affect our discrimination? I would guess that a white circle on a black background will look larger than a black circle of the same area against a white background. Is this so? How much bigger does the black-on-white circle have to be in order to look the same? If white-on-black circles look "bigger" than black-on-white, are there any other color combinations that look "bigger" than white-on-black? Of many circles of different colors on the same background, will some look bigger than others, and if so, which ones? If we have circles of the same color against different backgrounds, what differences will the backgrounds make?

This suggests in turn an experiment in color discrimination. Suppose we have some cans of commercial water-based wall paint. I suggest these because their quality is likely to be more consistent, and their colors better, than any paints we might mix in class. With older children, we might use some of the inks used in silk screening, which have very vivid colors. With younger children we would need paints or inks that, if spilled, could be washed.

At any rate, let us suppose that we have a can of red and a can of white paint. Into a number of small containers we put a carefully measured or weighted amount of red paint. Then into some of these jars we put a carefully measured amount of white paint—into one, 5 percent of the amount of the red; into another, 10 percent; into another, perhaps only 1 percent; and so on. Then we mix up thoroughly each of these jars of red-and-white, and using these mixes, paint some pieces of cardboard, or wood or masonite scraps—whatever samples we use should have a uniform texture. Then we run a color discrimination test, like the weight, length, and area discrimination tests we have been talking about. How much white paint do you have to add to your red to be able to tell it from pure red? Can you tell the 5 percent white from the 10 percent white? What change in percentage makes a noticeable difference? Does this change, needed to make a noticeable difference, itself change—that is, if we can tell pure red from red-5 percent white, can we tell red-20 percent white from red-25 percent white, or red-80 percent white from red-85 percent white?

Many variations are possible. Suppose we start with white and add more and more red. Or suppose, instead of adding white to the red, we add black. Or yellow, or blue. Suppose our beginning color is blue, or green, instead of red. Suppose we add yellow to red, or yellow to blue. Are the noticeable differences the same? Does the background make a difference? The classroom walls, at least in many schools, will be a kind of drab yellow. Is the experiment changed if the paint samples are shown against a white background? And what about the light in the room itself? Will our ability to discriminate between different colors vary at different times of day, or depending on the weather, or whether the room lights are on? Some students might be interested in seeing reproductions of the pictures that Claude Monet painted of the cathedral at Rouen in different lights. This might in turn lead to interesting discussions about color and color perception—about which many things are not yet understood. Or we might do something that art students often do, but that is almost never done in "Art" classes in school—use the three primary colors to make a color wheel, an array of all the varities of hues, tints, etc. (To do this, we will have to use good quality materials, which schools, in an unwise economy, almost never do.)

I would not expect a teacher or parent to do many of these experiments. To do only a few of them would take a great deal of work and time. I suggest so many only to give a surplus to choose from, and to show also something of the continuum of experience, the ways in which one thing leads to many others. From discriminating time with a stopwatch—and by the way, children who are used to hearing talk about our five senses may find it interesting to puzzle over the question, "What sense are we using when we estimate time?"—we have moved to discriminating colors. But all these experiments require us to *use* numbers—to measure, to record, to graph, to calculate fractions and percentages, to do exactly the kinds of things that people do with numbers in the larger world. With these ideas as a beginning, you and the children can probably think of many more of your own.

16

MEASURING SPEED

More things to do with a stopwatch. Children like to run, to know how fast they are running. With a yardstick and a piece of string we can lay out a running course. How long depends a little on how much room we have, and on the age of the children. For junior high and up, 50 yards would be good. For elemenary school, 30 yards might do for a start. Why the string? To give us a straight line along which to measure with our yardstick. Or we could measure with a long measuring tape. (Wolverine Sports Supply sells, 50-foot measuring tapes for $4.50 and some in even longer lengths.) Or we could use a splendid measuring device, the Measure Master, made by the Rolatape Corporation of Santa Monica, California. This costs about twenty dollars, and is a little measuring wheel on the end of a telescoping aluminum tube. As you roll the wheel along the ground, a counter attached to it tells you, in feet and tenths of feet, the distance rolled. As the counter reads up to 1000 feet, this is excellent for measuring long distances. It is perhaps too expensive to have one in every class, but any elementary or secondary school should have at least one of them.

When we have measured our course, we can see how long each child takes to run it. My system, when I did this, was to stand at the finish line, watch in one hand, other hand raised. I gave them the usual staring signal—Ready, Get Set, Go. On the Go I brought my raised arm sharply down and started the watch. I stopped the watch when the runner's head and upper body crossed in front of me as I looked across the finish line. Someone who is not running, or has just had his turn, can record the times. At first the children will all want to know each other's times. This will be all right *at first*—they will already know who are the fast runners and who the slow ones. But if some people in the class are much slower than others, there is a danger that if this comparing of times goes on too long, the slower runners will feel ashamed and will drop out of the activity. So it will probably be a good idea, quite early in the project, to get people thinking in terms of their own improvement. Each time a child runs, can he break his old record? By how much? We can keep note, somewhere in the classroom, not only of the children who run the fastest times, but of the ones who break their records by the largest amounts. Or we can begin to calculate the percentage by which children improve their running times, and note the ones whose percentage of improvement is greatest. This may have an added advantage, that it will often be the slowest runners who are able to make the greatest percentage improvement, since the faster ones are probably working nearer the limit of their capacity.

Keeping track of improvement can be done in all kinds of tests of strength, speed, quickness, agility, as well as more conventional tests of academic skill. It gives the children who are not very good at something, but improving rapidly at it, a chance to get the same kind of recognition as the children who are best at something. Some will say to this that we should not do anything in a class to encourage competition, of any kind. To me this is foolish and unrealistic. Children are naturally and healthily competitive. They are interested in knowing who does things best, and they are all deeply interested in doing whatever they do today a little better than they did it yesterday. This is a natural part of growing up. Growing up *means* getting, not just taller and heavier, but more competent and skillful. What is wrong with most schools is that we honor only a very few kinds of skills out of the great many that children possess, so that very few people get all the prizes. Also, we put too much emphasis on winning and too little on improvement, which is what children really care about, and what they can all share in.

Children are used to riding around in cars, and think of speed in terms of miles per hours. We can easily calculate their average running speed in feet/second, and from the fact that 44 feet per second equals 30 miles per hour, work out their speeds in miles per hour. We can compare this with the speed of the world's fastest sprinters. The world's record for running a hundred yards is 9.1 seconds. This is about 33 feet per second, or ¾ of 30 miles per hour, or 22½ miles per hour. We can compare this with the running, swimming, and flying speeds of other living creatures—most encyclopedias and almanacs have a table of these figures.

Children may be interested to know that as recently as the 1930's there was a commonly held assumption that the fastest living creature was an insect called the deer bot fly. It was supposed to be able to fly 415 miles per hour. If you have an old enough encyclopedia, you may be able to catch this myth in print. For a long time nobody questioned this figure. Then one day a scientist, Irving Langmuir, then working at General Electric, began wondering about it. He built a little model of the fly, its exact shape, size, and color. Then, in a brightly lighted, white painted room he whirled the fly around on the end of a wire. Even against this much better background the fly became invisible at speeds far lower than the fabled 415 miles per hour. Against the backgrounds in which people had seen him he would have been invisible at speeds of fifty miles per hour, or even less.

This should make us wonder about some of our other estimates of the speed of other creatures. How do we know how fast the cougar, duck, porpoise go? How could we find out how fast a dog can run? A cat? Rabbit? Mouse, squirrel, hamster. How fast do slow animals move?

Every few years someone takes out some electrical apparatus and measures the speed at which some of our fastest pitchers can throw a baseball. Boys might be interested in these figures. A few years ago Sandy Koufax of the Los Angeles Dodgers, then at the height of his career, had some of his fast pitches clocked at about 98 miles per hour. Some children might be interested in the ways in which people measure such speeds. This might lead to a discussion of the ways in which men measure very high velocities, like that of bullets and shells. If you don't know anything about this, don't worry. A nearby college physics department, or perhaps one of the popular science magazines on any newsstand, might be able to tell you or tell you where to find out. Talking about such things might lead to the question: What is the fastest thing of all? It is of course light, which travels at about 186,000 miles per second. Children will be impressed with that figure, but it will not mean much to them. We can talk about numbers of times around the earth in a second, but since children have no sense of the size of the earth, that won't tell them much. Still, it will be an excuse to play with some big numbers, which they like. Some children may want to know how anyone can measure the speed of anything that goes that fast. The explanation of this will probably be beyond little children, but some scientifically minded fifth graders and many junior high or high school students might find this interesting. Any good encyclopedia or good physics text will probably describe the Michelson-Morley experiment, and perhaps other ways of measuring the speed of light.

Children may be curious about why some can run faster than others. Obviously, being taller helps, or having longer legs. We might divide each child's running speed by his height or leg length and thus get a speed/height or speed/leg ratio. This might give us some new champions—who is the fastest runner in class in proportion to his height or leg length? At any rate, we would have some new figures to calculate, compare, and think about. We might also calculate, for each child, the ratio of his height to his weight. How would this height/weight ratio affect running speed? We would guess that the larger it is—i.e. the skinnier the child is—the faster he can run. So we could get a new set of figures, the speed divided by the height/weight ratio. Which children would be the winners here?

This leads to another question. The children will all know that big children can run faster than little ones. But is this because they are just taller? Or because they are older? Which difference makes the difference? Do tall first graders run as fast as older children of the same height? We could find the average speed/ height ratio for all the children in each grade in school. Would this be about the same for all grades? If this were so, we might think that it was greater height that made older children run faster. Would the height/weight ratios have anything to do with it? Do these ratios themselves get larger or smaller as children get older? Greater speed might come from greater strength. Does strength change proportionate to age? Will an average ten-year-old be twice as strong as an average five-year-old? How can we find out? More about this in another chapter.

As in other projects, the children could plot on graphs either their running times or their speeds. If they plot dates on the horizontal axis and running times on the vertical, the graph will slope down as they improve; if they plot speeds, the graph will slope up. Which do they like better? To make plotting speeds easier, we might make a conversion table, from which each running time— 4.7 seconds, 5.6 seconds, 7.2 seconds, or whatever—could be converted into speed in miles per hour. Older children might be able to do this by themselves. Given enough time, they might even think of it by themselves. They might also plot percentage improvement each week. What would this graph look like? Is improvement regular, or does it come in spurts? Is it the same for all children?

People obviously don't run as fast for long distances as for short ones. The world's best sprinters average 22.5 miles per hour over a hundred yards; a four-minute miler averages only 15 mph. How does running longer distances affect the children's running speeds? If we plot a graph for each child of average running speed against distance, what will it look like? Will it be the same for all? Will some children be better at dashes and others at longer distances? Can we find any connection between this and some of the ratios we have previously found, like height/weight? And what distance will give the highest average speed? Probably one hundred yards is too long, while five or ten yards will be too short—the child barely has time to get started. Is this best distance the same for all children?

If a child runs a dash several times, one right after another, how will his times compare? Chances are that his first time may not be his best; he will improve a bit as he warms up. After a while, as he tires, his times will fall off again. On which run is a child likely to make his best time? Is this the same for all children? Also, if he rests half a minute between successive dashes, how will his times compare? Suppose he rests a minute between dashes? Two minutes? Which will give the best results?

Perhaps I should pause here to make an important point. All this measuring and timing does not need to be done and should not be done by a teacher. Once one of these projects gets started, the more the children take it over and do it by themselves, the better. One of the reasons I have suggested a great many of these research projects is so that there will be more than enough projects to go round.

If the children are fifth or sixth graders or older, and some of them really get interested in running faster, they may want to try something that over the years I have found helps running speed, which is walking (and later, when you are used to them, running) in ankle weights. The best of these, in fact the only good ones I have yet seen, can be bought from Wolverine Sports Supply. Their very large catalog of sports equipment is well worth writing for. The ankle weights come in three sizes—5 pounds, 7½ pounds, and 10 pounds. I would recommend, in general, the 5's for fifth graders and under, the 7½ for junior high, and the 10's for high school students. But this depends very much on the strength and eagerness of the individual child.

As may be clear, I do not believe that sports, physical development, etc., belong to the physical education specialists, to be done in gym period and forgotten the rest of the time.

How should the children use these ankle weights? At first, they should just walk in them. They will be awkward, and walk with a stiff, leg-swinging, mechanical stride, rather like the monster in the old Frankenstein movies. Some children may comment and joke about this. They should try at first to attain a more natural way of walking. Doing no more than this will greatly strengthen many of the important muscles used in running. When a child can walk with some ease and naturalness, he can try some very easy jogging. Very gradually, as he gets more used to the weights, he can increase his speed, until finally he is trying to run as fast as he can. Here we can find a whole new series of measurements and experiments. Though children, who would rather run than walk, would ordinarily not want to see how fast they could walk a certain distance, they might want to see how fast they could walk with ankle weights —particularly heavy ones. And they could do some experiments, using children of about equal running speed, to see whether those who used the ankle weights improved faster than those who did not.

Other running contests. How fast can a child go a certain distance carrying piggyback another child of his own weight? How fast can he go hopping on one foot? Jumping with both feet tied together? Running backward? Running sideways, without crossing his feet? Going on hands and feet? On hands and feet backward? On hands and feet with his back facing the ground? Skipping? Skipping backwards? Going along a straight chalk line? A curved chalk line? A course made of bricks, in which he had to step only on the bricks, not the ground in between? A slalom course, in which he has to run a zigzag course around or between various kinds of markers? A back-and-forth course, in which he has to run a figure-eight type course, say ten times, around two markers five yards apart? For any or all of these we could do any of the kind of improvement experiments we have talked about. And the children themselves can invent many of their own special running events.

17

MEASURING STRENGTH

Our classrooms are bursting with the energy of children. We would like to turn it off, but we can't. We don't know what to do with it, so we think of it as a problem, and call it a problem. The things we do about it certainly *make* it a problem.

Energy. Children are full of it. We have only to look at them to see it. It bursts and squirts out of them in all kinds of exuberant noise and movement—what we adults, who rarely have enough energy, would call unnecessary. They fling their arms and legs about, take extra steps, jump, skip. This is part of what they are. Even the happiest and calmest child, secure and well-loved at home, at peace with himself, confident about his growing up, interested in the world around him, not fighting visible or invisible battles with the world or his parents or his brothers or sisters, not trying to work off fears and angers that he does not understand or know what to do with—even such a child has far more energy than almost any school or class will let him use or express.

The problem—as we see it—is made much more acute and serious because not many children these days are this healthy or happy. These are very tough times for children to grow up in. Most children, of whatever race, group, or class, grow up these days full of anxieties and tensions. This is not just true of poor kids. Over the years I have seen and come to know a good many children, in classes I have taught, in schools I have worked in or visited, in the homes of many friends, in various kinds of public places. Most of these children have been middle or upper middle class. By standards I have come to trust, hardly one out of ten of these children has seemed or seems to me in what I would call really good health of mind and spirit. They are more full than they ought to be of fear, and resentment, and anger. They are less trusting than they should be of themselves and others. But what troubles me most about many of them is that they have lost so much of their early naturalness, openness, spontaneity. They—above all, the good students—are much of the time far too calculating. They play games with people. They are sensitive to what is wanted of them, and therefore, to what they can get away with. When they have some freedom of movement and speech and action, they find ways, as is so beautifully shown in *The Lives of Children,* to work off their tensions and satisfy their deep needs. But in most schools, where they have no such freedom at all, these pressures build up until they explode, in constant and self-destructive rebellion (not all rebellion is or need be such, but constructive rebellion is hardly possible in most schools), anger, calculated meanness and cruelty, fighting.

What can we do in conventional schools and classrooms to let children use their energy, work off their tension, express their anger?

Let me start with a question and answer. Many teachers have asked me what they could or should do with the bad boy of their class. He teases smaller children, steals, breaks objects, hurts people, starts fights, disrupts the class and eggs other children on to do the same. To this question I always reply with a question of my own: "Is this boy one of the biggest and strongest in the class?" The answer is almost always Yes. I then ask, "Are there any ways in which this boy can gain legitimate recognition, reward, honor, for his strength, quickness, toughness, courage? Are there some things of which, because of these qualities, he can be the recognized class champion?" The answer is almost always No. In fact, I cannot remember when it was otherwise.

Many people have by now pointed out that the way to get along and get ahead in school, whether you are a boy or a girl, is to act as if you were a girl. It is sadly and dreadfully true. The very things that boys, real boys, the best boys, are most proud of, that make them feel most like boys, are exactly the things that are least acknowledged, admired, praised, or rewarded in school. In fact, these qualities are very likely to get them in trouble.

So let's see what we can do in our classrooms about strength—testing it, measuring it, noting its growth, finding ways to develop it. Don't think I am suggesting them just as a way of keeping children docile and quiet. These would be good things to do for their own sake, even if we never had anything in schools that we would call behavior problems. I suggest them because children are interested in strength and endurance, as they are in quickness and skill, and because nothing gives them more satisfaction, more of a sense of their being and growth, than gaining greater confidence and competence in the use of their own bodies.

One very simple strength-measuring device can be made from a bathroom scale and a doorway chin bar. Imagine a doorway in your classroom, or room at home other than the main entrance door. The chinning bar has rubber feet on the ends, and by a screw action is forced out against the door frame until friction holds it in place. We put the bathroom scale on the floor, right in the doorway. We fasten the chinning bar in place, at different heights depending on the exercise to be done or the strength to be measured. The child, whose weight we already know or now find out, steps on the scale and pushes or pulls up or down on the bar. Another child reads the scale, and notes the highest reading obtained (or, for some exercises, the lowest). The difference between that reading and the child's weight tells how hard a force he was exerting.

From any book on weightlifting or isometric exercises we can get ideas for a number of ways to push or pull on the bar. Here are some possibilities:

1. Bar is at elbow height (with child on scale). Grasp bar with both hands (can be done with either hand), elbows at sides, palms facing up. Push up against bar. Known to weight-lifters as the Curl.

2. Same as above, but lift with palms facing down. Slightly harder.

3. Bar at about height of forehead. Grasp with both hands (can be done with either one), palms facing up. Push up against bar. Known as the Press.

4. Same as above, but bar is behind head instead of in front of it. Press Behind Neck.

5. Bar at full arm's length overhead. Grasp bar in both hands, pull down on it. Children who can support their whole weight this way can try this instead with one arm at a time. Chin.

6. Bar at waist height. Grasp with both hands, fairly close to-gether, palms facing backwards. Pull up against bar. Pull-up.

7. Same, but with bar at height of armpits.

8. Bar behind legs, at height midway between ankle and knee. Grasp bar with palms facing backwards. With head up and back straight, pull up against bar. Hack Lift.

9. Same as above, but with bar in front of legs. Dead Lift. On both, back should be straight, pull steady.

10. Bar in front of legs, knee height. Grasp with palms facing backwards. With back straight and horizontal, head up and looking ahead, legs stiff, pull up against bar. Slow steady pull. Stiff-legged Dead Lift. Back must be straight, head well up.

11. Same position and grip, but pulling with muscles of arms in-stead of back. Rowing.

12. Same as above, but with bar about 6 inches higher. Bent Arm Rowing.

13. Stand sideways in doorway. Bar is an inch or so above knee height. Bend over sideways, keeping body in vertical plane. Grasp bar with one hand. Pull up. Do first one side, then the other. Side Bend.

14. Same position as rowing. Push down on bar. Invent a name for this.

15. Bar waist high. Standing on scale, squat so that bar is across top of shoulders. Keeping back straight and using legs only, push up against bar. Deep Knee Bend.
16. Bar at height of top of thigh. Standing a little bit back from the doorway, and holding the bar lightly for balance, bring one knee up against the underside of the bar, and push up against it. Knee Lift.
17. Bar at knee height. Stand sideways in doorway, straddling bar. Grip with one hand in front of you, the other behind you. Lift up. Straddle Lift.
18. Same position as Number 3. Pull down on bar. Children who can lift their weight this way do exercise with one arm at a time. Bent Arm Chin.

Children will probably be surprised to find how much stronger some muscles are than others. Some may be interested in knowing how muscles work, and which muscles are working in each of these exercises. There are many good books for children about the working of the body. One of the best is in the *Time-Life* Science Series —which has many excellent other things in it, as well. Even if you don't get into books, they may like to know that muscles work like rubber bands, that is, they can only pull, by contracting; they cannot push. When children think they are pushing, it only means that certain muscles are pulling. Some may want to try to figure out for themselves which muscles are pulling in any given exercise.

Children may want to figure out who is the strongest person in the class, or who is the strongest in proportion to weight. Here again are opportunities for improvement records. Perhaps we can find a connection between strength in certain exercises and running speed.

Let's suppose we have a child on the scale, doing a certain exercise. Another child stands by with a stopwatch, another reads the scale, and another records. At a signal the child on the scale begins to exert all his strength. Every two seconds the child with the watch says, "Mark!" The child watching the scale reads what it says at that instant, and the other child records it. They go on until the child on the scale is too tired to continue—probably after about 10 or 15 seconds. We can then plot each of those strength readings against time and get what we might call a strength decay curve. With these, we can think about many things. Are the strongest children the ones with the most endurance? How shall we define endurance? The children may want to discuss this. Is the one with the most endurance the one who can go on pushing longest without giving up? Or should we say that it is the one whose strength takes longest to drop to half its greatest value? Will the most enduring children by one of these definitions be the most enduring by the other? If we do these experiments with children of different ages, how does endurance vary with age? Are strength/weight ratios more or less constant as children grow older? How about strength/age ratios?

Another experiment, rather like one we did with running, is the following. A child is ready to do a certain exercise. He puts forth his maximum effort for a couple of seconds, and the scale-reader gets the maximum reading. Then the child rests for an agreed on time—say 15 seconds. Then the timer says Go, and he tries again. Another reading, another rest, another effort, and so on, for perhaps ten tries. What do we find out about these successive efforts? How rapidly do they fall off? What happens with a 5-second rest period? Ten-second? Twenty-second? How much rest does the child need to be able to keep equaling his best effort for ten tries? Five tries? How long does it take muscles to recover their strength? If we get tired past a certain point, do we find that we never get back to our peak, not on that day? What are the effects on strength and endurance of not having had enough sleep, or of having been sick? How long, after having been sick, does it take to get back to top strength? Are people stronger at some times during the day than others? What times? Are these times the same for all the children, or are there some morning people and some afternoon people?

There are other good exercise gadgets. The Voit Company, which makes rubber footballs, basketballs, soccer balls, etc., makes several of them. They have a grip strength tester, with a meter that records the maximum effort. They have another cable-type exerciser, available in sporting goods stores, also with a meter. My own feeling is that the best device, both for building and for measuring strength, is an adjustable barbell. The York Barbell Company, of York, Pennsylvania, makes two sets for children, the Little Hercules and Junior Hercules sets. The former, for small children, has a short light bar and, in different sizes, 13½ pounds of metal plates; the latter, for older children, a somewhat longer bar and 37½ pounds of weights. They are a good investment; they don't take up much space, they don't wear out, and they can't be broken. What other school equipment can make that claim?

The exercises I described were what are called *isometric,* which simply means that there is no motion, the muscles are exercised at one point. From them you can probably get an idea of what some of the *isotonic*—that is, moving—exercises would be that would be done with a weighted bar. In any case, the York Company, and other suppliers of this equipment, publish lists of exercises, with illustrations, so it is not hard to figure out what has to be done. There is only one thing to watch out for. Young children, and even high school students, are likely to have an exaggerated idea of their own strength, and may therefore try to do an exercise with a weight that is much too heavy for them. This may cause them to drop it, or to strain a muscle, A good rule, certainly with young children, and even with older ones until they have become very used to working with weights and skillful at using them, is to say that for any exercise they must use no more weight than will enable them to do the exercise twenty times.

Our strength-measuring now takes a new form. The aim for each exercise is to find the largest weight with which the child can do the exercise twenty times. We must reach some kind of agreement about the speed or rhythm of the exercise, or children will slow down more and more, trying to get their twenty by catching a little rest between efforts, while others shout, "That's not fair, he's resting in between, he has to keep doing it." One way of solving the problem might be to say that for each exercise there is a time limit within which the twenty repetitions must be done. It may take some trial and error to find what this time is. The exercises are best done steadily and rhythmically, but without hurry. Or, better yet, we could get a metronome, a very useful gadget, about which I will have more to say later, and for each exercise establish a tempo. Thus we might do each exercise in a count of four— Up-and-down-and-up-and-down-and—each word getting a click on the metronome, and the metronome set on an agreed speed. For arm exercises, like Press and Curl, a setting of 60 might be right; for exercises like the Deep Knee Bend or Dead Lift, a setting of 40 would be better. The point is for everyone to agree on a reasonable speed and stick to it.

From long experience with these exercises I can say that they have many benefits. They increase strength, endurance, and wind. If a good selection is done, they increase flexibility. They make for increased bodily awareness, at least in the muscular and skeletal sense, which is an important part of the elusive quality called "co-ordination." (In spite of what many coaches say, it can be developed enormously.) Not least of all, they are extraordinarily effective in reducing muscular and nervous tension. They are very relaxing, for perhaps two reasons. The first is that when a particular muscle group has been exercised to the limit of its strength, its natural tendency is to relax and rest when no further demands are made on it. The other is that someone exerting all his strength against a heavy weight must concentrate on it—he thinks so hard about what he is trying to do that he has no room to think about anything else, including what may have been bothering or worrying or angering him.

In *The Lives of Children* George Dennison describes how, from time to time, when a child got hysterical with anger or fear, he would take him by the shoulders and shake him, so that the child, in order to locate himself, would quite literally have to "come to his senses." These very specific and concentrated kinds of exercises have exactly the same effect.

So, I would imagine, does Yoga. I know next to nothing about it, but I do know that many young people are very much interested in it and good at it. It might be possible to find a high school or college student who could demonstrate some of its positions and disciplines to children.

There are other tests of endurance. One, used by the armed forces, is to have a man get on and off a chair a number of times in succession. In the classroom, again establishing a regular rhythm with our metronome, we could see who could do it most times before stopping or failing to keep up with the rhythm. Another test is a skiers' exercise. For this, you must have shoes that do not slip on the floor, or that failing, socks or bare feet. You take a sitting position, back flat against a wall, thighs horizontal, lower legs vertical, hands by your sides—you may not use them to push against your legs. Your whole weight is supported by your bent legs. The aim is to see who can stay in this position the longest. It is a stern test, not just of strength but of ability to withstand fatigue and, at the end, real pain. It is a way in which a smaller boy, unable to fight a bigger one, might still challenge him to prove his real toughness. Any child who held the class record in this would be sure to have the others' respect.

The first time I saw this exercise I was teaching fifth grade. One of the boys brought this exercise to the class—he had heard of it from a skier. A number of the boys, like all boys of that age, loved sports, and saw themselves as future all-Americans or all-Pros. One after another they took their places against the wall for their test. After about two minutes, teeth grinding, faces contorted, legs fluttering back and forth uncontrollably, they would sink to the floor. Two minutes was about the best time anyone could manage. Up stepped a skinny little girl who, as it happened, had been a very serious and talented student of ballet for a number of years. This meant less than nothing to the boys. They did not know what ballet required in strength, and thought it just meant twirling around in sissy-looking costumes. She sat calmly against the wall. A minute went by—not a flicker of expression on her face. Two minutes. She might as well have been sitting in a chair. The boys began to look at each other. What was this anyway? Was there any way to say she was cheating? They examined her position carefully. No luck; nothing to complain about there. Three minutes, and still no sign of strain. By this time they were furious. Wait till their next turn! By four minutes she was showing some strain, and at about five minutes she had to stop. The boys clawed their way to the wall. Let me! No, me! I'll show her! But they soon learned a hard lesson about the limits of will power in increasing strength. By a minute and a half their legs were burning and trembling; soon they were shaking again, and sagged to the floor, baffled and defeated.

I met another similar endurance test when at thirteen I first went away to school. Call it the crucifix. The aim was to see how long you could stand with arms held straight out at the sides. You could turn your hands over, palms up or down, but not otherwise move your arms. It seems to me that the record stood at about nine minutes. I did not hold it. It is a painful test, but it is the kind of things boys like to do, to test, show, and prove their manliness— what they are so seldom given a chance to do in school. It takes no space, makes no noise, except perhaps for the anguished muttering of the one being tested. Perhaps in many schools the mutters would be curses. Too bad.

Such exercises, tests, challenges, opportunities for honor and improvement should reduce markedly the tension and anger in many classrooms, and give many boys things to do more interesting than fighting. But they will not do away with all anger, and there is no reason why they should. There will still be anger, not to be appeased by challenges of endurance. There will still be fights. And why not? Fighting is for most boys an important part of growing up, particularly in the cultures in which many poor boys live. To try to forbid all fighting, or to act as if even to want to fight, even to be angry, was some kind of disease and crime, is foolish, ridiculous, self-defeating. The point is to manage fights so that they cause the least interference with the lives of those not fighting; so that people don't have to fight who don't want to; so that fighters don't do each other serious damage; so that the fight ends when one party has clearly won and the other is ready to quit, if only he can find a faintly honorable way to admit it; and so that there is a maximum possibility that after the fight the fighters will feel a greater respect for each other, and perhaps even the beginnings of friendship.

One way to accomplish this may be to introduce the children to wrestling, not professional, but amateur, collegiate style. Indeed, it is worth doing for many other reasons. If we start all matches kneeling down (I will explain the position later), wrestling doesn't take up much room. A couple of old mats and about 10 x 10 feet of floor space is enough. It is a quiet sport; except for grunts, wrestlers make no noise at all. Children doing it burn up an enormous amount of steam in a short time. High school wrestlers, strong, thoroughly trained and conditioned, wrestle nine-minute matches; it is enough. Elementary school children will probably poop themselves thoroughly in five minutes or less. It is a very aggressive sport; you are in close contact with your opponent, and you have very strongly the feeling of dominating him, or being dominated by him. At any instant of a match there is very definitely one who is winning and one who is losing. The nature of the combat makes it unlikely that the kind of blind, hysterical rage will develop that so often comes in boxing matches. You are very powerfully in your senses all the time, aware of yourself and your opponent, thinking about how to master him, aware of him thinking about how to master you. For this reason, even though it does less damage than boxing or fist fighting, it is more truly combative, and hence a more satisfying way to express and release anger.

It doesn't take much knowledge or skill to introduce wrestling. When I first showed it to fifth and sixth graders, I knew only a few rules; some prohibitions—no full nelsons, strangleholds, hammerlocks, scissors grips, or holds designed to inflict pain; a very few holds and escapes; and the wrestler's position. In this, the wrestler who does not have the advantage gets on hands and knees. The one with the advantage kneels beside him, one arm around his opponent's waist, the other hand on his opponent's near arm above the elbow. At the signal "Wrestle!" the one with the advantage tries to throw the other down, the other to escape from him. When the wrestlers go off the mat, the one had the advantage, who was in a commanding position, usually but not always the one on top—there are some pinning holds in which the dominator is underneath the dominated—takes the advantage in the wrestler's position, and they begin again. Scoring is more complicated than it used to be. You get several points for a pin—keeping your opponent's shoulder blades on the mat for three seconds straight. But you also get points for gaining a position of advantage, or for escaping from one—getting out from under.

If there are some high school or college wrestling teams in the area, you can probably get some of them to come to the school or class and demonstrate the rules and skills of the sport. If not, you can get started with no more than a book, like those in the Barnes Sporting Library. The children can look at the pictures, and from them figure out how the holds go. They will learn a lot just by doing it. There is a kind of inner logic to the sport that makes itself known, sometimes to rather surprising people. One of my fifth graders was small, slow of foot, not good at either kicking or bat and ball games. He turned out to be an extraordinarily gifted wrestler. He was quick, wriggly, determined, never gave up, and most important of all, he had the true wrestler's sense of his own balance and the balance of his opponent. If another boy, on top of him and trying to roll him over on his back, committed his weight too far, quick as a flash this little guy would turn under him, roll him over, and be on top of him, and this often with bigger and stronger boys. So the best wrestlers in the class may not always be the best all-round athletes.

Wrestling is a great developer of strength, endurance, persistence, and courage. A child can do well in the sport with nothing much more than the determination never to give up. Wrestling is a sport in which very often both opponents can gain a kind of victory. That is, even though one wrestler can dominate another throughout a match, unless he is very skillful, and if the other is determined, he may not be able to pin him. If the match is a kind of grudge match, the boy who is on top will get satisfaction out of showing that he is the better wrestler, out of mastering his opponent. But the one on the bottom may get almost equal satisfaction from not giving up, from continuing to frustrate the other's efforts to pin him. He may come out of the match with almost as much honor as the clear winner. And the wrestlers themselves may finish their match with a new respect for each other.

There are still other tests of strength, agility, and flexibility that don't take much time or space. A well-known one is arm wrestling. Here the two wrestlers are seated across a table gripping each other's right hands (or left), elbows on the table fairly close together and in a line. At a signal both try, without raising or moving their elbows, to force the other one's arm over until the back of his hand hits the table. This is a satisfying small-space combat. One who is better than his opponent can give him a beginning advantage by starting with his own arm bent over and the back of his hand near the table (or ground). A really strong kid can get satisfaction and honor by starting with his hand only an inch or two off the table, and challenging others to put him down. If they cannot, they will be impressed—and why not? Another good game is Indian wrestling, a good test of agility, balance, and deception, as well as strength. The wrestlers stand right foot to right foot (or left to left), gripping each other's right hands at about waist height. At a signal, they both try, by pushing and pulling backwards and forwards, or sideways, to get the other to move one of his feet, or to push him off balance. There is also leg wrestling. The wrestlers lie on their backs on the floor, side by side, the feet of one by the head of the other. Each raises his inside leg, the one closest to his opponent, to the vertical, and hooks his foot and ankle inside the foot and ankle of the other. At a signal, each tries to pull his opponent's leg over sideways, rather as in arm wrestling.

Another good contest is the standing broad jump. The jumper starts with feet together, toes on a line. Any amount of bobbing and swinging before the jump is okay. Measure the length of the jump to the point farthest back touched by the jumper's foot, or hand if he touches the ground with his hand to steady himself. Best results are had by keeping the feet together. If you have mats, this is better done on them, both to reduce noise and to cushion a little the shock of landing. You may be able to find some connections here between distance in the broad jump and height, or length of leg.

The standing high jump is also good. There are several ways to do this. The children can try to jump over a little stick or dowel balanced at different heights from the floor. Or they can see how high a point on the wall, or edge of a door, they can touch with their hands. Here the difference between that point, and the highest point they can reach while standing, gives the height of the jump. Boys may be particularly interested in this because of its use in basketball. There are experiments possible here, perhaps to find the connection or correlation between high-jumping distance and length of leg, or distance and strength in exercises like the Deep Knee Bend, or perhaps distance and a strength/weight ratio.

Another feat would be the standing broad jump, or high jump, off one foot. Are two feet more than twice as good as one? That is, are the records for one-foot jumps, both broad and high, about half the records for the jumps from both feet, or less, or more?

Other tests. How long can children stand on one foot with eyes tightly shut, or blindfolded? They will be surprised to find how hard this is. Why is it so hard? Why does having eyes closed make such a difference? Some discussion may come of this. Or they can do balancing feats, like balancing a broomstick or mop handle or yardstick on the end of one finger. How long can they do that? How long, without moving the feet? (This is harder.) And there are push-ups from the floor. Little children will not be able to do many of these, but older ones, particularly boys, will know about them. Who can do the most, at a specified metronome rhythm? Also, there are two harder varieties that many will not know about. In one, when you push yourself off the floor, you clap your hands together before coming down again. Not easy. And harder yet is to clap both hands against your chest before coming down. This is for strong ones only—and they won't be able to do many. Another hard stunt, and very good exercise, is to do a full deep knee bend on one leg. Few will be able to do this without holding something for balance, like the edge of a doorway. The problem of falling over backwards while doing this may be solved to some degree by putting a piece of wood, a quarter or half inch thick, under the heel. Or, if you have some weights in the room, a child can help his balance by holding a weight out in front of him at arm's length— though this means that his leg has that much more weight to lift. This is a very good exercise for runners, jumpers, skaters, skiers— anyone.

In these ways, and many others you and the children may learn about, or discover or invent for yourselves, the development and the testing and measuring of strength and endurance can become a central and vital part of the life and work of the classroom.

18

MEASURING OURSELVES

Another good thing to have in a classroom is a metronome. This is a little machine which we can set to make a clicking sound, or flash a light, or both, at a given rate—anywhere from 40 to 208 times per minute. Some metronomes are electric, some spring powered. Of the electric ones, some run off batteries, some off 120-volt AC (regular house current). An ideal one for a class would run off batteries, and would either click, or flash, or both. No such a one exists. The ones that run off batteries only click; the ones that flash use house current. There is a very small, battery-powered model called the Mininome, which has a little earplug with it, so that whoever is using it can listen to the clicks through the earphone and thus not bother anyone else. The most accurate spring-wound metronomes are made by a company called Seth Thomas. There is a slightly less accurate, but smaller and handier spring-wound model called the Taktelly Piccolo. My own Taktelly, set at 60 per minute, gives 59 clicks—not a bad error. The best of the electric models is the Franz. Most or all of these are sold at good music stores, and I would guess that any good music supply house, or the Sears or Ward catalogs, would have metronomes in them. My choice, if I could have only one, would be the Franz flasher, though I would like to have, in addition, either a small spring-wound model and/or a Mininome.

Also good to have is a stethoscope. Medical supply stores have them; Creative Playthings, of Princeton, New Jersey, sells one for about five dollars. (They also make many other good things for children and classrooms. Send for their catalog; it is full of pictures that children will want to look at and read about, and it may give you ideas.) Most children, and most adults for that matter, have never heard through a stethoscope the sound of their heart beating. Many young children do not even know that they have a heart that beats. In *How Children Learn* I described a little boy who, after jumping up as high as he could ten times, put his hand on his chest over his heart. What he felt there inside made his mouth drop open and his eyes practically pop out with surprise.

With stethoscope and stopwatch children can measure how many times in a minute their heart beats. This rate (which doctors call the pulse) can also be measured by feeling with the tips of the fingers the vein at the thumb side of the wrist or at the temple. Doctors and nurses use the vein at the wrist, as most children will know. But this little throb at the corner of the wrist is a delicate sensation, and little children may not be able to keep track of it and count at the same time. The thump of the heart through the stethoscope is more positive. Children can easily count the number of times it beats in a minute. One child can hold the stopwatch, say "Go" and "Stop" at the end of a minute. After a while a child can count and keep track of the watch at the same time. This, by the way, is good counting practice, for children who may need that. If they tire of counting for a full minute they can count for 15 seconds and then multiply by four. If they are not sure how to do it, there is an interesting problem to solve.

With a metronome we can synchronize (another good word) the beats of our heart with the clicks or flashes of the metronome. Thus we can measure our pulse directly, as it goes. When two beats of slightly different frequency—i.e., say, one at 70 beats per minute and the other at 75—are going together, it sounds as if the faster is either running away from or catching up to the other. If you have two metronomes, children can experiment with them, and see how two beats of different frequencies behave. From a time when they are together, how long does it take them to get together again? Children will find that this depends on the difference between the frequencies. The greater the difference, the less time needed to catch up. This raises another interesting problem. If we set one metronome at 60, at what speed shall we set the other so that it will take the shortest possible time for one to catch up with the other? What happens if one is going twice as fast as the other? Three times as fast? If the ratios of their speeds are three to two?

There is a very interesting but slightly more expensive musical device called the Trinome (available at some music stores or from Belotti-Trinome Corporation, New York City) which can make the sound of several rhythms going at once. On this electric box there is a lever with which I can set a basic beat, at up to 29 clicks per minute. Then by pressing other buttons I can get a click that goes twice that fast, by pressing another get a click three times that fast, or four, or five, all the way up to ten. The rhythmic patterns that we can get from this are very intricate and fascinating. Children may find it interesting to dance to them, or make chants or songs or rhymes around them.

A very good exercise in musical and rhythmic coordination is to beat one time with the left hand and another with the right. At first two beats (later three) with one hand for one of the other. Children who find these easy can try the much harder task of beating three against two. More complicated than that I cannot do. I have read that the conductor Pierre Boulez can beat five against seven. With two metronomes or the Trinome, children can find out what this would sound like.

Timing a pulse against a metronome, children may find it hard at first to tell which of the two different beats is slower, and to get them together. To do this, note when metronome and heart are together, and then see which one moves ahead. Soon the children will be able to take their pulse, using either stopwatch or metronome. This opens up many possible experiments. Sometimes when everyone is quiet and rested, we can measure the pulse of all the children in the class. Someone with a watch will give a signal, and everyone will count his own heartbeats until, a half minute or a minute later, he gets the signal to stop. Whose pulse is fastest? Slowest? Do these correlate (another good word that children may like) in any way with weight, height, age? If we rank the class by pulse, calling One the person with the fastest pulse, Two the person with the next fastest, and so on, and then rank them by height, or by weight, or by age, how do these ranks compare? Do they tend to go together?

If we get the average pulse for an entire class or age, and compare it with other classes or ages, we can ask if pulse varies with age, and if so how. How do the children's pulses compare with the teacher's? Some may be curious to know what are the fastest and slowest pulses that men have recorded. I have heard that some long-distance runners have pulses as slow as 40–45 beats per minute. (The average adult's is around 70.) We can find out from a doctor what is a very fast pulse, or what is the fastest that a person could have and still live. How do fever or sickness affect pulse? The children might make a point of getting their pulse, or having their parents take it, along with their temperature, any time they happen to be sick. Is there a correlation between pulse and temperature?

We might try to find the pulse of a relaxed baby. What happens if he is crying or angry? (If we put a cold stethoscope on his chest he may *get* angry!) If we take his pulse just before he is fed, and just after, is there a difference? With the stethoscope can we hear the heartbeat of a dog? A cat? A smaller animal? We might ask animal experimenters or veterinarians how they get the pulse of small animals. How would we listen to the heartbeat of a mouse or hamster? What are the pulses of various animals? What about animals that we are not likely to find in school—cow, horse, or, wilder yet, elephant, lion, whale? What is known about their pulses? How would one go about getting the pulse of a whale?

Perhaps if he was asleep, or sick, it might be easy enough. But what if he were healthy? Whom might we ask about this? How do all these animal pulses compare? Is there a correlation between the size of an animal and his pulse? What is the fastest known animal pulse? My guess is that it would be that of a shrew, an animal many children would like to learn about because of its almost incredible appetite and ferocity. What about the pulse of reptiles? Fish? Insects? If people have measured the pulses of these creatures, how did they do it? If nobody has done it yet, how do you think they might do it? What sort of instrument might we need?

Birds probably have a very high pulse, particularly the very small ones, like hummingbirds. How could we measure the pulse of a bird? Could we do it in a way that would not frighten him? What do the bird experts have to tell us about this? With electronic equipment getting smaller and smaller, it may be possible, today or soon, to wire a very small transmitter into a bird so that as he flies around it will tell us his pulse. Has anyone done this? Whom should we ask about these things?

Thinking about pulse opens up the whole question of frequency—that is, how many times something happens in a given space of time. In another chapter we talked about the running, flying, or swimming speeds of other living creatures. What about the frequency of some of their actions?

There are, by the way, some beautiful books of pictures of hummingbirds in flight that would make a fine addition to the library of a school or class. Some children might be interested in knowing how those pictures were taken. How does one get a close-up picture of a hummingbird in flight? This might lead to thinking about other kinds of very high-speed photography— bullets going through things, light bulbs exploding, drops splashing. All such things are interesting to many children, and lead to many ways of nibbling at the world out there. Are there other kinds of high-frequency animal actions? What about the noises made by crickets, or tree toads, or katydids? What is the wingbeat of flies or bees? Has anyone measured that? How did he do it? When I was in school a physics teacher told us that no one yet knew for sure how a fly landed on the ceiling, whether he did a half-loop or half-roll. When they put in bright enough lights to enable them to photograph the fly, he spent his time hanging around the lights and wouldn't land on the ceiling. I don't know if they have solved that problem yet. And then there are the extraordinary high-frequency sound beams the bat makes to hunt his food. Many children, after they had got over saying "Ick!" and "Ugh!"—the poor bat gets a very bad press—would be interested in the puzzle of how this little animal uses sound and sound echoes to catch flying insects in the dark, and the ways in which men have tried to find out how he did it.

Not all of these questions will be interesting to all children, or to all teachers. Some may want to explore some of these questions, some others, and some may not be interested in any of them. I make so many suggestions so that there may be something here for everyone, or better yet, so that people will join the game and think of new ideas for themselves. The other point is to show again, as I have tried to in so many other places, the many ways in which a study of one thing can lead to a study of many others, and in which in real life all the things that in school we call Physics, Mathematics, Biology, Physiology, and so on, are all tied together.

There is a whole list of experiments we could do to find the effect on our pulse of such things as sleep, rest, exercise, anxiety. We might ask children to take their pulse right after they wake up. At recess we could have people run a number of fast sprints, one right after another, until they were good and tired. Then we could measure their pulse, and measure it again every half minute or so. From this we could plot a curve of what we might call recovery— how long does it take the heart to get back to its normal rate? How does this vary from child to child? Does it vary with age? Since it has much to do with physical condition, we might measure it for some of the best athletes in the school, and compare their recovery curves with those of other children. Is there a correlation between time of recovery and height/weight ratio? We might guess that very fat children, being out of condition, would have a slow recovery rate. They might refuse to run the sprints; if so, how could we find out their recovery rate? We might also see whether pulse is affected by emotional states. The children might take their pulse just before a test, take it again during the test, take it again after the test was finished. How would these rates compare with each other, and with the normal rate? Do these rates correlate in any way with the results of the exam? In other words, do unsuccessful students, taking an exam, because of being afraid, have a larger jump in their pulse rate than more successful students? Do some people calm down once they start working, while others stay keyed up? We might see what the effect of anger was on the pulse. A student who is really angry might not want to take his pulse or let anyone else take it. On the other hand, if we are keeping records of pulses, a really furious student might let his pulse be taken in the hope of breaking a record, one of his own, or of the whole class. Such experiments might help children be aware of, and hence control not inhibit (the distinction von Hilsheimer makes here is most important) their anger.

Along with pulse we can also measure respiration, the rate of breathing. It is hard to say what we mean by "normal." If we tell anyone, adult or child, to breathe normally, he is almost sure to start breathing abnormally. Here children may be interested in the difference between the bodily actions that, at least up to a point, we can control, and those that we cannot, and in listing both. We can do an interesting experiment with breathing. What is the slowest rate at which we can breathe steadily without running out of breath? I tried this with a stopwatch. I began taking a full breath (inhale-exhale) every 10 seconds. This was easy. Then I worked up—12, 14, 16, 20, and then 24 seconds per breath. As the period gets longer, I had to take a fuller and fuller breath. This in turn means that I had to regulate very carefully the rate at which I took in air and let it out, so that at the end of one 12 seconds my lungs were full, and at the end of the next 12 empty. It should be a good exercise, not only for breathing, but also for bodily awareness, relaxation, and self-control.

We can also see how fast we can do this. If we set the metronome at 60, and take one complete breath, inhale-exhale, for each click, we are taking 60 breaths per minute. How high can we run the metronome up without losing the rhythm? I began at 60 and worked up to 200 breaths per minute. This raised many of the same problems as very slow breathing. As before, I had to be conscious of my breathing in order to stay in the rhythm and also to keep from getting too full or empty of breath. The two exercises might well be done together, first at the most rapid and then at the slowest possible rate. With a flashing-light metronome, the whole class could do the fast breathing together.

After children have run a number of fast sprints, or jumped up as high as they can ten times or more, how will their respiration rates compare? Can we find correlations with other measurements? Are fastest runners the slowest breathers? Do pulse and respiration go together? If we measure the recovery rate for respiration, how does that compare with the recovery for pulse? How do these vary with age? We might find that we have an interesting social experiment. My guess would be that down to a certain age children would be interested in the competitive and scientific aspects of this experiment. For much younger children all this will seem too remote and abstract to be worth bothering with. It seems unlikely that five-year-olds, for example, would be willing to run sprints so that older children can see how fast they breathe. But if they had seen the older children doing it, they might.

In all this, as in other experiments I have suggested, we may have a way to bring together children's great interest in themselves and the way they feel and work, and their interest in the kinds of things that older people do in the larger world. Many think that the child's interest in himself, what we might call his self-centeredness, is in conflict with our wish or need to interest him in the larger world outside himself. But this conflict is not necessary; if we are wise we should find many ways to resolve it.

Two more measuring instruments may help in this. One is a sphygmomanometer—the thing doctors use to measure blood pressure. They are not hard to get, or use. When we listen to a heartbeat through a stethoscope, we hear it has two parts, two thumps, one a bit louder than the other. To measure blood pressure, a doctor wraps a kind of inflatable cloth bag around the patient's upper forearm and, by squeezing a bulb, inflates the bag until the pressure is high enough to stop the flow of blood to the lower arm. He can tell if he's done this by listening to the pulse in the lower arm with his stethoscope. When he can no longer hear it, he knows the bag is blown up tight enough. With a little valve he slowly lets air out of the bag, reducing the pressure, until he can begin to hear the first part of the heartbeat—what doctors call the systolic. The doctor notes this pressure, which he reads on a gauge attached to the bag. Then he reduces the pressure still more until he can hear the second part of the heartbeat, and notes that pressure. These two numbers give him the person's blood pressure. Perhaps the high number is arterial, blood going out, and the lower number venous, blood coming back. Some children, perhaps many, will be interested in knowing how all this works, and perhaps in hearing how men came to discover it.

In all the conditions in which we have previously measured respiration and pulse, we can also measure blood pressure. We can then look for all kinds of correlations—pressure against respiration, against pulse, against age, how affected by exercise, fatigue, sleep, rest, sickness, anxiety. Which of all these three measurements is the best indicator of fatigue, or relaxation, or anxiety? Which are the most changeable? We know that temperature stays fairly constant, which is why doctors use it as a quick indicator of health, while pulse and respiration vary a good deal. What about blood pressure?

There is another instrument with which we can measure certain changes in the body. It is called a GSR indicator or meter, GSR standing for Galvanic Skin Response. Of all the instruments named here, it is probably the best indicator of emotional stress, anxiety, anger, fear. Two electrodes—electrical contacts—are put into contact with the skin. (Here are more big words for children to take home to parents. Here also are more nibblings at other parts of physics—air and liquid pressure, electricity, resistance, conductivity.) A very small voltage is applied across the contacts, which makes a very small current flow through the skin from one contact to the other. The amount of the current shows on a meter. As the electrical resistance of the skin changes, so will the current, and hence the meter reading. In general, as we become more tense or anxious our skin becomes less resistant, more conductive, so that the GSR reading tends to go up as we get more stressed and down as we get more relaxed. These GSR meters, with instructions and many suggestions for use, may be obtained (with many other interesting materials) from Humanitas, Orange City, Florida. Or the Psychology Department of a nearby university may have some to lend, or may be able to help you get some. Someone told me recently that a recent catalog of Abercrombie and Fitch, Inc., in New York City advertises GSR meters, but I have not yet been able to check that.

Of the instruments named, the GSR meter may be the one that can best help children who are always in a high state of stress —anxiety, fear, anger—to be aware of this stress, and being aware, to deal with it and in time to control and reduce it. Whole chapters or books could be written—perhaps have been written—about the ways in which the GSR meter, in connection with various stimuli such as sounds, pictures, words spoken or written, various kinds of touch, is used or might be used to help people to help themselves get over some of their crippling fears or angers. George von Hilsheimer and his colleagues, among others, have done much useful work on this, some of it described in his book *How to Live with Your Special Child.*

Here is one thing we might do with a GSR meter. Suppose we have a student who is very much afraid of doing something that he has to do in class—read, or do math, or take tests, etc. Let's assume the class, including this student, has used the GSR meter.

Perhaps they will have done experiments to see whether, by making loud noises or threats or showing scary pictures of snakes or spiders and the like, they can make each other's GSR reading (i.e. anxiety) go up. At some point, when he has played some such games and is used to the meter, our nervous student attaches the electrodes to himself and puts the meter on his desk where he can easily read it. Let's assume, too, that from wearing the meter while resting or doing things he likes very much, he knows what his GSR reading is when he is relaxed. We then say, "Here is one of these math problems or spelling tests or French lessons or books or whatever it is that makes you anxious. Start to work on it, and as you work, keep note of your GSR reading. As soon as it gets above a certain point, stop working. Do something you like, relax, dream, draw a picture, until the GSR reading gets down near normal. Then start working again, and keep on until the reading again reaches that high point. Stop again until it reaches the low point. And so on. Keep doing this. See what happens. As time goes on, does it take longer for the reading to get from the low point up to that high point? Or does it take about the same amount of time, or does it go up faster?" It might even be interesting to use a stopwatch to measure exactly how long it takes to go from low reading to high, then down to low, and so on. When we begin to take note of our feelings, observe them, measure them, think about them, we are less likely than before to be the helpless victims of them. Again, this is not at all the same thing as saying, as we often tend to in school, that fear or anger is "bad." What we say instead is that it is interesting and may even be helpful in learning something about the way our feelings work.

19

FRACTIONS AND OTHER
BUGABOOS

Let's look at two things in arithmetic that cause children endless and needless pain and confusion.

One is fractions—in particular, adding fractions of different denominators. The fifth graders I have known had little trouble understanding the idea of fractions, or with adding fractions with the same denominator. But when the time came to add ½ and ⅓— then the trouble started.

As is so often true, our explanations cause more confusion than they clear up. Most of us, when the time comes to "show" and "explain" how to add ½ and ⅓, say that they have to be changed into sixths "because you can't add apples and oranges." Something like that. (Perhaps the New Math has a different lingo for all of this.) The statement is both false in fact and absurd. Of course we can add apples and oranges. Every week or two I go to the supermarket, put a plastic sack of apples in the cart, then go down the counter and drop in a sack of oranges. I am adding apples and oranges. In the same way, a farmer may put some cows in a barn and then later some horses, thus adding horses to cows. Or a used-car dealer may drive six Fords onto his lot, and follow them with five Chevys, thus adding Chevys to Fords.

The trouble is that we haven't said what we meant, because

we haven't thought enough about what we meant. What truth are we groping for?

What is really odd is that many children know, or could easily figure out, the answer to this puzzle. I once asked some six-year-olds, "If I put three horses into an empty pasture, and then put two cows in, what would I have in the pasture?" After thinking a while, several of them said, "Five animals."

The first part of the truth we are groping for when we make our confusing statement about apples and oranges is that when we say that we can or cannot add this or that, we are really talking, not about the adding itself, but about the way we will express our answer. We can add anything to anything. The real problem is, how shall we talk about the result? The second part of our missing truth is this. It is because we want to find *one number*—hence numerator—to describe the collection of things we have made by adding apples and oranges, or horses and cows, or Chevys and Fords, that we have to find *one name*—hence denominator—to apply to all the objects in our collection. A name is a class, so we have to think of a class to which all the members of the collection belong. Simple enough. This is what the little children saw easily when they said that if I added three horses and two cows, I would have five animals. If I want to apply a single number—numerator—to all the apples and oranges in my basket, I have to think of a class to which they both belong, a name that I can give to all of them, a common name, a common denominator. So I call them fruit. If the used-car dealer, having put several Fords and Chevys on his lot, wants to say what he has there, he can say, "I have five Chevys and six Fords." But if he only wants to use one number to describe his collection, he has to have one name to apply to it, a common denominator. So he says he has eleven automobiles. If he was a dealer in farm machinery, and had in his lot, not just cars, but tractors, bulldozers, etc., he would have to say, "I have so and so many machines."

Now the case of fractions is only a very special case of this. If I put half of a pie on a plate, and then add to it a third of that same pie (or of another pie of the same size), what can I say about what is on my plate? I can say that I have half of a pie and one-third of a pie. Or I can say that I have two *pieces* of pie. In this case, "pieces" is a perfectly good common denominator. What it doesn't tell me, of course, is how much pie I have on my plate, whether the pieces are little or big. So I have to do two things. First, find names, denominators, for my pieces of pie that will tell me how much of the whole pie they are. Secondly, arrange things so that both of my pieces have the same name, a common denominator. I can do this by saying that the big piece is three-sixths of the pie, and the small piece is two-sixths of the pie. It is then easy to see that when we add these two together we can call our result five-sixths of a piece of pie.

Having talked about pies I will now say that it is a mistake to use pies and pie diagrams to introduce children to the idea of fractions, for the very simple reason that there is no way for a child to check, either by inspection or measurement (unless he can measure angles), whether his ideas about adding fractions make any sense or not. Give a child a 6-inch-long strip of paper and a ruler, and ask him to find what half of that piece of paper, plus a third of that same piece, would add up to, and he has a fair chance of coming up with the answer, 5 inches. He can see the reality of what he is doing. This is much less true, or not true at all, of pie diagrams. I remember once carefully making, on cross-ruled (graph) paper, a rectangle nine squares long by three squares wide, and then asking a fifth grader to show me one third of it. Into the middle of this narrow rectangle he put his old familiar one-third pie diagram, then looked at me with great satisfaction. Of course, I tried to tell him that pie diagrams only work for pies, or circles. This obviously seemed to him like one more unnecessarily confusing thing that grownups like to tell you. All his other teachers, when *they* wanted to illustrate fractions, drew pie diagrams; therefore, pie diagrams *were* fractions. Of course, in time I was able to persuade him that when he was working with me he had to use some other recipe, some other system, that I happened to like. But his real ideas about fractions, such as they were, did not change.

The last thing in the world I am suggesting is that we should throw at children all these words about cows and fruit and animals and cars, or that if we do, they will all know how to add unlike fractions. I do say that if we, unlike so many arithmetic teachers, know what *we* are doing when we add unlike fractions, and don't talk nonsense about it, we will have a much better chance of finding things to do or say, or materials and projects for the children to work with, that will help them make sense of all this.

It will be clear from what I have said already that I don't think children should be "taught" fractions, but that instead they should meet and work with them in the course of their real work with numbers. I have suggested some ways of doing this, and will suggest more. But if we feel we must try to "teach" children fractions, the proper time to begin is in the first grade. It is a dreadful mistake to wait until fourth or fifth. We should begin by understanding, and pointing out, that whole numbers, as well as fractions, are *ratios*—it is why they are all called rational numbers. A whole number, like a fraction, expresses a relationship between one quantity and another. This important idea, by the way, is not made clear, but obscured, by most of what I have seen written for young children about sets. There is no way of defining what we mean by "two" without at the same time stating or implying what we mean by "one." We should encourage children to think of two by saying that this * * , is two of this * , or that this ♯ ♯ ♯ ♯ is two of this ♯ ♯ , or that this ' ' ' ' ' ' is two of this ' ' ' , and so on. But if we do this, we can also look the other way, so to speak, and say that in each case the smaller quantity is half of the larger. In the same way, we should introduce together the idea of the ratio three and the ratio one-third. This & & & is three of this & , and this @ @ @ is one-third of this @ @ @ @ @ @ @ @ @ . And so for four, and one-fourth; five, and one-fifth, etc. From this it will not be hard for children to see that if you cut a candy bar into two equal pieces and take one, what you have is half of the bar; if into three equal pieces, one-third of the bar; and so on.

Shortly after typing this part of the rough draft of the book, I found myself in the company of a young friend of mine, a freshman at a local junior college. Though she is very bright, she has never been a good student, and was completely defeated by math. As for so many students, it was only by a kind of courtesy or default or exhaustion on the part of her teachers and schools that she "got through math." The fact is, as she admits, that she could probably not pass a math test today for any grade higher than second—if that. I showed her this part of the chapter, and asked her to read it and tell me if it seemed to make any sense, or helped in any way to clear up some old confusions. After reading it, she said Yes, it did make a lot of sense, she could see better now what fractions were about, and why you have to do what you do, and what confused her before. Then she added wistfully, "Why don't they ever tell you things like that?" The answer is that it is very hard for most people to think about things that they think are simple, just as it is often hard for people, unless they have had practice, to tell you how to get to where they live.

Another great mistake, which we start making in first grade and go on making for years, is to take statements like $2 + 3 = 5$ or $3 \times 4 = 12$, and call them "addition facts" or "multiplication facts." These statements do not describe facts about addition and multiplication. They describe facts about numbers. One fact is that the number we call 5, this many things * * * * * , can be separated or split into two smaller quantities, this * * and this * * * , which we call 2 and 3. The other fact is that the number we call 12 can be arranged in three equal rows with four items in each row, like this * * * *
　　　　　　* * * *
　　　　　　* * * *

These *statements* can perhaps be called human inventions, but the facts they describe, facts about the numbers 5 and 12, are facts of nature. They do not depend on man, though man may be the only animal that has yet noticed them or thought about them. (Do animal mothers with broods, say a mother duck, know when one of their brood is missing? Do they think, in some duck-like way, "We seem to be one short"? Or do they think, "Where is George?") But these facts were true before man noticed them. They are facts in the way that gravity—the attraction of masses for each other—is a fact. They are not true, as many mathematical statements are true, because man made certain arbitrary assumptions or choices that in turn made them true. They are not true only because man decided to make a particular invention called numbers or addition or multiplication. They are true *out there.*

This may seem to some a trivial or picky point. I don't think it is. For one thing, if these facts about numbers are true out there, then they do not have to be taken on faith and memorized by children, as they are now, like the Catchism or the Pledge of Allegiance. They can be looked for and found. Thus we do not have to make the beginnings of arithmetic into a mysterious ritual, like the start of a twelve years long initiation into a secret fraternity. We can instead make it one more way, and an exceptionally good and accessible way, of doing what all young children like to do and are good at doing—finding out things about the world out there.

What are some things we might ask them to look into and what might they find? One question might be, "How many pairs of numbers can you find that combine to make 5 (or any other chosen number)?" Another might be, "How many different ways can you put numbers together to make 5?" Children using Cuisenaire rods investigate such problems, in many cases *even before they know number names,* when they do what is called "making the pattern of the green (or blue, brown, black, or whatever) rods." They find that the longer the rod is, the greater is the number of possible patterns to make it. This is a very important piece of mathematics. After a while, children may find, with or without Cuisenaire rods, that there is a definite relationship between the size of a number and the number of ways that it can be made by adding together two smaller numbers.

Teachers who teach children of widely varying skills often ask me for mathematical games or puzzles that can be played or investigated at many different levels of skill. This problem, of finding all the pairs of numbers that add up to make a given number, is a good example. Consider a fairly unmathematical student, trying to find as many pairs of numbers as he can that add up to (for example) 12. He is likely to work on it in a most unsystematic way. He may start with a number picked at random—say 5. Subtracting, or working with his fingers, or however he wishes—this is not an arithmetic test, but a research project—he finds that its complement is 7. He writes $5 + 7 = 12$, or perhaps just $5 + 7$, or 5 and 7. Then he looks around for another number to try. Perhaps he thinks of 3. Soon he has $3 + 9 = 12$. After a while, by this random process, he has a number of pairs. Does he have them all? He does not know. To find out is in itself a mathematical problem of great importance and generality, and when he solves it, he will have taken a great mathematical leap forward. He may see after a while that when he has $3 + 9 = 12$, he does not need to bother with 9; it is already taken care of. He may see after a while that the largest number he has to consider is 11. After a while he may see that when he has used up, in all his pairs, all the numbers from 1 through 11, he has completed the problem. Perhaps he will look over his random pairs, counting his way up from 1 to 11, and mentally checking numbers off as he sees he has used them. Perhaps he will write down the numbers 1 through 11, and check them off when he finds he has used them. It may take him a long time to work this out. *We must not rush him.* Above all, *we must not tell him.* We must resist the temptation to say, "Here is an easier way." In looking for that easier way he is doing mathematics, real mathematics. The search, the finding of the treasure, is a thousand times more important than the treasure itself, in this case the easy way we want him to know. Any ground he gains for himself in his search will be ground really gained, not to be lost soon if ever.

When he feels sure that he has found all the pairs for 12, we can ask him to try the pairs for 13. Being as yet rather unmathematical, he may see this as a completely new task, a whole new bunch of pairs to find. But he may think, wait a minute. If I already have a bunch of pairs that add up to 12, it will be easy to make each of them into a pair for 13, by adding 1 to one of them. Thus, if 5 and 7 add up to 12, 5 and 8 will make 13. Perhaps at first he will add 1 sometimes to the larger of the pair, sometimes to the smaller. If so, some of his 13-pairs will be duplicates. (Note in passing that though I have not explained what I mean by "13-pairs," it is clear. The work itself has made it clear.) After a while he may see that if he adds 1 always to the smaller number of the 12-pair, he will have all his needed 13-pairs, with one duplication, and with the 1-12 added in. Here he may think, "13 has the same number of pairs as 12. Does 14 have the same as 13? Does 11 have the same as 10? These are truly mathematical questions. He may find that when you go from an even to an odd number, your number of pairs does not increase, but that going from odd to even, it does. More mathematics.

While he is slogging along, slowly seeing similarities and short cuts, which *are* mathematics, some other student in the class, in a minutes or less, may write down all his pairs for 12. 1–11, 2–10, 3–9, 4–8, 5–7, 6–6. No need to go any further, that's all of them. He may notice that the total number of pairs for this even number is half of the number. Is it true for 10? 1–9, 2–8, 3–7, 4–6, 5–5,—yes, it is, and it is easy to see why. Must be true for all odd numbers. So the number of pairs to make any given number is equal to the number divided by two, and if you have a remainder, ignore it. So he comes up to us and says, "Have you got something else for me to do?" Putting down as silly and unworthy whatever in us may feel threatened by children who are much brighter than we are, we express our pleasure and admiration. But we must not forget that that slower or less mathematical student plowing along at his desk is making mathematical discoveries of his own that are just as real and legitimate. What difference does it make if the

orders that he is seeing for the first time, in the world or in numbers, are orders that some other student found long before, or was
aware of even without looking for them? Above all, we must not
let ourselves forget the very real possibility that the "slow" one, if
we let him go on making his own real discoveries, may one day
make some that the "fast" student has not made and will not make
at all. After all, Einstein's teachers, including his science teachers,
considered him a "slow" student.

Along with this work, we can gradually introduce children to
the idea of what mathematical symbols and statements are and do.
They are not mysterious symbols that fell out of the sky, and that
some remote and forgotten wise men learned how to translate.
They are ways that men worked out to write certain things down,
because they were convenient, saved time, paper, thinking, remembering. They are not the only ways that could have been worked
out; indeed, as some books show, our own numbers and mathematical symbols are the latest products of many inventions and
much change. So children should be encouraged to invent their
own ways of talking and writing about what they find out.

In my mind's eye I can see—I have seen it so many times—
first graders painfully copying out their "addition problems" or
"addition facts." First the 3, carefully and wavering, then the plus
sign, then the 2, then the two lines, not long, not too far apart,
keep them pointed the same way, then the 5. Every single mark that
that pencil makes on that paper is a mystery, done because They
tell you to do it, done that way because They tell you it can't be
done any other way.

When we find out how many pairs will make a certain number,
and when we try to find or invent shorter and easier ways to write
down what we have found, we come naturally, though from one
particular angle, to algebra. We don't need to call it that, or indeed
call it anything. Better *not* call it algebra; children with older
brothers and sisters groaning about their algebra will be needlessly
frightened. But algebra is the study of those statements about numbers that are true of many or all numbers. We have found that the

number of pairs to make a given number is equal to that number divided by two. Can we find shorter ways to write it? *We* could write: No. of pairs to make number equals half of number. P to make N = N/2. P $\quad$ = N/2. Part of mathematics is just inventing $\quad\quad$ N

short language. Abbreviations of words is a kind of mathematics. So is shorthand. Can children invent short languages, not just for numbers, but for other things they know and can do? A formula is a piece of short language. So is a map, or a plan, or an engineering drawing. All symbol systems are ways of condensing reality, or parts of it. Are photographs a kind of short language? The children may be interested to hear—I was—that there are primitive peoples who cannot recognize anything, even themselves or their family or their village, in a photograph. Are line drawings a kind of short language? Stick figures?

Let us think some more about the properties of numbers. How many ways can we find of combining numbers to make a given number? For 2 we have 1 + 1. For 3, we have 2 + 1, and 1 + 1 + 1. For 4, 3 + 1, 2 + 2, 2 + 1 + 1, 1 + 1 + 1 + 1. And so on. (Let's agree that the order of the numbers added does not make a difference, so that 2 + 1 is considered the same as 1 + 2.) How many ways can we combine numbers to make 5, 6, etc.? This problem or project is more interesting and less easy than it looks. For small numbers, it is simple enough. When we work with larger numbers, two problems come up. How can we be sure we have all the possible combinations, and have not left some out? How can we be sure we have no duplicates? To solve these problems, we have to think about ordering, arranging. If we ask children to see who can find the most ways to add numbers to make a given total, with no duplications allowed (and perhaps points taken off for duplications), they may find many interesting solutions to the problem. Is there a formula, or can we discover or make one, by which we can tell in advance how many different combinations of numbers will add up to a given number? If we know all the combinations for, say, 9, can we tell how many combinations there will be for 10, without having to write them all down?

Working on such a project we soon see that there is in it a great deal of the kind of work that teachers ordinarily call "drill"—the figuring and writing down of sums of numbers. But this drill, dull by itself, is not being done just because the teacher said to do it. It is being done in connection with a real mathematics project, a genuine investigation. Some may ask—people asked me this, angrily—"If the children have to learn these numbers, why not go at the matter directly, why all this fancy beating around the bush?" One answer is that, because drill is dull, children use only a small part of their attention and intelligence doing it, hence learn inefficiently if at all, and forget quickly. Another is that since only by threats can we get healthy and sensible children to do this kind of donkey work, we have to put fear into the classroom in order to get it done. But this fear defeats its own ends, by making many of the children too afraid to think or learn or remember at all, and in a longer view, by making them fear and hate all of mathematics, and indeed all of school. But the most important reason of all for having children meet and work with numbers in connection with larger projects is, of course, the one I have already spoken of. Instead of doing a lot of drill now so that years later, if all goes well, they may do some mathematics, they are doing the mathematics *now,* real mathematics, the kind of thinking and working that real mathematicians do.

This sort of research into the properties of numbers may help us avoid other kinds of mumbo-jumbo and mystification. One of the many things wrong with talking about "addition facts" or "multiplication facts" is that children will soon be asking us, or at any rate wondering, why 7 + 3 gives the same answer as 3 + 7, or 4 × 5 the same as 5 × 4. In the old days the answer to this question might well have been, "Because that's the way it is." Today, I'm afraid that many teachers with a little training in the New Math might say something like, "Because addition (or multiplication) is commutative." This is no help at all; the old answer, though not much good, was better. What does it mean, after all, to say that addition is commutative? It means that $7 + 3$ gives the same answer as $3 + 7$. But the child knew that. He was wondering why it was so. What was already mysterious is now a little more mysterious, though if he is one of the children who likes big words he may have fun talking about "commutative." A more sensible and helpful answer would be to say that $3 + 7 = 10$ and $7 + 3 = 10$ are two ways of writing down a fact about 10, that it can be made (among many other ways) by adding the numbers 7 and 3. Why, then, doesn't it make any difference which way we add them, the 7 first or the 3 first? Because if, for example, we are putting a group of seven marbles and another groups of three marbles into a bowl, it doesn't make any difference which of the groups go in first—eventually they all get in. If we want to talk more generally, we can say that this particular property of numbers comes from a property of matter, things in the real world, that numbers were invented to represent.

To this sort of talk I have often heard the reply that numbers are abstract and must be taught abstractly. I have heard this used as a criticism of the Cuisenaire rods. People who say this do not understand either numbers or abstractions and abstract-ness, or the rods. Of course numbers are abstract, but like any and all other abstractions, they are an abstraction *of something*. Men invented them to help them memorize, record, certain properties of reality—number of animals, boundaries of an annually flooded field, observations of stars, moon, tides, etc. These numbers did not get their properties from men's imaginations, but from the things they were designed to represent. A map of the United States is an abstraction, but it looks the way it does, not because the map maker thought it would be pretty that way, but because of the way the United States looks. Of course, the map maker can and must make certain choices, just as did the inventors of numbers. He can decide that what he wants to show on his map are contours, or climate, or temperature, or rainfall, or roads, or air routes, or the historical growth of the country. Having decided that, he can decide to color, say, the Louisiana Purchase blue, or red, or yellow—whatever looks nice to him. But once he has decided what he wants to map, and how he will represent it, by colors, or lines, or shading, or whatever, reality then dictates what his map will look like. So with numbers. The time may come when it is useful to consider numbers and the science of working with them without any reference to what they stand for, just as it might be useful to study the general science of mapping without mapping any one place in particular. But it is *illogical, confusing, and absurd* to start there with young children. The only way they can become familiar with the ideas of maps, symbol systems, abstractions of reality, is to move from known realities to the maps or symbols of them. Indeed, we all work this way. I know how contour maps are made—in that sense I understand them; but I cannot do what my brother-in-law, who among other things plans and lays out ski areas, can do. He can look at a contour map and instantly, in his mind's eye, feel the look and shape of the area. The reason he can do this while I can't is that he has walked over dozens of mountains and later looked at and studied and worked on the contour maps of areas where he was walking. No amount of explanations will enable any of us to turn an unfamiliar symbol system into the reality it stands for. We must go the other way first.

There are other properties of numbers that we and children can investigate. We can find out whether any given number is prime or composite, and if it is composite, we can find its factors, in other words, the numbers which when multiplied together have the given number as a product. The words "prime" and "composite" stand for something very simple, which even very young children can investigate. (This is something else that children can do, and in many places are doing, with the Cuisenaire rods, though it can also be done in other ways and with other kinds of materials.) A number is composite if we can arrange it in more than one row, with the same number of items in each row. Four is composite because we can arrange it like this $^{*\ *}_{*\ *}$; 6, because we can arrange it like this   * * *   ; 12, because we can arrange it like this * * * * or like this * * * * * * . 1, 2, 3, 5, 7, and many others, are prime because we cannot arrange them that way. So a good project for children is, starting with the smallest numbers and working up, to find which are composite and which are prime.

The children are very likely to discover after a while that they can say that 6 can be arranged in three rows with two items in each, or two rows with three items in each. Some may say something like, "It's really the same, it's just the way you look at them." We must not force this discovery, or try to hint them toward it. There is no rush. They will see it eventually, and anyway, it is not on the Achievement Tests (though, alas, if enough people read this book, it may someday be—unless we have enough sense to do away with Achievement Tests altogether). We must let the children talk about their discoveries in language that is natural to them—rows, lines. Young ones may want to make families or armies out of them. Okay. After a while, without making a big deal of it, we can say that if 10 can be arranged in two rows with five in each row, or five rows with two in each row, we say that 2 and 5 are factors of 10. We can also write that as $2 \times 5 = 10$, or $5 \times 2 = 10$.

We can now expand our research project by asking them to find, not just which numbers are composite and which are prime, but what are the factors of the composite numbers. Which composite number under 20 has the most factors? Can we guess in advance? Which composite number under 50 has the most? Under 100? What is the smallest number that has the factors 2, 3, and 4? Or 2, 3, 4, and 5? When I studied arithmetic, this problem was asked, "What is the Lowest Common Multiple of 2, 3, and 4?" The trouble is that we were told in advance "how to do it," so that it was not research, but only drill. A similar problem is "What is the Highest Common Factor of any two (or more) given numbers?" In short, given, for example, the numbers 72 and 60, what is the largest number that is a factor of both of them?

Working on these things, the children may make some interesting and important discoveries. One might be this, that if 6 is a factor of some number, say 12, then the factors of 6 must also be factors of 12. Some child, looking at ****** , will suddenly see that you could arrange it like this *** *** , which in turn you could arrange like this

```
* * *
* * *
* * *
* * *
```

The children will see that for each factor there is another factor that goes with it. That is, when we find that 2 is a factor of 12, we also find that 6 is. When we find that 3 is a factor of 12, we also find that 4 is. If we write out our pairs of factors, like this

$$2 \times 6$$
$$3 \times 4$$

we see that we don't have to look any further for factors of 12; we have found them all. If we went any higher we would get 4×3, but we already have that. This can save us from wasting time hunting around when looking for the factors of larger numbers. Suppose we are finding the factors of 36. We have found these:

$$2 \times 18$$
$$3 \times 12$$
$$4 \times 9$$
$$6 \times 6$$

Because anything bigger than 6 must have as a companion (or complement) something smaller than 6, we know we have found them all.

The children may notice that certain numbers are what the Greeks called square numbers. (We still call them squares.) That is, they can be arranged in a square, the same number of rows as items in each row; or one of their pairs of factors is a number times itself. Thus 4 (2 × 2) is a square, also 9 (3 × 3), 16, 25, etc. We can offer this as another property of numbers that the children can look for. Or, particularly if the children are testing their rows by putting marbles into a grid, like a Chinese Checker board, or are using Cuisenaire rods, or are even working with graph paper, we might wait to see if the children notice this. Of course, we have to remember that little children may not know the words for the distinction between a square and a rectangle.

Another property of numbers that interested the Greeks— and, by the way, the children might be interested to know that the Greeks attached mystical or religious attributes to these properties —is that of being what they called triangular. A triangular number is one that we can make by putting one item in the first row, two in the second, three in the third, and so on. Thus 1, 3, 6, 10, 15, 21, etc., are triangular numbers. The Greeks discovered—if you arrange these numbers on some kind of grid it is not hard to see this —that any two adjacent triangular numbers added together make a square number.

At this point, as I wrote, I was diverted in my work by a little problem. Having written down a number of triangular numbers, and noticed that none of them was prime, I began to wonder whether it was true that *no* triangular numbers were prime. The first thing to do was to write down some more, and see if I could find one that was prime. When I wrote 253 I thought, "Aha!" It had a kind of prime look about it: 3 is not a factor, nor 5, nor 7. But 11 was. So I decided to assume that triangular numbers were *not* prime, and see if I could find a proof that they were not. In a little while I found one. (I don't claim to be the first; I'm sure this proof is as old as the Greeks.) But I did not know the proof, and had to work it out for myself. In Appendix I, I have written all the wandering steps by which I did so. I hope you will read it. It may give you a sense of what one small piece of mathematical exploration and discovery was like. Some of you may want to try to work out this proof for yourself. To do so, you don't need to know anything more about mathematics than is already included in this chapter. Indeed, there is no reason why some mathematically minded children could not work it out, and it might be an interesting open-ended, no-time-limit problem to suggest to them.

Let's look a little more at our factors of 36. We know that if 18 is a factor of 36, then the factors of 18 are also factors of 36. So we could say that $36 = 2 \times 18 = 2 \times 2 \times 9 = 2 \times 2 \times 3 \times 3$. Those are all primes, so we can't go any further. Since we call 36 a composite number, we might say that we have decomposed 36 into its prime factors. When we do this with $36 = 3 \times 12$, we get the same result— $2 \times 2 \times 3 \times 3$, which is what we would expect. We also see that by recombining these prime factors in all possible ways, we can get all the factors of 36. Thus we have 2, 3, 4 (2×2), 6 (2×3), 9 (3×3), 12 ($2 \times 2 \times 3$), and 18 ($2 \times 3 \times 3$). This gives us an easy way to find all the factors of larger numbers.

One more question. Is there some other group of prime numbers that will compose to make 36? No, there is not. Can we prove it? Yes, though it would be a difficult proof for most children to work out, or even to understand if we showed it to them. But we can prove that the product of two prime numbers cannot be the product of any other number, and from that it follows quite easily that for any number there is one group of primes, and one only, that multiply together to make the number.

Prime numbers have always been fascinating to mathematicians. Indeed, an important part of number theory, itself an important branch of mathematics, has been devoted to primes. Children may find it interesting to do some research into primes. What are the prime numbers from 1 to 100? What are the primes from 101 to 200? From 200 to 300? One of the things they will notice is that a lot of primes seem to come in pairs, two apart, like 29 and 31, or 71 and 73. How many primes are there up to 100, or in the next 100, or in the next? How many of these prime pairs are in the first 100? In the second? The third? What about the last digits of primes? They have to be odd (why?) and they can't be 5 (why?). But in the final digits of primes, do the 1's, 3's, 7's, and 9's occur in equal numbers, or are there more of one than of the others?

Children will make many mathematical discoveries while they are looking for primes—which, by the way, involves plenty of work with numbers. They may see, first, that they don't even need to think about even numbers, since no even numbers are prime. No need, either, to think about numbers ending in 5. Since there is almost no chance that a child would discover it for himself, it would be okay to tell him—but not essential—that if the sum of the digits of a number is divisible by 3, then so is the number. So, if we are testing some number like 173, we don't need to try to divide it by 2, 3, 4, 5, 6, or any other even number. The first number we must divide by is 7. Do we need to divide by 9? If not, why not? Then by 11, then by 13. That is as high as we need to go. The reason? Because, since $17 \times 17 = 289$, it follows that *if* 17 were a factor of 173 (obviously, it isn't—why is it obvious?), the complementary factor would have to be something *smaller* than 17—and we have already tried all those numbers. So for any number less than 289, we don't need to divide by anything larger than 13. This is something that children might very well see for themselves, after a while. So don't tell them, or hint them toward it.

If some child gets really interested in primes, write, or better yet have him write, to the Mathematics Editor of the *Scientific American,* Martin Gardner, to find out where he can learn more about them. As a matter of fact, Mr. Gardner's regular mathematical column in the *Scientific American* is a rich source of ideas, puzzles, and problems. Many of them are too difficult for most children, but some are not, and would give them ways to do much genuine research.

20

FROM TALKING TO WRITING

Schools and teachers are much concerned with helping children to write well. So am I. But by "good" and "bad" writing I don't mean what most schools and teachers mean, and I have quite different reasons for feeling that good writing is important. We are deluged these days with bad writing. This is a serious problem. Bad writing is a kind of sickness of society. It pollutes thought. It makes it hard or impossible for us to think clearly and well. It destroys our trust in ourselves.

The bad writing from which we suffer is of two kinds. One comes from our promoters, our advertising and public relations men, our official spokesmen, our image makers, our propagandists, and, worst of all, because more than anyone else they have the duty of being clear and truthful, from most of our politicians, officeholders, public servants (who think they are masters). The other kind usually comes from our experts, our intellectuals, our academics—and, sadly enough, from many of their most angry and radical young critics, who too often write exactly like the professors and administrators they oppose.

The first kind of writing is bad because those who use it do so only to exploit and manipulate. They do not use words to help us to know and to do what we need and want, but only to make us do what they want, or even worse, *to make us think we want what they want us to want.* The second kind is bad because the men who use it are not really talking to us at all. They are quite literally talking over our heads, as if to someone more important, someone who really counts. They talk for display, to show something about themselves—how learned they are, how wise, how clever. Sometimes they may talk to show how brave they are, how angry, how defiant. These people do not use words to get us to do something, but to tell us in different ways *that it makes no difference what we do,* that we don't count. As Dennison said, they do not mean to empower us, but to hold us at a distance, "to stand over us and manipulate us."

The effect of all this bad writing on us is just what one might expect. We feel mystified and manipulated. As Paul Goodman pointed out in *Compulsory Mis-Education,* knowing how to read often makes a man not more informed, but only more gullible. All this print makes us feel small, weak, confused, stupid. As Erich Fromm puts it, we feel impotent, and quite naturally react by looking for power symbols and power figures to identify with, submit to, and serve—hydrogen bombs, tough-talking generals, proefssional athletes, hard-nosed politicians, astronauts, moon rockets. (We are conned into thinking that *we* are exploring space when we see on our TV sets a picture of men walking on the moon; but space is not the sea, it is not for you and me.) Worse, we look for scapegoats and victims, people we can look down on, treat with contempt, push around when we feel more than usually pushed around ourselves, so that from pushing them around we get a sense that we are, after all, *somebody.* All successful tyrants and dictators know that one of the most important tricks of their trade is the art of giving most people somebody they can safely push around. This was the function of the Jews in Nazi Germany. In our society, it is for many people an important function of children. (If we can't push kids around, who *can* we push? And if we can't push anyone, then that must mean that *we* are the ones on the bottom.) It is certainly a major source of our racism, our contempt and hatred for black people—and red, brown, and yellow as well. It may be a reason why so many people approve of wars like the one in Vietnam, if they don't last too long (where is that victory we were promised?), or cost too much money or too many American lives (Vietnamese lives don't count).

Good writing, on the other hand, makes us awake, aware, informed, competent. It helps us to know ourselves—our experience, our wants, our needs, our hopes, our fears—and to make ourselves known to others, and to know them. That this is important is not a new idea. The command to Know Thyself comes to us from the Greeks; so does the statement that the unexamined life is not worth living.

Indeed a life not examined, not *known,* can hardly be said to have been lived at all. In an excellent letter in the Autumn 1969 issue of *This Magazine Is About Schools* (good reading for teachers), George Martell writes that "manhood requires the development of an articulate self-consciousness." Speaking of a teen-aged boy, living in a Toronto slum, of whom he had written in an earlier issue, Martell also says that "Charlie MacDougal's words were one final reality, one part of his humanity, no matter how articulate he may be in love and violence. Without his words and his knowledge that they are in some important sense true, he is a slave and has no chance of becoming a man." The great and unmet need of young Studs Lonigan, in James Farrell's novel of that name about a boy growing up in a Chicago slum, was that only once in his life, and then not for long, did he ever have anyone that he could truly talk to. Because of this lack, this unmet need, he could not grow up a whole man.

By what we do in school as well as what we say, we convey to children that words, talk, writing, are not an expression and extension of oneself, but things that one uses to influence, to manipulate, to get things out of other people. This may be an important reason why so many young people, particularly among our best students, are turning so angrily away from the written word, or even words altogether. Even more than the unsuccessful students, they have been using words dishonestly in school, to manipulate their teachers and to get whatever rewards were to be had. Many of them now believe that it is hardly possible to use words honestly at all, that to speak is to lie. It is not just that so many people have used words dishonestly to them, to lie or manipulate or threaten or coerce. It is that they themselves have done so much of the same thing.

This calls to mind Dennison's words, in *The Lives of Children*, about children feeling that things heard in school belong not to them but to school. Our official users of words, our writers of bad writing, and perhaps above all our schools and teachers, have in a very real sense taken away, *stolen* from most people, words, talk, language, with all its power and possibilities. For they do not say to children, "Language, words belong to you, for you to use, for your purposes, your growth, your needs." On the contrary, they say, "You may not talk (or write) except when we tell you, and then only about what we want you to talk about, and in the way we want you to talk about it. All other talk and ways of talking are illegal, to be repressed and punished." (It may be worth noting here that in parts of the country children from Spanish-speaking families are still beaten in school if they talk Spanish there.)

Our fundamental knowledge and understanding of things, our mental model of reality, is, despite the obvious importance of words, not made of words, and the trouble with the word models we make, or that schools try to get us to make, is that they may have very little to do with the more real non-word reality below them. But it is no remedy not to have a verbal model at all, never to try to put our subconscious and non-verbal feelings and understandings into words. The trouble with the non-verbal mental model of reality is that it is so hard to get at. I once said about my fifth graders that they were quite good at thinking, but no good at all at thinking *about* what they were thinking. Because they were not good at putting their thoughts into words, they had no way to examine and reflect upon these thoughts, to check them against later experience, to refine them and improve on them. To put it still another way, they had no way to get outside of them the things they had inside. All of us, working on problems we could not solve, or trying to remember something just out of the reach of memory, have felt vague hunches and thoughts, swimming as it were like fish just below the surface of consciousness. We have thought, "There's an idea there, if I could only get hold of it." (In a similar way, there are tunes that I can hear in my head, but that I can't quite get enough of a grip on to sing or whistle; when I try they slip away.) This is what words—or symbols of some kind, mathematical, musical, the artist's or architect's or engineer's sketch—do for us. They enable us to get hold of the idea, so that we may then think about it, or even think of something else without the danger of losing it. Often, too, the act of getting hold of the idea will enable us to get new ideas from it.

The honest use of words, then, in talk or writing, is an act first of self-awareness, and then of self-expression. First we get hold of what we have inside; then we put it in such a way that someone else may share some of that feeling, experience, understanding. Which comes first? Do we need self-awareness in order to write, or do we write in order to gain self-awareness? Neither comes first; they grow together. We need some self-awareness in order to speak, to talk or write well, but through speaking we can become much more self-aware. We speak that we may know ourselves, and the better we know ourselves, the better we can speak.

But, as I said before, self-expression is only part of good writing and talking. What we want, as Dennison says, is communication and change. We must therefore be sensitive to the effect that our words are having on our hearer, we must be aware of and be able to hear and understand what he shows and tells us, in his words, or simply by his gestures and expressions, about the feelings and meanings he is getting from what we say. I once heard a prominent American educator talk to a large group of teachers, to whom I was to talk next. Waiting for my turn, I sat in the audience and looked around me, to get a sense of the people I would be talking to. While the expert droned out his mimeographed speech, teachers all around me slept, talked with their neighbors, read, drew pictures. They and the speaker might as well have been in different rooms. To talk to people in this way is not only arrogant but stupid. We must pay attention, not just to what we are saying, but to the one to whom we are saying it. Is he getting from our words the meaning we wanted to convey? If not, we have to find other words, find out as much as we can about the connections between *his* words and *his* meanings, so that we may better know what words to use to get *our* meanings over to him. In short, there can be no real talking without listening. The bad writers of whom I have spoken, the experts, intellectuals, academics, may be expressing themselves, and as honestly as they can, but they write badly because they are *only* expressing themselves. They do not care whether we, who hear them, grasp their meanings. Many of them think, and sometimes say, "If you do not understand me, it is because you are too ignorant or stupid; I will not struggle to understand the source of your misunderstanding, or to speak in words meaningful to you." Of course, there are notable exceptions, men like Bertrand Russell, true philosophers, who because they work hard at it can put difficult ideas into words that a great many people can understand.

A writer, therefore, needs a strong sense, awareness, not just of himself, but also of his listeners, readers. It follows from this that no one can write well who has not learned, and many times, what it is like to talk long and seriously to a trusted friend (or friends) about things deeply interesting to both of them. Such friends need not be of the same age; one such friend, when I was a boy, was an uncle. What is vital is mutual trust, respect, and concern. To get or encourage good writing, we must start here. We must make schools and classrooms where there is plenty of time, and spaces large and small, and above all encouragement, for the civilized art of conversation, some public, in groups, much of it private. Edgar Friedenberg has often pointed out how in all but a few schools there are neither times nor places where students can legitimately be by themselves. This would be a bad mistake, if only for its effect on students' writing—and this is among the least of its bad effects.

21

RECORDING TALK

There are many things we might do in the classroom to interest children in talking, and to record and preserve, and so make them aware of, their talk. One helpful piece of equipment is the tape recorder. It is one of the best machines that our technology has made available to the schools, a teaching machine that children themselves can use in many ways. The earlier open-reel machines were a bit difficult for children to use, but the new cassette-type recorders can be easily operated by any child, and the portable battery-operated models free us of worries about extension cords and children getting electric shocks. *Consumer's Reports* recently strongly recommended the portable cassette recorder made by Sears Roebuck. I have one, and it works very well.

Often, when visiting the early grades, and particularly in schools where I thought children might be a bit shy, I have brought the recorder with me. What I do is sit or squat, with the tape recorder going, near where some little children are busy. It is never long before someone asks me what the thing is that I am carrying. I say that it is called a tape recorder. Sometimes the children know what this is, sometimes not. If not, they ask. I say, "Well, the sounds we make with our voices go into the microphone here, and then into the machine, and onto this little tape that is going around, and then when we play back the machine we can hear what we said." The children consider this a while; then someone usually asks, "Is the machine going now?" I say that it is. They ask, "Is it taking down what we say?" Yes, it is. Soon someone asks if they can hear the voices; if no one asks, I suggest it. I rewind the tape and play back our voices speaking. The children, like everyone who for the first time hears his own recorded voice, find their voices a bit strange. But they recognize my voice, and other voices on the tape, and so know when their own voices are speaking. They react to this in different ways. Some look surprised and delighted, some are excited, some turn away with a shy smile. As soon as we have played back the voices, I begin recording again. Usually children talk about what they have just heard. After a while, I play back some more, then record again. Some children ask if they may talk into it. I say they are already talking into it, that it is taking down what they are saying. Some children then make a loud noise, some sing or show off or say silly things, many crowd in close but without saying anything. Some children are quickly turned on by the machine. Far from being shy of the mike, they want to talk into it all the time. They tell stories, make up songs, and so on. But in time even the shy ones get bolder. Soon all the children want to say something, and ways must be found to have people take turns.

In another class I visited, in Leicestershire County in Great Britain, the children, perhaps because they were interested in my American voice, perhaps because they like to hear stories read aloud by anyone who will read them, asked me to read them "Thumbelina," one of their favorites. I did, and recorded it, with their and my comments. When I finished, I played back some of the tape. They were charmed to hear again what they had just heard. Later, returning home, I had a recording made of the tape, to give them on a later visit. It would be easy for a teacher who liked reading stories to make recordings of each story read, so that children could play them again later by themselves—perhaps looking at the book as they listened, and in so doing, learning some things about reading. As other willing visitors arrived, parents or otherwise, they might be asked to read and record stories. One friend of mine, Roy Ilsley, now head of the Battling Brook Primary School in Leicestershire, has made a number of tapes in which he weaves together his reading of a story with appropriate selections from classical music. The children like these very much.

A few years ago I visited a wonderful combined fifth-sixth-grade class in one of the schools in the black community in Philadelphia. One of the big events of the day was a visit from the music teacher, a most gifted and imaginative woman. She played the guitar, and led the children in a number of songs, which they sang with skill and gusto. The songs were wonderfully chosen. Of them, I only remember "Everybody Loves Saturday Night," which they sang at the top of their lungs and in several languages. The songs were very different, some fast, some slow, some gay, some reflective; but all of them, like the "Saturday Night" song, carried a gentle message about our common humanity.

When the singing was over, she and the children did something they call Interview. This was a regular part of her work with the class, and one the children looked forward to. After some talk about whose turn it was, one of the girls was chosen to be interviewed. She stood at one side of the classroom, the music teacher stood at the other. This was part of the game, to make the child speak loudly and clearly enough for the teacher, and hence all the other children, to hear. The music teacher then began to ask the child a number of questions, as if interviewing her for a newspaper or radio or TV show, and the child answered. The first questions were: What is your name, Where do you live, and so on. These served to break the ice, and to get the child used to talking. As the interview went on, the questions became more personal and involved, requiring longer and more thoughtful answers. One rule of the game was, of course, that the child could decline to answer any question, though since the teacher was both tactful and trusted this did not often happen—not at all the day I was there. At the end of the interview the child could then ask the interviewer any one of the questions that she herself had been asked. This was exciting for everyone.

All the children clearly liked this game, which had done much to help shy children speak clearly, and with poise and conviction. There are many possible variations of this game, and ways to use them with the tape recorder. Children are used to seeing and hearing talk shows and interviews on TV and radio. We might invite them to plan and record their own talk shows for the class, taking turns at being the interviewer and the guest. In these shows they could appear and speak as themselves, or they could pretend to be other real people, perhaps other children in the class, perhaps adults—well-known personages of our time. Or they might pretend to be historical figures, or fictional characters from stories or TV shows or comic books. (Most children would find an interview with Superman quite interesting.) Or they might play characters invented entirely by them. Or the visitor might be from another planet, or might be an animal able to speak, or a dinosaur, or an automobile, or a tree, or a cliff, or the ocean, or the moon.

Some chlidren, particularly in very poor rural communities, may come to school with very little experience in talking, and so be very shy and hesitant. Even talkative children (like many adults) are often struck dumb when they find a mike in front of them. There are things we can do to help them get over this. One of the advantages of these tape recorders is that the mikes are so sensitive that a child can talk into one in a whisper so soft that nobody, not even near neighbors, can hear what he is saying. Then, listening with earphones, he can play back what he said, again softly enough so that nobody else can hear. Thus he can use the tape recorder even at times when the class is very quiet or silent, and without disturbing anyone else. Also, he can say things into the tape, and then listen to himself saying them, that he might not want anyone else to hear. In *The Underachieving School* I wrote about what I call Private Papers—papers written by a student for his eyes alone, papers that no one else will read. In the same way, it might be a good idea to let each child make a private tape, on which he could say whatever he wanted, safe in knowing that nobody else would ever hear it.

In my last fifth-grade classroom I had a tape recorder which, at least during our many open periods, any child who wanted could use. Interestingly enough, the children who used it most were those who most of the time were quite shy about speaking in class, or unwilling to speak at all. They liked to imitate radio announcers, to do commercials, to imitate and improvise science-fiction shows. One boy, a great hockey fan, whenever he got the chance would announce long imaginary professional hockey games. After a while one of the children—I think I know which one started it— invented a new game, of whispering taboo words (to call them "dirty" is silly) into the tape and then playing them back very softly for others to hear. Naturally, the game was popular. Soon the children began to spread the word around among their friends. One of them, perhaps trustingly, or perhaps deliberately trying to get someone in trouble, told an adult. Soon the story had made its way back to the authorities, and from them to me. So I gave the children a talk about taboo words and the dangers of using them in our society, and also about why it is a good idea, if you have a secret pleasure, to be sure to keep it secret. This more or less took care of the problem. At any rate, there was no more static about it.

With this in mind, when I began to invite students to write Private Papers, I took the precaution of saying that they really had to be private, they could not be for everyone in the class *except* me. Either a paper was not private, in which case I could read it, or it was private, in which case nobody else could read it. This, of course, applied only to school papers; if they wanted to write letters to their friends, that had nothing to do with school—they could put into those letters whatever they wanted and show them to whomever they wanted. But a private paper done as a school assignment, or on school time, or in school, had to be really private. We could make a similar rule for tapes, saying to the children something like this, "If you are going to use a school machine to make a private tape, then that tape must be truly private, for your ears only. If you want to make a tape to play for other people, then you mustn't put anything on it that you wouldn't be willing to have everyone else in the class hear, including me. Otherwise we might have people saying things to hurt other people's feelings, or other things they shouldn't say. Too much of this, and we might not be able to make any more private recordings, and might even lose the tape recorder altogether." The children would probably understand very well what we meant.

Some children may feel, at first, that we are not sincere in saying that private tapes will remain private, but instead may try to hear what they have said. It might reassure them if we show everyone that anything put on a tape can be erased by recording something else over it. Indeed, it would be a good idea to get, along with the recorder, what is called a bulk eraser—a not very expensive electrical device that will erase everything on a tape all at once. Thus a child who feels that he has exposed himself rather dangerously on tape may, if he chooses, quickly erase his whole recording. Or the teacher himself, if working in that kind of school or community, might feel safer if before the end of a school day he could erase all private recordings made during the day. It would be better if we could avoid this, and let each child keep everything that he had privately recorded, so that some months after the start of school he might, if he wished, go back and hear what had at first seemed very important for him to say. From such experiences children can get a very vivid sense of their growth and change.

I think again of young Studs Lonigan, who did not dare talk to his friends, or at least his companions, the other boys in his gang, about the things closest to him, fearing with good reason that they would make fun of him or later take advantage of his confidences. Perhaps many children feel this way, particularly in schools and communities where toughness, coolness, non-involvement, stoicism are seen as heroic virtues. Would such a child be willing to exchange tapes with another child, perhaps about the same in age, sex, and background, but again perhaps very different, in another and distant town or city, far enough away so that nothing he said about himself could be used against him? Would such children have enough trust in their schools and teachers—

hard to blame them if they did not—to let them be the medium of such an exchange? If not, how else might we put such children in contact with each other, and make available to them recorders on which to make and play back their tapes? Perhaps this could be done in learning centers, or street academies, or free universities and schools, or independent public schools—open admission, no-tuition schools outside the state-run system. Despite such difficult problems, this idea of tape exchange between children is one we might do well to explore further.

To help children get over their shyness there are other games or contests that we might play, with tape recorder and stopwatch. A beginning might be to ask all the children to talk, without stopping, for a given length of time. At first, this time should be very short. Children unused to talking much, at least in school, might find it hard to talk for even as long as five seconds. (Even some of my most talkative fifth graders, and much to their surprise, found it impossible at first to talk without stopping for only one minute.) When everyone could talk without stopping for 5 seconds—this could be done all together, without recording anything—we could raise the time to 10 seconds, then to 15, and so on. Once the children had got started, we could invite them to have a contest with themselves to see how long they could talk without stopping. As in the Composition Derby (see "Making Children Hate Reading" in *The Underachieving School*), the rule would be that the talk had to be about something—you couldn't just say "dog dog dog dog" or something like that. Though perhaps even this rule is not needed. Understanding this, a child could get ready, get his story well in mind (a good thinking practice in itself), then start the stopwatch and start talking. When he ran out of words and had to stop, he would stop the watch. In a book or on a graph of some kind, he might keep a record of his times, so that he could see improvement. In such an exercise, a child would do three things that we want him to do when we ask him to write: (1) think about what he was going to say; (2) say it; (3) go back and hear what he said. We could expect children not only to become more fluent, but to be able to keep longer and longer stories or talks in mind.

Let's take a second here to consider the arithmetic of children talking in school. When a child may only talk if he is called on by the teacher, and when all his talk is to a teacher, how much talking will he get a chance to do? Suppose we have thirty children in a class. Suppose we have a teacher who believes that it is important for children to talk. Suppose he curbs his own talking so that he is only talking half of the time. (Such restraint is very rare.) This means that in an hour class we have thirty minutes to divide up among thirty children. One minute per child per class. Perhaps six minutes a day. Not enough. Yet the picture is usually not even this good. Most teachers—this has been very carefully measured—talk much more than half the time in their classes, and the time that is left is not all used for children talking. Moreover, it is probably true that most of what talking the children do is done by a few of the best students. We can be sure that there are a great many children in schools who do not get a chance to talk even as much as one minute a day. We can't expect good writing to come from such a situation. What is the remedy? How are children to become fluent and skillful with words? The remedy is simple enough. The teacher cannot control, or even hear, all the talk. The children must be able, for large parts of the day, to talk either to themselves on a tape recorder or to other children. A silent school or classroom can only be a factory of stupidity.

To return to our class, children might challenge each other to talking contests. This could be done in different ways. At a signal, they might both begin talking at once, perhaps into recorders, perhaps to impartial judges. It would be the duty of the judge to signal, and to stop the watch, if one of the talkers stopped. This will start some lively arguments. How long a pause counts as a stop? Perhaps a fair rule might be that a pause, or an "Er," "Ah," or "Hm" of more than one second counts as a stop. They might take turns, first one talking as long as he could, then the other taking a turn, then the first one trying to beat the new record, then another turn for the second, and so on. Chances are that they would get ideas from each other's talk—like jazz musicians—and would be able to talk more and more as they went on. There might be one such contest going on in a class, with the other children watching. Or there might be many contests going on at once. Perhaps some children, or many, might do this outside of class.

Children might also be interested in measuring speeds of talking. How many words a minute do we speak in ordinary conversation? If we make up our own talk as we go along, who can say the most words in a minute? To judge this, we will have to record the talk, then play it back slowly, writing it all down, then count up the words. How does this compare with the number of words that a child can read aloud in a minute? Here we can count in advance the words in a given passage, then give it to different children to read aloud, timing each one. (There is good arithmetic involved in turning time to read a given number of words into a rate of words/minute.) Are the fastest at talking also the fastest at reading aloud?

From this point the children may be interested in comparing the speeds at which we can in various ways write down talk. How fast does a fast typist type? Perhaps one of the secretaries in the school office could come to class and show her skill. How many words a minute can she copy? What is the world's record? How does this compare with the handwriting of the fastest writer in class? (Though my handwriting is fairly rapid, a number of my fifth-grade students, to my surprise, could write faster than I could.) From this, children may see some of the advantages of learning to type. How fast can an expert at shorthand take dictation? Again, it would be a good idea, if an expert is available, to have him come and demonstrate. Some of the children will be interested in the shorthand. How can those funny little marks stand for words? Some may want to start learning how to do it.

The Early Learning Center in Stamford, Connecticut once asked an expert in Chinese calligraphy to come to school to show his skill to the children. To everyone's surprise, it was so popular that before long he was coming in once or twice a week to teach a regular class. Children are fascinated with skill, competence, particularly when it seems to have some relation to the real world. We could also show them Speedwriting. Some might want to try to invent their own forms of shorthand or speed writing—a very useful skill for people who have to take class notes. I often use it myself when I am away from a typewriter and have thoughts I want to write down. If you can find someone, perhaps a court reporter, who knows how to Stenotype, invite him to come to class with his machine. The children, particularly if they are used to typewriters, will be interested in how the Stenotype works, and the ways it differs from a typewriter. They will find it hard to believe that an expert in shorthand or Stenotype can record as fast as they can talk. We could show this by having them read, as fast as they can, a passage from a book. The stenographer would then read back from his notes, and the children could compare this with the original passage. Older children might be interested in getting a Stenotype machine for their class, and in learning to run it.

All this is just a beginning. With sound equipment of higher quality we can make the business of recording voices and playing them back much more exciting. With most tape recorders, we can plug the output into an amplifier and then play it out through a speaker. The voices will then sound much more natural, so that children will more easily recognize their own and each other's voices. Also, they can be made much louder. A child can murmur or whisper very softly into the mike, and later hear his whispering voice made loud enough to fill the room. This will certainly be very exciting for children, and may help them get a stronger sense of themselves. With a stereo mike and recorder, and good stereo playback equipment (which schools should have anyway for good reproduction of classical music—there is no excuse any longer for the kind of thin and scratchy sounds that are all most children ever hear of it), we can get an ever greater sense of realism, the sense of space and location in space that we get on good stereo recordings. This may lead them to think of many new ways to use this quality of space, to work out sound effects, to make up and produce plays for taping and replaying, and so on.

Let me quote here from a short article "Aurally We're Illiterates" by James Feeley, again in the Autumn 1969 issue of *This Magazine Is About Schools.*

> . . . At school you write, and write, and write. You sit still and quiet and you write. . . . It doesn't matter what the words are. . . . You pull many of those words out of the air off the lips of teachers . . . You copy many of those words from books. You even write some of those words "yourself." . . . in the present society the major technology for transmitting and preserving information is changing, and so too are the learning and education processes.
>
> After you get out of school you get a job. And you talk, and talk, and listen, and talk. You spend the rest of your life talking, and sometimes listening, but seldom writing. Sure you have to write letters, and memos, and reports, but never again in a sixteen year period will you write five million words. At school you learn [my note: at least they try to make you] how to handle the *written* word, but you never learn how to handle the *spoken* word. You never do for the spoken word what you do for the written word. Aurally you're illiterate. What would happen to you during your sixteen years at school if you learned about tape recorders, dictating machines, mikes, tapes, and splicers? What if you work with them and with amplifiers and filters and voltage regulators? What if you tape, edit, and re-tape the spoken word just as often as you write, edit, and re-write the written word? Wouldn't you be a different person with a different way of looking at the word and the world? And isn't that what learning is about?

The point is important. We talk of preparing children for what many like to call the Real World. But in that world, even today, the whole technology of recording, preserving, and retrieving the spoken word is of enormous importance. I don't happen to agree with the extreme McLuhan-ite position that electronic technology has made print obsolete; print is still by far the cheapest way to distribute certain kinds of information, and, since we can read much faster than we can talk, by far the faster way of retrieving it. I can skim *The New York Times,* looking for what interests me, but there is no way to skim the conversation of a bore, or to know what is on a tape short of hearing everything on it. But at the same time I would say that a child who goes through school and does not become familiar with the technology and techniques of recording sounds is a great deal more illiterate, and worse prepared for life in these times, than one who does not know multiplication tables, how to divide fractions, or the dates of historical events.

22

MAKING LETTERS

In our work with children, there are a couple of good rules to keep in mind. One is that it is always better to say to a child—instead of "Do it this way"—"How many ways can you think of to do it?" The other is to let children find, by experiment, trial and error, and imitation, which of the possible ways of doing a thing is best for them. This best way may often be our way, the way we would have "taught." This is what Dennison means by "the natural authority of adults." But even if in the end children do come to *our* way of doing things, we should let them do so in *their* way. Some might say, "Why waste time? If we know that a given way of doing things is best, why not just tell the children to do it that way?" But our way may not be the best way, but only the way we are used to. Also, the best way for us, or for some children, may not be the best way for all. Finally, it is *always* better, if he can do so at not too great cost or risk, for a child to find out something for himself than to be told. Only from making choices and judgments can he learn to make them better, or learn to trust his own judgment.

A scene comes to mind. While I was visiting a college, giving several talks and observing different parts of the school's work with children, someone asked me to come to a seminar, run by some operant conditioners, behavior reinforcers. In general, I don't like this way of dealing with children, or for that matter people of any age. This seemed all the more reason to see some of what they were doing. Perhaps what they were doing was better than it had sounded. Perhaps it was worse.

The leaders of this seminar were telling about some of the work they had done teaching four- or five-year-olds to write—that is, to make letters. They explained reinforcement theory and their own methods. I believe they generally gave the children tokens or points. Soon one of the leaders said, "Now the first thing we have to do is teach the children the right way to hold the pencil." We all nodded agreement. But then, as they told about the prizes they gave to children who held their pencils correctly, I began to wonder. Suppose we *didn't* teach children how to hold the pencil? What would happen? And then an even more subversive thought crept in. Is it really true that the way we all hold our pencils is the only way, the best way? Might some other ways not work as well? So, sitting on the floor in my corner of the room, I began to experiment. Soon I found five other ways of holding a pencil. One was at least as good as the conventional grip. The others were a bit awkward, but with them I could make a legible handwriting recognizably my own. Switching to the left hand, where I was starting from scratch with all grips, I found one of my new grips much more comfortable for me than the conventional grip, though it made my handwriting slant the other way.

Now, as I write, I have done the same experiment again. Results are the same. There *are* other ways to hold pencils, and some of them, for children with small and weak fingers, might at first be a good deal better than the one we try to teach them. Given the right kind of pencil or pen (like a ball-point), it is really very easy to write with the pen gripped in the whole fist. Writing with the left hand, for me at least, the fist grip is considerably easier and more controllable. Also, my hand doesn't have to touch the paper, which might do away with the problem of smearing the ink. I suspect that the fist grip might be much less cramping and tiring for little children. But anyway, why not let them learn to hold a pen the way they learn to ride a bike or whistle or do a thousand other things far more complicated and difficult than holding a pen? Children want to learn to write—watch any two-year-old with pencil and paper. If we give them pencil and paper, they will try out different grips to see which works best for them. They will certainly look to see how we do it, and will probably do it our way if they can. But if something else is more comfortable for them, where's the harm?

I did not raise this issue at the seminar. I had come to hear their story, not to tell them mine. I left the meeting feeling as strongly as before (and much more strongly now) that getting children to do things by rewarding them every time they do what we want is unnecessary, harmful, and even in its own terms inefficient.

Men, and above all little children, have much more intelligence than, say, pigeons, and it seems unwise, to say the least, to treat them the same. Even if efficiency is all we are interested in—and it ought not to be—the efficient way to teach any creature is to make the fullest possible use of his capacities.

We have such a passion for uniformity and control! One might think we had all come off one of our own assembly lines. In classrooms all over the country we can see, tacked up over the chalkboards, the same letter chart—on green cardboard—capital and lower case A, then capital and lower case B, then C, and so on. On some of these charts, and these I would really like to rip off the wall, there are even little arrows and numbers to show in what direction and in what order the child must make the strokes of the letter! Must children feel that they have to make their letters in *exactly* the shape they see on the chart? This might make sense if it were true that only the exact shape of the A could be recognized by other people as an A. But this is not true. Even the books in our classrooms have many different kinds of A's. Typography is one of the great crafts or even arts, with a long history of its own. Why not give children a glimpse of this part of the continuum of experience? Why not get, from any maker of type, or printer, or commercial artist, or art supply store, some sheets of samples of type faces, so that children can see some of the many ways in which we make our letters? Better yet, why not invite the children, using old newspapers, magazines, labels, and so on, to find as many different kinds of A's (or other letters) as they can?

By the way, we ought to make sure to use the words "capital" and "lower case" instead of words like "big" and "little" or "large" and "small," or anything else suggesting that the difference is a matter of size. The difference is a matter of shape; size has nothing to do with it. We can make any capital or lower case letter as small or as large as we wish. Some of the children may ask why we call some letters Capital and others Lower Case. The word "capital" may come from the fact that the Romans (who invented our alphabet) used those letters on the capitals, that is, across the tops, of buildings. I'm not sure of this. Lower case has to do with the ways in which printers arrange letters in a font, or case, of type. If there is a printing shop around that you can visit, the children can see what lower case means. Or perhaps someone could bring a font of type to the class for the children to look at. And this raises other questions, to which I don't know the answers. Who invented lower case letters, and for what reason or purpose? When did men start using capital letters for the rather special purposes for which we now use them, with lower case used most of the time? Do other alphabets, and if so which, make the distinctions we do between capital and lower case letters?

We might start everyone thinking about the number of ways we can make a capital A. We could make it tall and thin, or short and fat. We could make it slant to the right or to the left. We could make the strokes thick (heavy) or thin (light), or a mixture of the two. We could put feet (serifs) on the legs, or leave them off. We could put the bar high in the letter, or low in the letter. We could weight the lefthand stroke, as in the type face Ultra Bodoni. Or we could weight the righthand stroke. We could make our strokes hollow, or fill them with cross-hatching, or dots. We could make our strokes out of wiggly lines, or right-angled steps, or dots, or short dashes. Or we could make our strokes out of the letter A itself, or some other letter—why not an A made out of B's, and a B made out of A's? Children like such novelties. They suggest that the world is a fascinating place, full of possibilities. Why not tempt children with the idea of making A's (or other letters) in as many different ways as possible? Making letters would then be an exploration, an adventure, not a chore. The chances are that they would make a great many more letters. Also, by making a variety of shapes they would train and coordinate the writing muscles of hand and arm far better than they could with the old, laborious, wrinkled-brow, tongue-sticking-out-of-the-corner-of-the-mouth drill.

This is just a beginning. Suppose we have a collection of A's. There are at least two things we can do with the collection. We can consider for each pair of those A's what the significant variable is. An example will make this clear. In the first pair of A's the variable might be called Proportion—the ratio of height to width. (Some good new words here—as I say elsewhere, the idea of ratio is fundamental to the idea of number.) In the second pair of A's the variable is the direction of slant—Right or Left. Another variable could be the amount of slant. Who can draw the slantiest A? In the next pair the variable might be called Weight (or Thickness) of Stroke. Naming the variables may suggest new variables to us. Or it may suggest ways in which we can combine variables. Thus, we might have an A which is thin, slightly slanted, slanted left, and heavy stroked. Children play a lot of these classifying or categorizing games in school as it is—why not combine them in an interesting way with the world of letters? For older children there are mathematical possibilities in this that I won't even go into here—the total number of kinds of A's you could make combining all these variables, and so on.

Another game would be, given a particular A, to make a similar B, or C, or some other letter. (Again, we are in the field of likes and differences.) Or make an entire matching alphabet. Or, given a certain A, make a B in all respects the opposite— given a Heavy, Right Slanting, Fat A, make a Light, Left Slanting, Thin B. We might put these letters on cards and have various ways of sorting them—put similar letters together, or opposite together, or all the ones together that have a given variable in common. We might play with these letters some of the kinds of matching and sorting games found in the excellent piece of classroom equipment called Attribute Blocks (McGraw Hill Corporation, Webster Division, St. Louis, Missouri). Or we might invent a color code, assigning a color to each variable. Thus if to the variable of Proportion we gave the color blue, and agreed that a large number indicated a tall thin letter, and a small number a short, fat letter, we could use color and number to designate a certain kind of A. How might we designate slant by using a number? What do people mean when they say a highway has a slope of 1 in 10? What kind of people, in the course of their work, have to interest themselves in such matters? What is the steepest grade usable for a railroad? An auto road? Or we could use degrees to measure slant, and thus introduce children to the protractor, and also to another part of mathematics, the measurement of angles in degrees.

Children can make letters out of other things than pencil and paper. Why not letters you can feel as well as see? There can be many advantages in this. Children who have become so anxious about reading that they can hardly even *see* letters, let alone tell one letter from another—see my remarks about this in *How Children Fail,* or Dennison's moving description of José trying to read in *The Lives of Children*—can regain their sense of the shape by feeling it. The Montessori schools have letters made of sandpaper or cardboard or wood backing, which the children feel, and learn to know by touch. A good idea; but like much Montessori equipment the letters are expensive, and because sandpaper is hard to cut, they are hard to make. We can find cheaper and easier ways to do the same thing. How about gluing heavy twine to cardboard to make the shapes of letters? How about putting rough crepe paper, or perhaps strips of masking tape, on a background of glossy paper? How about using double-sided Scotch tape, and then putting salt or sand on the top? How about pegs in a pegboard, or round-headed map pins pushed into cardboard? How about letters made of grooves pressed into clay, or out of glass beads pressed into clay?

Recently I visited the Children's Community Workshop School in New York City, a wonderful independent public school —that is, a school open to all and charging no tuition. Many of the children in one of the early age groups were sticking oranges full of cloves, to make a scent ball to hang in a clothes closet. As I helped one little boy with his clove orange (he asked me to), an idea came, and I stuck cloves into an orange to make my name, J O H N . Quite a number of children came round to watch as I made those letters. It seemed hardly possible that one *could* make letters with cloves and an orange—letters were made with pencil and paper—and yet, there they were. The boy asked me if he could keep the orange. I said sure, so at the end of the day he took it home, wrapped up—bundled up might be a better word—in tissue paper.

Why not mobiles of letters? Letters hanging from the ceiling? It would be easy to make them of pipe cleaners. Or papier-mâché, on a core of rolled or crumped paper. What could be more handsome than papier-mâché letters, printed in bright colors? Or we might make letters of the cardboard cylinders in paper towels. Or letters of rubber tubing. Or of spaghetti, bent when wet and then allowed to dry. Of plasticene or clay. Of wire from coat hangers, or, for schools in farm country, of baling wire. Of cloth cylinders stuffed with more cloth. Huge letters, tall as a child.

Another project. Using only one sheet of paper, how big a letter can we write? How big, if you can use more than one sheet? What is the largest letter that can be made, keeping inside the classroom? Outside the classroom? In the schoolyard, can we draw huge letters with chalk? Write them in the snow? Make them out of snow? Or could we make letters out of children themselves, like marching bands at a football game? If the school building has several floors, someone might take photos of these child-letters from an upper window. Which letters can we make with our fingers? I don't mean drawing with the fingers, I mean using the fingers themselves for the parts of the letter. Some letters are easy —T, C, etc. Others are not so easy. Can we make them all? How many letters can we make, using our whole body—arms, legs, etc.? If two or more children work together on this, how many can they make? Can you have a dance of letters? Children might be interested to know that in many languages all words have gender, that is, are boy-words or girl-words. If letters had to be boy-letters or girl-letters, which would be which?

We might show children how to use the lettering rules that draftsmen use to get uniform lettering on their drawings. From these, a child would learn through his hand, his muscles, what it felt like to make a letter of a certain shape. Stencils, rubber letter blocks, any kind of printing material, are all popular with children. Let children who are starting to make letters begin by tracing. Write a letter with heavy strokes, using a black felt-tipped pen; then let them put it under their paper and trace from it, over and over, perhaps in rhythm, until they get the feel of it. From drugstores, get Magic Writing Pads—write on one, lift up the paper, and the letter disappears. This is good for beginners—if they make a bad one, they can get rid of all traces of it immediately. No erasing, smudges, holes in the paper. In certain kinds of import stores, more on the coasts than further inland, we can often get the kind of small slates that all children use in countries where chalk is cheap and paper scarce. Children like to write on these, and again, erasing is easy, which is important for nervous beginners.

From these beginnings, I am sure you can think of many more ideas of your own. I have written at such length on a very simple subject to show that *nothing,* not even a task as seemingly cut-and-dried as making letters, needs to be monotonous, frightening, dull, cut off from the rest of learning and of life, or from the possibility of imagination, experiment, invention, play.

23

PHOTOGRAPHY AND WRITING

One useful, exciting, and important piece of equipment we can use with children is a camera. Photographs are a major part of the day-to-day experience of all of us. We are surrounded by photographs of the world around us, still, or on movies or TV. Much of what we learn of that world we learn from photos of it. For all of us, the camera is a kind of extra, long-range, Superman-like eye, a way of seeing much that we might otherwise not see. So nothing could be more exciting or real for children, or rich in ways of moving out into the world, than learning how to use and using cameras.

There ought to be at least one camera in every well-equipped classroom; at the very least, one for every two classrooms. Unfortunately, many schools will not have them, and will not get them. Then we will have to get one ourselves. There may be many ways to do this. Many commercial photographers have old or rarely used cameras which they might be willing to lend, or sell very cheaply. In middle-class areas, where people own many cameras, some parents or friends might be willing to lend one. If there is a college or university nearby, or even a well-equipped high school, we may be able to work something out with their photography department or students. If all else fails, we can buy a camera ourselves. Perhaps one or more fellow teachers or parents of children would be willing to share the expense. Most large cities have secondhand camera stores where very good older models can be bought for very low prices. Cameras that a few years ago would have cost two hundred dollars or more can now be bought for fifty to one hundred dollars. Those not in or near a city should check some of the photography magazines, on newsstands all over the country; many of the big camera stores advertise in them, and since they do a large mail business, they probably can be trusted.

Among cameras, there are several kinds to consider. One is a Polaroid camera. Its big advantage is that you can see your picture right away. Little children particularly like this. The Polaroid company makes Colorpak models that will take quite good pictures in color, which young children also like. There are some disadvantages. There is no negative, so enlargements and prints must be copies. The Colorpak models are almost certainly too bulky and stiff for the youngest children to use; it takes quite a bit of strength to pull out the film after a picture. Also, though the cameras are designed to be almost foolproof, they are somewhat limited in what they can do. They don't have as fast lenses as conventional cameras (which means that you can't use them as well in dim light) and their film is less versatile. They are purely and simply snapshot cameras. Their cheapest model, the Swinger, might be very good for a beginning camera. If the children became really interested, and wanted to go further into photography, one of the other types would be better.

Here we have a choice of three kinds—35 millimeter (mm.), split-frame 35 mm., and 120 size, which gives a picture of 2¼ x 2¼ inches. The advantage of the 120 is that the pictures are big enough to be looked at and used as they are developed, and do not need to be enlarged. The disadvantages are three: the film is more expensive, with fewer pictures per roll; the slides, if we make them, won't fit in many slide projectors; and the cameras are more bulky. The 35 mm. camera is probably the best bet, particularly if you know amateur photographers, whether older students or adults, who will do developing, enlarging, and printing at cost. Most cameras now sold are of this type. With them you can get faster lenses (a fast lens is one with a wide opening, which lets in more light and hence exposes the film faster), a wider variety of film, color slides for projecting on a screen, which is very exciting for children, and the possibility of making many prints for low cost. The disadvantage of 35 mm. is that the pictures are so small. With color slides, we can look at them through a viewer, or use a projector. Black and white prints will have to be enlarged to be big enough for the children to see them.

Since with 35 mm. we must use either a viewer or projector for color slides, or enlarge black and white pictures, it may make sense to consider the split-frame 35 mm. camera. This uses 35 mm. film, but takes twice as many pictures, of half-side. The advantage is that film costs less and there are more pictures per roll, so that the film doesn't have to be changed so often. Also, the cameras are smaller and handier. I have one, which is a pleasure to use. Since they are quite new, they may be harder to find secondhand, and there may be better bargains in 35 mm. cameras. Some 35 mm. cameras use conventional roll film, giving a small oblong picture. Some use drop-in cartridges, easier to load, but which give a slightly smaller picture, and which are more expensive than ordinary film. I would tend to stay away from super-automatic-foolproof cameras. Part of the point of a camera project is that children will learn how to use cameras, and in the process learn other things about light, film, time, and so forth. If the camera itself always decides exposure and lens openings and shutter speeds, the children will not be able to think and learn about these things themselves. Also, the cameras are less versatile. To get a foolproof camera we have to give up flexibility, the chance of making the picture come out the way we want instead of the way the camera designer wants it.

Buying a secondhand camera, we should find out whether an instruction booklet comes with it. If we cannot get a booklet, we must make sure that the dealer can supply some other sources of instructions. For most of the major makes of cameras, there have been published handbooks, costing a dollar or two. A photographer in your area may be able to show you how to use the camera. It would be a good idea, anyway, to ask an expert's advice about what and where to buy.

Let's imagine that we have our camera, and an instruction book, and that we are going to work with it in a class of young children, four-, five-, or six-year-olds. It would be a good idea to bring the camera to the class in its box or carton. Children like to see how things are packed and shipped. Part of the continuum of experience is that some people go to great trouble to put things into a box, and other people have to go to great trouble to take them out. There will be writing on the boxes and cartons, and some children may be interested in what it says. Unpacking anything is exciting. The empty cartons, cardboard, etc. may be useful. And the children will learn from whatever thinking we may have to do to take that box apart and get the camera ready for use. It will be tempting to practice enough with it beforehand, so that we come to the class as an expert, but it is better not to. As much as possible, we should ourselves learn to use the camera before the eyes of the children.

Of course, experienced photographers, familiar with the camera they will use in class, can't pretend otherwise for the children, though we can talk about whatever we do as we do it. But if we have not used a camera before, or the one we will be using, then we should let the children see us doing the kinds of things we all have to do when we learn to use something new. Think aloud as you find the instructions and do what they say. "Let's see, there must be some instructions somewhere. Ah, here they are. 'Instructions for Using the XYZ Camera.' " . . . "Well, let's find out first how to put film in it. Yes, it says it goes into this, we turn this knob, yes, I see, now we put this here." And so on. There will be photographs of the camera in the instructions. We should show them to the children. The parts of the camera will be labeled on the photographs. We should show the parts on the photographs and also on the camera. If some child says, "Let me see," then we let him see. We must try not to keep saying, "Be careful." The children may be offended, and rightly, by our assuming that they would not be careful unless we told them to be.

What shall we do if we meet something we do not understand? The first thing to do is to define as closely as we can what it is we think we do not understand. Next we must try to state in what way we don't understand. Is the problem that someone is using words or symbols that for us have no referents, nothing they refer to? This would be the case if the instructions told us to attach something to a certain part, but we did not know what the part was. Or is the problem that one thing we are told seems to contradict something else we are told? Or is it that when we try to follow a particular instruction the thing that is supposed to happen does not happen? Or is the problem that we have not been told something we need to know?

In the first of these cases we have to find something in the instructions that will tell us where that unknown part is, or what the unknown word means. We should talk about these difficulties as we go along. Thus, suppose the instructions say, as they will for any camera with any kind of built-in exposure meter or automatic exposure device, that somewhere we must set the film speed into the camera. Someone inexperienced with cameras may not know what film speed means. If this is the case, we should say so. "Film speed. I wonder what that means." It has to do with how quickly the film takes the picture. A fast film gets exposed more quickly than a slow film. That means in turn that in dim light we must use fast film, or that when we are using fast film we can use faster shutter speeds. We might say, "Film speed must be about the film, so maybe it's somewhere around the box the film came in." We can read aloud some of the things written on the box. If the speed is not there, it will be on some piece of paper inside the box. We take the paper out, show it to the children, read some of it aloud. We skip around, looking for film speed, reading a bit here, a bit there, thinking aloud as we look.

From all this children will see that people don't always understand everything, and that a man who makes something has to tell someone else, a long way away, and much later, how to use it. He does this by writing things down. The other person finds out what he said by reading. Therefore, people can talk to each other, learn from each other, help each other, even when they are far apart. The children will feel themselves part of the continuum of human experience because they are *with you in it.*

If we find that we cannot figure out how to run the camera, it will not be bad, but good, because it will give the children a chance to see us coping with a human problem. If, even though we try not to be, it still makes us nervous to be confused before others, then we should talk about that. "I hate not being able to understand things, do things, when other people are around. It makes me feel so silly and stupid and embarrassed." The children will nod; they know what we mean, they are in this boat all the time. Some of them might decide right then to tell about something like this happening to them. If so, good; if not, we should not try to coax some such story out of them. If a discussion starts on this, we can let it run. If not, that's all right too. The real business of the moment is the camera, and how to get it working as soon as possible.

To this some may say, "This is all very well, but how do I do all these things with a class of children to look out for? Who is going to be taking care of the class? The children will be running all over the place." If these children are young, they will like mysteries, surprises, watching grownups do things, and will probably be very interested, at least for a while, in getting the camera working, all the more so if we tell them that as soon as we know how to work it we will take some pictures of them. If we sit on the floor, or on a low chair, so that all the children who want can come close and watch, this is probably what many of them will do. Those not interested can find things to do by themselves, or we can suggest something for them. Or we could begin when everyone was working on some project of his own, and then start opening the camera. Those inclined could come and watch, while the rest went on doing whatever they were doing. If learning to use the camera is going to take long, we might plan work on it in fifteen- or twenty-minute stretches, perhaps once or twice a day. If it should happen that none of the children was interested in seeing how to work the camera, we could take it home and learn to work it there. The signal will come from the children.

It would be fair to say as we started something like: "Now you children can watch me open this and figure out how to work it, but please be rather quiet and peaceful, as I have to concentrate." This is not a threat, simply a matter of fact. If many of the class are not interested in the camera, and are running around or doing something that seems to demand attention, we could say, "Well, I'll have to work on this some more later, when things are a bit calmer." Again, this is just a statement of fact. We should not make it into a reproach or rebuke.

If you fear that while you are learning to use the camera, the children will explode, bring your worries into the open. Bring the camera to class in its box. The children will ask what it is. "It's a camera, and I'm going to take your pictures with it as soon as I can take it out and figure out how to work it." They will ask when that will be. Say something like, "Oh, as soon as possible. But it will have to be sometime when things are very quiet and peaceful in here, nobody running around or fighting, because I'm going to have to think hard to figure out how to use this camera, and I can't do that if I'm worrying about what everyone is doing." No reproach; after all, the children haven't done these bad things *yet*. But tell them what is on your mind. One way or another, they will react to the promise of the camera and to your fears about classroom disturbance. What they do will tell you how to proceed. Or, if your class usually runs on a very tight schedule, give a minute or two every day to Camera Time, tell them that during this time you will gradually open the box and learn how to work the camera. If these minutes work out well, stretch them out to five minutes or ten.

If the thought of doing all this in the classroom just seems impossible, the best thing will be to learn to work the camera at home, then put it back in its box, bring it to school, and show the children how you unpacked it and learned to work it.

Let us assume now we have a camera—let us say a Polaroid Swinger—all loaded up and ready to shoot. A good start is to take a picture of all the children, or at least as many as want to have their pictures taken. Some may be shy of this. Like some primitive people—and in a sense little children are primitive people—they may feel that the camera is going to steal their spirit away, do something to them. But the shy children will probably get over this quickly when they see the other children looking excitedly at their pictures. Even the children who are at first most shy of tape recorders soon want to talk into them.

On the camera, or in the book, there will be instructions about how to take the picture and get it out of the camera. We should read these directions aloud, talk about what we are doing as we do it. "Now we count up to ten seconds. Now we carefully pull out the film. Now we pull away the backing—let's see how it came out." When the picture is ready, we can mount it on a piece of cardboard, shirt cardboard, oak tag, or something like that, leaving plenty of room around the edges for writing. There we can begin to write some information about the picture, saying it as we write it: the names of the child or children; the class—Kindergarten, or First Grade; the name of the school; the teacher's name—"picture taken by Mr. Brown"; perhaps the day and the date, or even the time of day; perhaps other information about the picture, things in it, the background against which it is taken. The children themselves may suggest some things they would like written about the picture. If the picture is of one child, he may want to take it home. This is okay, but after he has had it at home for a while, he should bring it back, so that everyone can look at it. These pictures with their writing will be very valuable reading texts.

Children will cling to their pictures for a while. When they bring them back to class, they may still want to keep them in a place they feel is theirs. In time, the pictures should be displayed, at least for a while, somewhere in the room where everyone can see them. Or we might collect them into a book—a kind of photographic journal of the class. Mounting pictures on 8½ x 11-inch oak tag or cardboard, and then putting them into a loose-leaf notebook, would be one way. Any time the class goes anywhere, or does an interesting project, or someone makes something interesting, or brings something to class, or there is a visitor, or anything out of the ordinary—a big storm, a deep snow, a fire drill, or whatever—that's a good time to take a picture, ask the children for ideas on what to write about it, and put it in the book.

Pictures taken with non-Polaroid cameras must go somewhere to be developed and printed before the children can see them. So we will have to write down somewhere all the vital information about the picture before we forget it. For this, we might make what could be called a Photo Log—another notebook, listing photos by number and giving for each one of them all the important information. Suppose three children want their picture taken with a gerbil or other pet. We can say, "All right, but we must write down in the log our information about the picture before we send it to be developed or copied." When the copies come back, which will be exciting, the children can look up the information in the log and transfer the information to the picture mounts themselves. Such reading and writing will of course be very real and interesting to the children, strongly linked to their experience. From it they will get a strong sense of what reading and writing are *for*.

The children will want to use the camera themselves. Nothing could be better. Some might assume that little children are too small or clumsy or careless to handle cameras, above all very good ones. It is not so. In many places right now, six-year-olds and under are using good cameras and taking good pictures with them. A friend of mine, Karen Halbfinger, who runs a most interesting small nursery school in Israel, sent me not long ago many wonderful pictures taken by six- and five-year-olds, using a 35 mm. camera. In some ghetto schools I have heard of, young children have used cameras to make photographic essays of themselves and their neighborhoods. Children have the skill. In Japan, thousands of four- and five-year-olds are expertly playing the violin. Using cameras is easier.

If the children are not used to the idea that adults in school will actually let them *do* things, we may have to convince them that they really can use the camera. We might start by printing in large letters, with felt-tipped pen, all the necessary directions for using the camera, and posting these direction on the wall. From time to time we could show all the children, or those interested, how to use the camera, reading aloud each step of the directions and demonstrating with the camera, then letting certain children demonstrate. From this the children would learn, not only how to use the camera, but also all the words in the directions. If some of these words are large, so much the better. It will impress anxious administrators and/or parents. Some of these will be so pleased to hear a child using a word like "exposure" that they may be ready to overlook or accept the fact that he is also enjoying himself.

Some years back, when many non-academic high school boys were interested in hot rods (as many still are), people were surprised to find that boys who were "non-readers" could read and spell words like manifold, carburetor, ignition, distributor, differential, etc. People remember what they use, what is important to them. With this in mind, let's think about some of the words that children will meet and use as they learn to use a camera: lens, aperture, opening, shutter, focal, advance, rewind, emulsion, field, focus, expose, exposure, counter, intensity, image, viewfinder, rangefinder, adjust, battery, pointer, indicator, negative, positive, enlarge, contact, enlargement, overexposed, underexposed, composition, contrast—and many more. These are all part of the everyday language of photography. Children who are interested in and use cameras will naturally use, and therefore know, these words. Doing so, they will begin to nibble, in Mrs. Hawkins' apt phrase, at many pieces of the world of physics and chemistry and mathematics.

When children start taking their own pictures they may soon want to write their own words in the Photo Log, the class journal, and on the picture mounts themselves. If they are very young, at first they may simply tell us what to say, while we write it. Later they may ask, or we might suggest, that we write whatever words they want on a separate piece of paper, which they can then copy wherever they wish. If there is a typewriter in the class or available, the children may want to type their picture captions. Soon they will be ready to write directly into the log or journal themselves. We should not use this as an occasion to correct their spelling. They will soon see that spelling is a convention, and that if they want other people to be able to read what they have written, they will have to spell it in a conventional way. This is sensible and does not need to be hammered in with bribes and threats.

A camera—either 35 mm. or Polaroid—can be used in many other ways in connection with reading and writing. Sylvia Ashton-Warner wrote for the children, on word cards, whatever words they most wanted. A problem with word cards, though, is that a child who does not know what the word says may have no way of figuring it out. Some teachers have made self-explaining word cards by using pictures cut out of magazines, catalogs, etc. If we can't find in a magazine the picture we want, we can take a picture of it ourselves. In a class that had many pieces of equipment for children to use, we could take a photograph of each one, label it, and so have a kind of catalog. If children wanted to know what a particular thing was called, or how to spell it, they could find out by looking up the picture. Or the children could take pictures of other people in the school, or of other places—gym, cafeteria, auditorium, music room, art room, etc. Or perhaps of places of interest around and near the school, or in the city or town itself. Famous cities have guidebooks; why not let children make these for their school or neighborhood or town?

24

WRITING FOR OURSELVES

Good writing, writing that is a true extension and expression of ourselves, helps us to know ourselves, to make ourselves known to others, and to know them. It gives us a way of getting hold of our thoughts and feelings, so that we may think about them, learn from them, build on them. It can help us break out of the closed-in quality of our own experience, and share that experience with others. And it is still, and will be for a long time to come, one of the most powerful ways to reach other men, and so to make and change the reality we live in.

How do we make available to children the experience of writing, putting down on paper some of the real thoughts and feelings they have inside? One thing we must not do. We must not treat writing as a "skill," something that can be exercised all by itself. As Wendell Johnson put it, "You can't write writing." We cannot teach children "the skill of writing" in a vacuum of ideas and feelings, by having them write exercises or essays that we think are good for them, and then expect them to take that "skill" and begin to use it to write something important. They can only learn to write well by trying to write, for themselves, or other people they want to reach, what they feel is important. It is not much help to say, "Write about anything you want." This freedom of choice is essential for children, but it may not help them much if they have no idea what the possible choices are. And it won't help at all if the writing they have already done in school has made them feel that all writing is painful and dull or that they can't do it.

If we begin early enough, beginning may be quite easy. In *The Underachieving School* I describe one such beginning:

> Once when substituting in a first-grade class I thought that the children, who were just beginning to read and write, might enjoy some of the kind of free, non-stop writing that my fifth graders had done. About 40 minutes before lunch one day, I asked them all to take pencil and paper and start writing about anything they wanted. They seemed to like the idea, but right away one child said anxiously, "Suppose we can't spell a word?"
>
> "Don't worry about it," I said. "Just spell it the best way you can."
>
> A heavy silence settled on the room. All I could see were still pencils and anxious faces. This was clearly not the right approach. So I said, "All right, I'll tell you what to do. Any time you want to know how to spell a word, tell me and I'll write it on the board."
>
> They breathed a sigh of relief and went to work. Soon requests for words were coming fast; as soon as I wrote one, someone asked me another. By lunchtime, when most of the children were still busily writing, the board was full. What was interesting was that most of the words they had asked for were much longer and more complicated than anything in their reading books or workbooks. Freed from worry about spelling, they were willing to use the most difficult and interesting words that they knew.

This class of children had learned to make their letters, or most of them, by the time I came to them. If they had not known how, what would I have done? At first, I would have done just what I did. That is, I would have written on the board, perhaps in somewhat larger letters, whatever words the children wanted to write on their papers, and asked them to copy them just by looking at them. After all, if they must copy letters from those letter strips that we see over most chalkboards, they can surely copy from real words, which are more interesting. If a child was too anxious about this to try it, I would make for him, using bold letters made with black felt-tipped pen, a capital and lower case alphabet. Then I would say, "When you see a letter on the board that you are not sure how to write, find that letter in your own alphabet, and either copy it on your paper, or put the letter under your paper and trace it." If a child couldn't do this, I would make one more change, after the example of Sylvia Ashton-Warner. I would say, "When any of you ask me for a word, I will write it on the board. Copy it if you can, using your own alphabet if that helps. If you feel unsure of that and want more help, I will write the word on a card for you. Then you can either copy it or trace from it." With this much help it seems almost certain that all the children would be able to write something. And from the very start they would get the idea that writing is a way of saying something that you want to say.

We may make it harder for children to write by having them make their letters too small too soon. Even the wide-lined paper that many schools use does not allow the size letter that many children would be comfortable making. Why not let children make letters two or more inches high? And why not in colored crayons, which they like anyway? Pencil is not very exciting. For that matter, why not use felt-tipped pens for beginning writing? The letters are bolder and handsomer. True, felt-tipped pens are more expensive than pencils. But, at least in black, it is possible to get the liquid to refill them, which makes them inexpensive enough to be worth using.

In *The Underachieving School* I also describe the Composition Derby, which I invented to help fifth graders get over their dislike of writing and the fear that they could not do it, that anything and everything they wrote would somehow be judged bad or wrong.

> I divided the class into teams, and told them that when I said, "Go," they were to start writing something. It could be about anything they wanted, but it had to be about something; they

couldn't just write "dog dog dog dog" on the paper. It could be true stories, descriptions of people or places or events, wishes, made-up stories, dreams—anything they liked. Spelling didn't count, so they didn't have to worry about it. When I said "Stop," they were to stop and count up the words they had written. The team that wrote the most words would win the derby.

It was a success in many ways and for many reasons. The first surprise was that the two children who consistently wrote the most words were two of the least successful students in the class. They were bright, but they had always had a very hard time in school. Both were very bad spellers, and worrying about this had slowed down their writing without improving their spelling. When they were free of this worry and could let themselves go, they found hidden and unsuspected talents. . . .

In our first derby the class wrote an average of about ten words a minute; after a few months their average was over 20. Some of the slower writers tripled their output. Even the slowest, one of whom was the best student in the class, were writing 15 words a minute. More important, almost all the children enjoyed the derbies and wrote interesting things.

The Composition Derby evolved into the somewhat less competitive Non-Stop paper. I stole this idea from Professor S. I. Hayakawa (*Language in Thought and Action*), who in his freshman English classes at Roosevelt College many years ago had his students write in class for a half hour without stopping. He asked them, if they ran short of ideas, to write over again the last sentence they had written, and keep copying it until more ideas came. They found they seldom had to copy the sentence more than once. In the winter of 1969 I and my students at Berkeley did ten to fifteen minutes of this non-stop writing in almost every class. We found that we became much better at it with practice, so that before long thoughts came much faster than we could put them down. After a while, to keep up with the speed of our thoughts, I suggested that we write in a compressed, telegram or shorthand style. This was still not fast enough. Even when we condensed each thought into a key word or two, thoughts came faster than we could write them. This is a very good exercise for writers; indeed, I often use it as a first step in my own writing.

Another idea of mine, new to most schools, is the Private Paper. This is a paper written by the student *for his eyes alone*, not to be handed in, or even seen by anyone else. Such papers are useful and important for many reasons. One is simply mechanical. If what students write is limited to what teachers can correct, or even read, the students don't write nearly enough. Also, writing privately they will write about many things they would never put in a paper to be handed in. Of course, it may take a while to convince them that private papers really will be private. When they believe it, they are likely to begin to write the things that are really on their minds. Once, to some eleventh graders, I said, "I am not going to ask you to do this, your private papers are private, but just out of curiosity, *if* I asked you to take your private papers, censor out everything you did not want me to see, and then hand them in, how much of what you have written would you want to censor?" Some said only 10 or 20 percent; one student laughed and said about 90 percent. His writing was probably very useful to him.

At Berkeley after we had done some private papers, I asked my students how many of them had, in their schooling, had the experience of writing, not for someone else's credit or approval, but for themselves, and how they felt about the experience. Hardly any of them had ever done it before. On the whole, they found it interesting, often surprising and absorbing. Many of them found, as I often do, that after only a few minutes they were writing things that they had not planned or expected to write, sometimes things they had not even known they thought. I urged them to do more of this writing at home, and some of them did. I do this myself. I often write a quick paragraph or two on the typewriter, thinking that someday I may expand it or work it into something or somehow make use of it. And I always carry in a pocket a little pad on which I can jot down, in a kind of personal speedwriting, thoughts that come to me. This is one of the things any writer has to learn to do, let thought flow quickly and unself-consciously from mind to paper. Get it down now; worry later about cleaning it up, ordering it, figuring out what to do with it.

Many teachers, when I talk about private papers, say, "How do you make sure the students are writing them?" First of all, why do we have to make sure? Why not trust them? Some students, at least, will probably do private writing, and some of them, at least, will find it worth doing. If so, they will tell others, and the word will get around. There is no big hurry. We are not running a writing factory, trying to turn out a certain volume of papers. The papers are only a means to an end. The end is that students will find that discovering and writing their thoughts is something so worth doing that they will want to do it. We don't have to make this happen or expect it to happen in weeks, or months, or even years. After all, as things are now, it hardly ever happens at all. We can afford to be patient, and let the pleasures and satisfactions of good writing slowly work their way into the lives of the students.

Of course, this answer does not and will not satisfy many teachers. Some will have to deal with their own anxious feelings that the classroom is a place where they *make* things happen, that they have a duty to make sure that private papers get written. Others may have the tactical problem of satisfying administrators or parents that things really *are* happening. And it just might be possible that some students, who had been completely turned off by school, never would write anything.

For those with such worries, there are mechanical ways to see that some writing gets done. The first is simply to do some in class. This may be a good idea for other reasons. A student in a roomful of children all busily writing away may feel, "If they can do it, I can do it." Or he may simply feel less foolish doing it. Also—and this is *essential*—the teacher can also write with the students. After ten or fifteen minutes of writing, everyone can stop and talk a bit, not about what they wrote, but about what the experience was like. I have asked students, "How many of you found that you wrote things that you weren't thinking about writing or didn't expect to write when you started?" Almost everyone finds he has done so. I say, "How many of you felt that thoughts were coming much faster than you could write them down?" Again, most say they found it so.

Even with students who have been writing on their own, it is a good idea to use class time to introduce them to new kinds of writing experiences, for just the reasons given. It will keep many of them from being frozen by self-consciousness, from feeling, "This is silly, nobody else could be doing this." And it gives everyone a chance to talk later, if they wish, about their reaction to the experience. When the writing is not very personal, as when we are experimenting with verse forms like Haiku or other syllable patterns, or simply playing with words, students can read to the class what they have written. If people are self-conscious, it may help to say something like this, "Some of the time—I will always let you know this in advance—we will write things that many of us will read to the class. Just the thought of doing this may make some of you anxious. If so, let's talk a bit about this. It really will help us in our work with writing if we can develop enough confidence and trust in each other so that we will be able to do some writing for each other, and draw on the ideas and opinion of all of us."

But when we ask students to write Private Papers out of class, how can we be sure that they get written? In one class, when I was worried about that, I asked students to bring in their papers, and simply hold them up in the air so that I could see them, wiggling them slightly if they wished so that from a distance I could not read their writing. They didn't seem to mind doing this. Some might say, "How do you know you weren't being shown the same paper over and over?" I didn't know. But if this seems a problem, there is a simple remedy. Have each student write at the top of each paper his name and date, in felt-tipped pen, in letters large enough so that we can read them at a distance. Or, as they show us a paper, have them put a large check across the top, to show that we have seen it, and so that they won't be able to show it again. Perhaps, if we discuss this problem with students, they may be able to think of other ideas, safety devices. On the whole, the best answer to this problem, if it is one, is to get students interested in a particular kind of writing *in* class before asking them to do it outside of class. Try always to give a choice of assignments, so that students who don't like one variety of writing may work on another they do like.

Once in a while it may be hard to get the writing started in the first place. It happened once to me. The Composition Derby had worked so well that it seemed to me that any children, once freed from the worry of making mistakes and being wrong, would write just as freely. This proved not to be so. For a few summers I taught English in the Urban School, a small, privately run and financed, evening summer school for high school students, many of them from the black community. One summer, I had a class of these students, almost all of whom were black and had not had much success in school. I told them about non-stop writing, about writing down thoughts as they came, about not worrying about spelling or grammar, about the papers being private, and so on. Then I started them off. Before long a number of them had stopped writing and were gazing into space. I caught their eye, made writing gestures in the air with my hand. Seeing this, some would smile and start writing again. Others just looked at me, shook their heads. I would say, "Write anything at all, write the last sentence you wrote over again, but keep writing." No reaction. Things weren't working.

It might have been smart to do what Daniel Fader, in *Hooked on Books,* describes doing to get boys writing in the reform school where he was teaching. He told them that if they wanted they could copy from books or magazines. Also, he told them that if they wanted they could write one word over and over again. Indeed, on one occasion one boy covered eleven pages with one four-letter word, and with good reason, since it was not a bad one-word description of what his whole life up to then had been like. Later, at first in secret and then publicly, this boy began to write some excellent poetry. But I didn't think of either of these tactics.

Looking back, I can think of many reasons why these children found it so hard to write, even under my conditions. Perhaps I shouldn't say "even"; the conditions may have been more threatening than I thought. I can think of things I might have done about this non-writing, other than what I did. Some of these things might have worked better. In any situation in which action is blocked by feelings, it may help to talk about the feelings, and perhaps I should have tried this. On the other hand, these children were shy, at least of me, no more ready to talk than they were to write, and probably least of all about their feelings. So that might not have worked either.

At the time, it seemed to me that these children had not had much practice in thinking about their own thoughts, had not done much daydreaming or speculating or talking to themselves. When I asked them to write down their thoughts, the only thought that came may have been that they couldn't think of anything. Perhaps this froze them into some kind of anxiety or shame or perhaps defiance. I don't know. What I decided to do was to try to find some games or exercises that would give them a glimpse of their own minds at work, the ways in which their thoughts came one after another. The idea that popped up in my mind was the game of word associations.

In my early teens I used to love to read rather old-fashioned British detective stories. It was once a very popular literary form. We all know about Sherlock Holmes, but he was only one of a tribe of master thinkers. I don't know why these stories pleased me so. Like the Poor Sap in Stephen Leacock's parody of Sherlock Holmes, I was content to admire the detective's brilliant thinking without competing. I wanted to see how the story came out. One of the things that some of these gentlemen-detectives used to do to find the guilty man was to have all the suspects in a case play the word-association game. It works like this. Detective and suspect face each other across a table. Before him the detective has a long

list of words that he has prepared. Most of these are innocent—
ordinary words like dog, cat, sun, sky, and so on. But some are
loaded—clue words like knife, bell, midnight, etc. The detective
tells the suspect that he will read the words on the list, one at a
time. When he reads each word, the suspect is to say, as quickly as
he can, the first thing that the word makes him think of. The detective begins reading, looking as he reads at the second hand of
his pocket watch. He then writes down each word the suspect says,
and the number of seconds it took him to think of it. Naturally the
guilty man hesitates when it comes to words like "knife," "safe,"
or whatever may have been involved in the crime. Or he says
words that give him away. Either way the detective gets information that helps him close in on the criminal. (A great way to solve
crimes, if you can only get the suspects to play.)

I told my students about this game. I don't remember whether
I told them how and where I learned about it. If I didn't, I should
have. It would have given them a stronger sense of the continuum
of experience, the way in which my life was linked to theirs.
And the students, when they came to make up their own lists,
might have had fun pretending that they were detectives trying to
catch a criminal. Anyway, I made up a list of ten or twenty words.
I said I would read a word every five seconds, and that as I read
each word they were to write the first word it made them think of.
They liked the idea, and off we went. When I had read all the
words on my list, I went back and read each word again, this time
asking them all to tell me the word that my word had made them
think of. They were glad to do this. Most of their words were
about what one would have expected, but every now and then a
surprising one would come along. I would ask, "How did you
come to think of that?" The student was always willing to tell us.
We all found this interesting. The game was among other things a
good ice-breaker, a way of getting kids to talk who were new to
each other, to me, and to the school.

Looking back, I see that I could have found better ways than
I did of using and developing this game. The words on my list

were commonplace and neutral—dog, cat, chair, etc. They didn't have much meaning or emotional content for the students. It would have been wiser to make up lists that had more meaning. Better yet, I should have drawn the students into the making of the lists. I might have asked each one of them to contribute a word to a new list, with which we could all then have played the game. Or I could have asked each one of them to make up his list, and then let each of them in turn be the detective with the rest of us, including me, playing the game. Many good things might have come out of this.

But I didn't think of this. I had a different plan. I soon asked them to play a new game. In this we all began with the same word, which someone suggested. We wrote it down, then wrote the first thing it made us think of, then wrote the first thing that next word made us think of, and so on, in a chain of associations. As I wrote this paragraph, I played the game for a moment or two. I began with dog. Dog led to bone. For an instant this led to nothing; then I got a flash of bleached bones in a desert in the West. This made me think of sagebrush. This made me—still in the same Western scene—think of the sky. This made me think of jet planes. At this point I went back to writing. Try the game yourself. It is a good exercise for writers, however practiced or fluent.

We began to play this game. The students liked it. As I wrote my list, I could see others busily writing theirs. After a while we stopped and read some of our lists. I asked them if, as they read over their list, they could remember the way in which each word led them to the next. After a while, they said they could. I don't remember whether I asked anyone to give us a ride, so to speak, on his train of thought. If I didn't, I should have. Perhaps the best way for a teacher to get students to do this is to do it first himself.

There are many ways to play this association game. Years later I played it with my students at Berkeley. I found that my associations were very likely to be visual, as in the short example I have given. Other people associate in very different ways. We might play the game with sounds. Think of a sound—the slam of a certain door, screech of brakes, bark of a dog, etc. Then write the next *sound* that it brings to mind. Think of that sound, and write down the next sound it brings to mind, and so on. We could do this with music, songs, tunes. Or perhaps with smells, textures, tastes. I haven't tried these, but they might be interesting. Even as I write I find myself thinking of the feel of sand underfoot, or gravel, or hot pavement, or the feel of velvet, or snow.

As I turned the On switch on my typewriter, I decided to play an association game with touch. Turning the switch made me think of turning the steering wheel of my car. From there the associations went as follows: steering wheel; the feel of the shoulder safety belt in the car; feel of seat belt in airliner; feel of tipping back the seat in airliner; feel of reclining chair in my living room; feel of shiny chrome arms on that chair; feel of sweat suit that I sometimes put on those arms as a kind of arm cushion; feel of lying on the floor for a short rest after hard exercise; feel of trying to relax and sleep when restless; feel of a kind of psychosomatic itch that tries to interrupt this relaxing process; feel of having hay fever. At this point I ended the game and went back to work.

Some may wonder whether these association games in my Urban School class led to more fluent writing. I don't know. We had very little time to follow this up. Classes met only two nights a week for six weeks. Even those few students who came to all classes had only a total of about ten hours' class time. Most students had only about half this much, and even in that short time we did other things besides write—discussed this or that, talked a little about books or issues of the day, and so on. The association games did give the students a way of looking at the workings of their own minds, and they seemed surprised and interested by what they found. In later classes I carried this kind of work further, but with older and more school-successful students. I can't be sure that I would have had the same results with the summer school students, but I think I would. I do feel that these exercises are promising and worth pursuing further.

One other writing game proved very popular with Urban

School students. This was in another class, where the students could write a little more freely. I suggested that everyone write a few lines of a story about someone, or a description of someone, or anything they wanted. After a few minutes of writing everyone would pass his paper on to his neighbor. Each person would then try to continue, on his new paper, the story that the person before him had been writing. This was a great success, but not in the way I had expected. I had thought that picking up on someone else's story and continuing it might be an interesting challenge, and that the jointly written stories might evolve in an interesting way. Seeing all the students writing away, many of them chuckling or laughing as they wrote, I felt very pleased. When the time came to read the stories, I got a surprise. The students had not seen the task at all as I had meant. Instead of trying to continue the story that the one before them had been writing, they continued the story they themselves had been writing, and the more violently it conflicted with what had gone before, the funnier they thought it was. And it was funny. One boy made up his mind to write about a baseball game, so every character who came along, no matter who he was or what he had been doing, found himself thrust willy-nilly into the middle of that baseball game. Everyone found this hilarious.

Again, I didn't have time to pursue this very far. It might have been interesting to do so. Would the students at some point have grown tired of the game as they were playing it, and instead tried to write more cooperatively? Or would they continue to see how wildly and grotesquely they could change each new story as it came to them? Either way would have been fine. Or could they learn to play, and would they like to play, by both sets of rules? I leave it to others to find out.

25

VARIETIES OF WRITING

Some may be surprised by my talk of making available to children *a variety* of writing experiences. Writing is writing, isn't it? How can there be a variety of writing experiences? The forms of writing are few. One can write stories, or novels, or poems, or plays, or essays, or reports, or letters. What else is there? Reports, except in a school newspaper, aren't usually what we do in school. Neither are letters—though this is a serious mistake. Letters are a very natural and important kind of writing, and one of the best kinds of training for writers. I wrote millions of words in letters before I ever thought of writing for any other purpose, and my first book and part of my second were first written *only* as letters. We would be wise to let students use school time—class, study hall, whatever—to write letters if they wanted.

Plays and novels are too long and hard for most students to write. This leaves stories, poems, and essays. Most schools quickly boil this down to essays. If they are old-fashioned, they tell the students what to write about. If they feel more modern, and want to encourage "creativity," they may say, "Write about anything you want." But beyond giving the students this choice, there doesn't seem to be much to say.

This is where my thinking was, a number of years ago, when I first met James Moffett, then teaching English at Exeter. He gave me a copy of a long piece he had just written called "A Structural Curriculum in English." The title put me off a bit, but from our talk I knew I liked him and found him interesting, so I read it. He has just written two books called *Teaching the Universe of Discourse* and *A Student Centered Language Arts Curriculum Grades K-6* (published by Houghton Mifflin). The first is about thought and language in general, more with reference to older students. The second is more specific and deals with younger children. I have only had time to read parts of each, but have seen enough to recommend them both strongly. About many things I do not altogether agree with Moffett; he is a more traditional teacher than I am. But his books contain many interesting specific suggestions for classroom work, and his main idea or insight is so powerful that it should help many people think of many new ideas of their own. He also edited the paperback short-story anthology, *Points of View,* used by many schools, and a good short introduction to his thought.

Let me try to sum up what I learned from him. In all talking or writing (which is a special form of talking) there are three elements. Someone is talking; he is talking *to* someone; he is talking *about* something. How he talks, or writes, depends on whom he is talking to, and what he is talking about. By changing these two variables, we can get an almost infinite variety of kinds of talk.

One way of thinking about the *someone* the talker is talking to—it can be one person, or many—and the *something* he is talking about, is in terms of near and far. If I am talking face to face with an old and dear friend, I am talking to someone near. But so am I if we are talking on long-distance telephone. If I am talking to an audience of a thousand people, or to a stranger or client or customer or judge, I am talking to someone further away. If I write a piece of philosophy or a religious tract, something that seems to me true for all time, I write for a very distant audience, many of them still unborn. Clearly the nearness or farness of the audience has to do not just with actual distance in time and space, but also with the relation I have to the audience and the spirit in which I speak to them. Gandhi often spoke to crowds of as many as half a million people, many of whom, though they had come to hear him and knew he was speaking, could not in fact even hear his words; but he was very close to them, much closer, say, than was Gladstone to Queen Victoria, who complained once that he talked to her as if she was a public meeting. (We all know people like that.)

In the same way, the *something* that the talker is talking about can be near or far. If I talk to you about my toothache, or hay fever, or worries, the subject is closer than if I talk about my plans, and much closer than if we are talking about someone else, or the weather, or politics, or the fate of man, or the nature of truth. On the whole, men don't talk to distant audiences about near subjects, but not always so; we have memoirs, like the *Confessions* of Rousseau, *The Confessions of an English Opium-Eater* (De Quincy), and so on. The method of the great pioneers in depth psychology was to explore truths about all men by revealing very intimate truths about particular men, including themselves. Two books on my recommended reading list (see Appendix), *Operators and Things* and *I Never Promised You a Rose Garden,* are accounts, one told as autobiography under a pen name and the other as fiction, of a person's own experience with schizophrenia.

When we think about it a bit, we see that the closest kind of talk, in which both audience and subject are as close to the speaker as they can be, is a man talking *to* himself—in his mind, or aloud, or in writing—*about* himself. When we think further, we see that this kind of talk, most of it silent and private, must be very common. There is probably very much more of it than of all other kinds of talk put together. It is this kind of talk that we allow and encourage when we give students the choice of writing private papers.

From this beginning, Moffett made some very important points. One is that almost all the writing we ask students to do in school is of a very distant kind—writing to a far, almost a non-existent audience, about far subjects. No matter how wide a variety of essay topics we may assign, no matter how often we tell students that they may pick their own topics, the student—the talker or writer—is always in the same position. What Moffett calls "the discourse" is always of one kind. This makes writing dull for the students, and makes their writing dull for those who have to read it. But Moffett's further point is that it is very unlikely, almost impossible, that someone will be able to do good *far* writing if he has not first learned to do good *near* writing. From this came his idea of a structural curriculum. What he meant was that students should be given a carefully worked out series of assignments, beginning with very near kinds of writing and working up to more distant kinds. When we met, he showed me some writing that his students had done, using such a curriculum. It was easy to see how the directness and freshness of their near writing carried over into their more formal essays. Again, the way in which nearness or farness affect writing form and style is clearly shown in Moffett's anthology *Points of View*.

I have not altogether used Moffett's ideas in the way he used them or, I think, meant them to be used. I am not convinced at all that we need to use a carefully chosen *sequence* of assignments to lead students from near writing to far writing. This seems to imply that far writing is somehow better or more important, and that the proper aim of any writing curriculum or class must be to turn out students who can write good essays. I don't agree. What I have learned from Moffett is quite different—a number of things. One is that if we want to give students a sense of many possibilities in writing, it is not enough just to give them different writing "topics." We have to vary the kinds of discourse, the distances between them and their audiences and subjects. We have to give them the choice of talking in many ways to many kinds of people, not always put them in the position of having to give a formal speech to a remote and invisible audience. Another is that when we start thinking in terms of varying distance, we begin to see varieties of writing experience that we had never dreamed of. Most of the ideas I have already talked about, as ways to help children be more aware of their own thought, have come to me as a result of Moffett's work. But these are just a beginning.

The closest kind of discourse that we can have is someone talking to himself about himself. Moffett calls this an Interior Monologue. An even more restricted form of this is the Sensory Monologue. In this you simply write down what you are receiving through your senses—sight, sound, smell, taste, muscular tension, pressure, temperature, touch, an awareness of breathing, heartbeat, other body functions. This can be an extraordinarily interesting exercise. Even here there is a great variety of possibilities. When they first do this, students may begin by looking around the room and writing down, as in a catalog, everything they see. This is fine to begin with. If they do it too long, they will get bored and resistant, so after a while it may be a good idea to rule out sight. They are likely to write next about what they hear. This calls for a different kind of awareness. If some students get into a rut of listing sounds, try ruling out sound as well as sight. They will have to become aware of other things. We might carry this to the point of one day asking them to make a distinction between what they feel from outside their skins and what they feel from inside. I recall Leopold Bloom at the beginning of Joyce's *Ulysses,* and the kidney he cooked and ate, and the vividness of the sensations it conjured up, both outside him and inside.

We can use memory, play this game in time. Thus we might say to students, "Imagine yourself in a place where you have been, where your sensory impressions were at one time very strong— walking on a hot day, or a very cold one, lying under the sun, being in the water, exercising hard, doing something you like very much, or perhaps dislike. Put yourself there, and then give me your sensory impressions as they might occur." A girl in one of my classes sent herself far back in time, to when she was very little, playing on a beach in the summer, lying in the sand, trickling it through fingers, throwing it, digging in it, tasting a little of it, spitting it out—most of it—feeling a little left in her mouth. As I thought of this, I had a sudden clear recollection of eating quite a lot of sand, when I was very small, and soon afterward throwing it all up, painlessly as children do, along with the eggs I had had for breakfast, not yet much changed by their short stay inside me.

If we let this monologue include thoughts as well as sensory impressions it becomes the Interior Monologue. This is what most people write when they do non-stop private papers. Such writing, because of the restless and ever-changing nature of our thought, can hardly ever grow monotonous. Yet it too can be made more varied. I once asked my students to imagine a character, imagine him in a particular situation, and then, without telling me directly anything about either the character or the situation, to tell me as much as they could through his thoughts as he might think them. The students, most of whom had never written any fiction and would probably have said that they could not write any, wrote some remarkably powerful and beautiful things. We can vary this situation still further by specifying that the imagined character shall have certain kinds of feelings, perhaps embarrassed or ashamed, or disappointed, or afraid, or joyous, or angry, or perplexed.

I want to stress here a point of great importance, which is that by limiting the imagination in some directions we can very often free it to move in others, and that quite often it is only by limiting it that we can free it. This sounds like a contradiction, but it is not. Art teachers know this very well. There is no use saying to people, "Be Creative; write or draw anything you want," when in their hearts they think, "I'm not creative, and I can't think of anything to write or draw, and even if I could think of it, I couldn't write or draw it." Many good art books, art teachers, schools of art or design, begin with very restricted exercises. Make a desgin on a page, using nothing but lines, or dashes, or dots, or squares and rectangles, or circles of different sizes. Don't even think of it as a design; just put the lines, etc., on the page. Now do it again, another way. Now another way. How many ways can you think to do it? Do you like some better than others? Which do you like best? Now make the lines wiggly or curved. Make some heavier than others. Fill in some of the white spaces between lines. And so on. Gradually the novice finds that he *can* make some of these designs, and that some of them are really quite nice to look at. So he gets a growing sense of the possibilities in the medium and in himself.

The trick is to find writing possibilities that are quite sharply limited in some ways, and completely open in others. From the Interior Monologue we can go to the Exterior—someone telling a story, talking without interruption, or at least so that we cannot hear the interruptions. A lovely example of this is the short opera *La Voix Humaine,* by Francis Poulenc, in which from beginning to end the only voice we hear is that of a woman talking on the telephone to her lover, who has left her. With the Exterior Monologue we can vary the person or persons that our speaker is talking to. We can work out the almost endless possibilities of having someone tell the same story on two different occasions. Thus we might have a politician or other public figure giving a speech to an audience, and then later on telling his wife, or some political cronies, or a friend, what he said. Or a man who has been in a dispute might first describe it to someone in a position of power over him, his boss, or a judge, and then later to a friend. Or a man might tell about something that he did or that happened to him, first to people he knew slightly, and then to someone that he felt he could really rust. In how many different ways might a given man tell a particular story? How might his telling of the story change with time? Suppose, as we write the words he speaks as he tells the story, we also write his thoughts—an Interior-Exterior Monologue. What new possibilities does this give us?

From the Monologue we can go to the Dialogue. More possibilities appear. The two people can be in different relations to each other. We could have parent and child; older child and younger one; teacher and student; employer and employee; lovers, married or otherwise; married un-lovers; ex-lovers; salesman and customer; doctor and patient. We can vary the situation in many ways. A wants something that B has, but doesn't want to give him. Perhaps B knows he wants it; perhaps it is part of A's task to make sure that B doesn't find out he wants it. Perhaps A knows something that he thinks B doesn't know, or that B doesn't know he knows, and wants to keep it secret from B. Perhaps it really is a secret from B; perhaps it is not, but B chooses to pretend that it is. I find myself thinking of the conferences that Roosevelt and Churchill had with Stalin during World War II, in which they thought they were keeping secret from him the fact that they were trying to make the atomic bomb, while he knew all along that they were working on it, but didn't let them know he knew. What thoughts were those men thinking behind their spoken words?

We can put our A and B into many situations. A is trying to persuade B to do something; B is willing to do it, but doesn't want A to know that he is willing; or perhaps he isn't willing but wants A to think he is willing. Perhaps A and B are seeing each other for the first time after a long absence, or after a quarrel, perhaps recent, perhaps old, or after a joyous and shared experience, or a tragic one. Perhaps A likes or admires or loves B, but B does not feel the same way; perhaps B is trying to show this to A, who won't see it; perhaps B is trying to conceal this from A; perhaps A only thinks that B doesn't like him, and B is trying without success to show him that this isn't true. From all the situations can come many different dialogues. They can be both Interior and Exterior. To one class I suggested that they write a dialogue in which the spoken conversation was accompanied by the unspoken thoughts of the speakers. Everyone leaped on this with joy, and wrote essentially the same paper—two people are pretending to be polite, but secretly are thinking cruel thoughts about each other. This may well be a popular paper among children. But if we rule out this particular combination of polite talk and cruel thoughts, more interesting possibilities begin to appear.

Two things occur to me as I write. One is that though I have been thinking of high school or junior high school students writing these papers, there is no reason why younger children could not write them as well. If they wanted to let their characters be animals or ghosts or dolls or elves or toys or monsters or anything else, that would be fine. My other thought is that in exploring the possibilities of these combinations of characters, situations, and feelings, children might be able to learn much more about the complexity of human feelings, their own and other people's, than in most of what now passes for talk about this in school. There is a growing movement in schools to have times and occasions in which children can discuss with each other and the teacher various kinds of feelings. This is all right, but I suspect that this might be done more interestingly and profoundly, and without violating anyone's privacy, through the kind of writing experiences that I have suggested, and through discussing some of the writing itself. Thus, if students wrote dialogues about a child talking with a parent, in which the child was trying to get the parent to let him do something the parent didn't want him to, they might later discuss whether they themselves, in the same situation, thought and felt and talked like the characters in the various stories. In short, in trying to decide whether their writing was true to life, they would be thinking and talking about their own lives.

As we explore possibilities for writing, we begin to see some of the choices a writer has to make when starting to tell a story. If we are going to write the words and perhaps the thoughts of some characters, do we report them as if we were an invisible and all-knowing person in the room? Or do we report through one of the characters themselves? What is good or not so good about each of these methods? If we write a particular scene or dialogue in two ways, first as reported by an invisible person, secondly as reported by one of the characters, which makes the better story? If we are going to report through one of the characters, which shall we pick? Does it make a difference? Do we make our hero the narrator, or someone else? John Knowles, in *A Separate Peace,* makes his narrator not the hero, but the closest the story has to an anti-hero. In this case, is it necessary? What might make it necessary? If we write an argument between parent and child, or an older and younger person, first from the point of view of one (we see here the reason for the title of one of Moffett's books) and then of the other, what difference does it make? We might begin with a conversation, just the words spoken by a group of people, and then have different students, without changing the spoken words, write the scene as it might have been experienced by each of the people in the conversation. What sort of contrasts might we get? Which person's point of view gives us the best story?

In all the examples given so far, the suggestion is that students write what their invented characters say or think. But there are other possibilities. One is to describe a character wholly through his appearance—what he looks like, what he wears, how he moves, what we can see him doing. Another would be to write what our made-up characters write. In other words, we could invent a character, put him in a situation, and then tell his story as he would later write about it, either in his diary or in letters. Many stories have been told this way, including my favorite of all ghost stories, M. R. James's horrifying "Count Magnus."

We can also describe a character as someone might see him who likes him, and as someone else sees him who does not like him. We can ask students to invent characters, and then have them described, or thought or talked about, by a friend, or an enemy, or by a variety of people—wife, husband, child, parent, boss, employee, former lover, rival, admirer from afar, etc. Or they might describe, as if by a friend and then by an enemy, but without naming him, someone they know, perhaps the teacher himself. Or, as a private paper, we might ask students to describe themselves, as someone might see them who liked them very much, someone else who loved them, someone else who disliked them.

I have by no means given all of Moffett's ideas about writing or explored all the possibilities in them. This is just a beginning. Let me close with two quotes from his book about the curriculum. Speaking of grades K through 3, he writes:

> A general problem of writing at this age is: why write it when you can say it? To whom would the child be writing? And for what reason? Why do adults ever write? And why record? Why not just observe? Let us grant that elementary schoolers in general have a competence motive—to learn to do and become good at all sorts of crafts and skills valued by their social world and practiced by adolescents and adults. The competence motive is based on every individual's need to think well of himself, enjoy success, achieve things, and strengthen ego and identity. But, like game motivation, it can easily be abused, and when children discover that they have worked hard at something that is not "real" after all but just a teacher's invention for his own purposes, they feel cheated and resentful. This is a great source of cynicism among students of all ages.

This is a very good point, and reminds me of something that happened when I was working on a Composition Derby with the fifth graders. We began doing the Derby for ten minutes; as the students grew more fluent, and liked writing their stories, I stretched the Derby to fifteen minutes, twenty, sometimes thirty. One day one child suggested that they do an overnight Derby, writing a paper at home and seeing who could write the most. Everyone liked the idea, and they wrote their papers, the longest being about 3,000 words or so. The thought came into my mind that here was a device by which I might "get out of the children" an enormous amount of writing—as if I were running a writing factory. So a week or two later I suggested another overnight Derby. But the children must have sensed that in a way they were being used or exploited, or that they soon would be, and they refused, so flatly that I knew that I had to forget the idea altogether. And indeed, no child ever suggested an overnight Derby again.

Later, Moffett says:

Second- and third-graders soon lost interest when asked on un-related occasions to observe animals and merely say what they saw. But when they kept animals in the class for several weeks, cared for them, lived with them, and experimented with them, they not only observed them closely but they talked constantly about them, and wrote more about them than the teacher could have hoped for.

The lesson I learned—and this is why I have dwelled so long on this whole issue—is that a familiar, pleasurable, and well motivated activity can provide the context that will in turn motivate a new, different, and more advanced activity.

What he means by a well-motivated activity is something *not* just done to please the teacher, but done to give the child a sense, to use Dennison's phrase, of advancing himself into the world. This kind of true learning *always* leads to more learning, whereas even children who are very good at playing school games for rewards in time grow bored with it and cynical about it.

In my English classes at Berkeley, I asked the students, as part of their work of self-exploration, to make up lists. I said, "These will be private. You don't have to finish them by any par-ticular time; in fact, they can't be finished, so don't think of finish-ing them at all. As you think of things to add to them, add them. Also, don't feel that they have to be complete and exhaustive, don't rack your brains trying to think of things to add to them. Add to them whatever comes easily to you, if and when it comes." Some of the suggested lists were:

1. Places you like. These can be big places, like a part of the mountains, or the coast at Big Sur, or the Southwestern desert. Or they can be little places, a certain spot on the campus, a house, a room in a house, even a part of a room, a chair, a bed. You can like them for different reasons, because they are beautiful, because you associate them with something good that happened to you, or with people you like, or simply because you feel happy and com-fortable there.

2. Places you dislike. From here on I will only name lists on the positive or like side, but for every one of them there is, of

course, one on the negative or dislike side. These are also useful to make up.

3. People you know and like.

4. People, not known to you, but public figures, alive or dead, that you admire or like.

5. Books, plays, stories, etc.

6. Periodicals, newspapers, or columns that you regularly read.

7. Movies, plays.

8. TV shows or other spectacles you regularly see and enjoy —sports events, concerts, etc.

9. Pieces of music—classical, jazz, folk, rock, blues, etc.

10. Poems.

11. Performing artists—musicians, actors, dancers, comedians.

12. Paintings, sculptures—or painters and sculptors.

13. Other works of art, or artists—perhaps architects, designers, fashion designers.

14. Other made objects—automobiles, skis, cameras, boats, hats, etc., owned or not owned, perhaps wanted, perhaps not wanted but just admired.

15. Things to eat and drink.

16. Places to eat and drink.

17. Things you like to do. Can be trivial, like putting on newly shined shoes or cutting fingernails when they are too long or sneezing when you have to, or not so trivial, like playing the piano or running a good class or skiing or writing a good article. Anything the doing of which gives you pleasure.

18. Sounds you like.

19. Smells.

20. Things to touch.

21. Things you feel strongly about. Again, they may be trivial, like "I hate the sound of the busy signal," or "I look terrible in orange," or "Miniature poodles give me a pain," to not so trivial, like "We should get out of Vietnam" (or stay in), "There

should be a guaranteed annual income," "Mankind has not many years left on earth, as he is going," "Keep cars out of our cities," and so on. Any kind of statement of belief or prejudice can go in here, provided only you feel it strongly.

22. Places you haven't been to and would like to go to.

23. People you don't know, but would like to know.

24. Things you haven't done, but would like to do, or be able to do—catch a trout, fly a plane, conduct an orchestra, be President.

25. Different lives you would like to live, if you had many lives to lead.

These will suggest what is possible. Some of these lists could be broken down into sub-lists. You may think of others I have not thought of. If you are fortunate, many of your lists will be too long to write. It would take me many pages, or chapters, to list the music or books I like, or the places, or many other things. This is one good measure of a person's education—the length of the lists of things he likes. In any case, the lists of young children will not be so long, and it will be possible, and in many ways interesting and useful, for them to write them down. They may even want to try to rank some of their lists, to decide which places or people or foods or activities they like better than others—though they may also find that this is often difficult. The lists, if they do write them, should be private, though even as I say this I realize with dismay that most children have no privacy nor even the right to any. There is no place they could put a list that would be safe from the eyes of some prying adult. Anyway, let's say that the lists should be private as far as the teacher and school are concerned. But there may be things on some of the lists that the children would be willing to make public—some of the places, foods, books, stories. Are there some things on everyone's positive lists— ice cream, staying up late, presents, visiting, hiding places, spending the night at someone else's house? Are there some things on everyone's dislike list—disappointments, unfair treatment, being patronized by adults? Are there some items that some strongly like and others just as strongly dislike? All of these may give children, or a class, interesting things to talk or write about.

Other people, in other books, have made other good suggestions. George von Hilsheimer's book I have already mentioned and strongly recommended. There are many good ideas about writing in Herbert Kohl's *Thirty-six Children.* Kenneth Koch has recently written a book—*Wishes, Lies, Dreams,* a wonderful book about teaching or helping children to write poetry. Another good source of ideas, and a very good book in many other ways, is Postman and Weingartner's *Teaching as a Subversive Activity.* One of the best of all books on the subject of discussions with and among children (though there are other things in it I don't at all agree with) is William Glasser's *Schools Without Failure.* He has been particularly successful at getting children to talk publicly and honestly about things they don't often talk about, least of all in school. Some of his stories about the things he and the children talked about, and what was revealed in those discussions, are quite extraordinary. The one that sticks in my mind is his account of a discussion in which a large group of middle-class children, after much talk about lying, said that they would not undertake to go for even as short a time *as one day* without lying, since to do so seemed to involve far more risk at the hands of adults than they were willing to run.

There are by now, besides the periodical *What's Happening,* a number of good books of writing by children, among them the poetry collection *Miracles;* Stephen Joseph's *The Me Nobody Knows;* the books *Mother, These Are My Friends, Talking About Us,* and others. Since children are interested in what other children write, all of these should help to stimulate writing. In fact, the independent newspapers that students are beginning to publish all over the country, usually in the face of heavy school opposition, may create more interest in writing, and more good writing, than anything we English teachers have been able to do. If for no other reason than this—and there are many other reasons—we should encourage, rather than discourage, such independent efforts, no matter how angry or irreverent or rebellious they may happen to be.

26

WRITING FOR OTHERS

People say, how will the students ever learn to write if we don't correct their mistakes? When I started teaching English I was a very serious paper-corrector. In my work with the world government movement, I had done some editing for a small magazine we published. I enjoyed trying to clear up unclear ideas and to make writing more plain and strong. At the Colorado Rocky Mountain School I found time to do twenty minutes or so of editing on just about every paper that my students wrote. I filled the margins and the spaces between lines with what I hoped would be helpful remarks about style, choice of words, clarity of ideas, continuity of thoughts, and so on. The writing continued about the same.

Some years later, when he was a senior at Harvard, I saw a good deal of one of my former students. One day he told me that of all his teachers, in school and college, none had corrected his papers as carefully and completely as I did. For an instant I swelled up with pleasure and pride. Then I asked, "Just out of curiosity, did you read the corrections?" He laughed and said, "No." I laughed too—by this time I had begun to learn a few things—and asked if any of the other students had read them. He said No, not as far as he knew. He went on to say, "Of course, we used to skim through looking for wise remarks, EYF's [note: that stands for Elongated Yellow Fruit, from a story by Thurber about his early newspaper days], steam shovels, and anything else that might get us a laugh. But study the corrections the way you wanted us to? Never."

Not long after I talked about this with a good friend, also an English teacher. Later I wrote him a letter. Here are some parts of it:

... Children do not see school as we teachers do, as a place where they are going to learn things that will someday be useful or valuable or interesting to them. They see school in terms of the day to day tasks they are given to do. Some children do their best to do them, so as to earn the respect and approval of people they care about, and even more, perhaps, so as not to cause them pain and disappointment. The tasks may sometimes even be interesting. But it is not primarily interest in the work that moves the children to do it. I liked to get A's on papers for the same reason I liked to win squash matches; it was tangible proof of my competence at something; but it had little to do with interest in the subject or the teacher.

Motivation being what it is, 99 out of 100 children, when they have finished a paper and handed it in, say in their mind, "There, it's done." They have done what they were told to do; they have got the mark, good or bad, that the paper supposedly earned them; the whole business is in the past. We may think that, by means of our corrections, the students may learn something further from the paper. In other words, we may see in it further opportunities for learning. *But the student did not see it as an opportunity for learning in the first place.* He did not do it so that he could learn something by doing it. He did it because he was told to.

Such is the injustice of the universe that corrections, while they seldom do good, seldom help children to write better, often do harm. Here I am singing an old song, so will sing briefly. When a child sits down to write something with his mind on what the teacher is going to say about it, his work will suffer. If his concern about what teacher thinks and wants does not paralyze him, it almost surely inhibits him, keeps him from plunging deeply into his own thoughts and the material itself, keeps his mind up on a shallow and Right Answer level.

This leads to the question, "If kids don't become good writers through having papers corrected, how do they become good writers?" I'll be brief. Kids who read a lot, for pleasure not duty, pick up writing styles, as I do, by osmosis, imitation either conscious or unconscious. Also, practice makes, if not perfect, at least better. More writing tends to make better writing. That is, if the writer is saying something that *he* wants to say, something important to him, that he needs to make clear to himself or others. A man writing hack stories for cheap magazines does not get to be a better writer by the exercise. But is not the position of the student in the classroom often much the same? I know the comparison is unflattering to us teachers. The point is that in both cases the writer is grinding out, under some kind of compulsion, something that he thinks someone else wants. Writing for marks, or writing for money; are they not very nearly the same, as far as the spirit of the writer is concerned?

There has to be more writing for love, if writing is to improve, and I don't see how this can be done unless at least a good part of each child's writing is wholly outside the area of corrections, approval, criticism, marks. Conversely, a child who writes something because he deeply wants to say something on his mind will want to express it clearly, and will probably be eager to hear anything you or I might say about parts that we could not understand.

This reminds me of something. Even at school, I found that if I read aloud, to them, the papers of some of my friends who were having trouble with English, they could often see their own mistakes and bad writing. But I could never get them to read their own papers, carefully, as if they were seeing them for the first time. It took me years to find out, or guess, why not. They had written those papers for someone else, not for themselves. They were a kind of excreta, which they wanted to be rid of, done with. It is probably true of many students that when they have struggled and sweated to the end of a paper, they not only are bored with it, they actively hate it, and don't want to have to look at it again. In this frame of mind, how can they learn from what they have written, or from what we have written about what they have written? Whereas the child who, like a true artist, writes for love, for the sake of what he is writing, cannot but help learning as he works, and will learn every time he re-reads what he has written.

This happens to me, as I think it must to every serious writer. When I read over, now and then, some of what seems to me my best work, I often think, as if seeing it for the first time, "But this is good!" I sometimes think, "Did I really write that?" It is almost more as if it was written through me than by me, if that makes any sense. The effect of this is to make me very dissatisfied, as I write, with anything that seems much less good. From what I feel is my best writing in the past I get a standard that I want all my work in the present to reach.

Not long after I wrote the letter from which I have quoted, I began to teach English again to secondary school students. I told them my experience with correcting papers, and my feelings about it. I then said I would make a bargain with them. I was willing to do the work of an editor if they, in turn, were willing to do the work of a serious writer. I said, "On anything you write, I will do as much or as little editing as you want, including no editing at all. But where I edit, you have to be willing to rewrite, to try to put into practice whatever suggestions or criticisms I have made. If you don't want to rewrite, that's okay, but then I won't edit."

Reactions to this were mixed. One class generally went along with this offer. Two or three times during the year they asked me to do detailed editing on their papers, which they then rewrote. Most of the time, they just wrote. On the whole, they were at least competent writers to begin with. They did not have many or serious problems with structure, grammar, or usage. Their writing, if anything, was too wordy and ponderous, too academic, too abstract, and most of what I tried to do was to get them to write in a more simple, direct, and personal way. A few resisted this strongly. Most of the class, though, before the year was over wrote many papers that by my lights were very good.

A later class resisted my offer. They claimed it wasn't fair. If I try to put into plain English what I think I heard them saying, I get something like this: "We are English students, and part of being students is that we have to go to the trouble and unpleasantness of writing papers. You are an English teacher, and part of being a teacher is that you have to go to the bother and unpleasantness of reading and correcting our papers. If you won't play your role, we won't play ours." The argument seemed petulant and silly, and still does. But I sensed that if I didn't at least begin by playing the part of an English teacher as they understood it, they would not cooperate with me in things I cared about. So at first I did edit their papers, though in much less detail than I had done some years before. As the year went on, and they grew less dependent on me, I edited less and less. Like the students the year before, they wrote many fine things during the year. But my editing had nothing to do with it.

Were I to teach English again, there are two things I would try to do that I did not do in those classes. One I did not do because, though I knew others had done it with good results, I couldn't see how to do it in my setting and with my students. This was to have students comment on and judge each other's work, to use the class itself as editor. Teachers that I know have done this with great success. In a school and class where there is not much dog-eat-dog competition, where the students know and trust each other, and are used to treating each other with some kindness and respect, they could be the best of all editors of each other's work, much better than any adult teacher. But though I was very fond of almost all my students, I felt that many of them were too aggressive, to vain of their own cleverness, and too competitive to be able to help each other in this way. The fault was not theirs; this school, like many secondary schools, graded students not only by letters but also by their class rank, a figure which was sent on to college admissions offices—to my way of thinking a truly disgusting practice, since under it nobody can gain except at everyone else's expense.

It seemed to me, at any rate, that one thing I had to try to do in my class was to create an atmosphere of mutual courtesy, respect, and trust, and that it would be hard to do so if the students were correcting each other's written work. Perhaps I unfairly misjudged them; they might well have been more kind, generous, and sympathetic than I gave them credit for. It may also have been true that in a class where I was doing almost everything for the first time, in ways new to me, this new and difficult task was more than I felt ready to undertake. I had never done it or seen it done and knew nothing about how to do it or even get it started. I am not sure, either, that it would not have been resisted by the students. In any case, I didn't do it. I still feel that, in the right kind of a class, and with a teacher who feels confidence in it, using students as editors might be very helpful.

Ken Macrorie's *Up Taught* shows how this might be done. At the beginning of the year he gave all his writing students the following memo:

> Every student in this class who stays with the program will write at least one paper that knocks out the other students. Most will write several that deserve publication on campus.
>
> You will write, and your papers will be read around this table. The class is designed to move you from success to success. For the first month neither you nor I will talk about anything weak in the papers. Only the strong places. I will reproduce sentences or passages I think are strong and you will say why you like a passage, or just that you like it and don't know why. If you are not moved by the writing, you will say nothing.
>
> Keep your papers in one folder. I will not grade them until the end of the semester. In the meantime you will be getting more responses to your work than you ever got from a grade. Good writing will be reproduced and read. And praised. Later in the semester we will comment on weaknesses as well as strengths. If at any time you feel desperate for a grade, because Dad has promised you a new car if you get a B or you need a grade for application to Harvard Law School, bring the folder and I will give it a grade as of the moment.
>
> In this class I'm asking for truth, not Engfish (I had explained the fish, through examples). To ask such a thing is dangerous. It implies the asker habitually tells the truth. I don't. Nobody does.

But in this class I will make a hard try at it, and I want you to, also.

This is what I should have said to my students. In this spirit, as Macrorie's book shows, the students can be a tremendous help to each other.

What I would now try to do in any class of my own, and recommend to others, is publish what might be called an open journal. This publication would be distributed to all the members of the class, or perhaps even a wider audience—the entire school, or school and parents, or the community itself. It would come out whenever there was enough material for an issue. There would be no selection; the journal would be open; anyone who wanted to publish something in the journal could do so, and it would be published *as they wrote it*. Should articles be signed? If the journal was for people outside the class, articles would, I think, have to be signed; if it was for the class only, articles might be anonymous. In either case, it would be up to the writer to find ways to correct his spelling, grammar, etc. Perhaps, for obvious tactical reasons, the teacher-publisher would have to be free to cut out certain taboo words, if they appeared. Otherwise, the journal would be unedited and uncensored. People could write as little, or as much as, and in what form, they pleased. The teacher-publisher could fairly ask that writers make their own ditto stencils (or mimeo, if that was used), and even, for large pieces, that they help to run off copies, collate, staple, etc. Or the students might produce the journal entirely by themselves.

Such open journals might be useful for many reasons. One has to do with our continuum of experience. Writers in the world out there write for others to read; it is why they write. A child writing for an audience, not just a teacher, becomes a real writer, part of that world out there. Also, the chance of writing for an audience will surely make many children want to write, as it has done for the many children in New York City ghettos who have written for *What's Happening*—which goes to schools and other subscribers all over the country. (See the reading and information list in the Appendix.) Finally, knowing that his writing will appear in public, under his name, will make a child feel *responsible* for his writing. He will want it to be his best, and will go to some trouble to make sure that things like spelling are right, and that his manuscript is neatly printed or typed.

The journal might hold, among other things, open correspondence columns, like those of many British newspapers and weeklies. Thus A might write a piece or a news story in one issue; in another issue B might answer it; in a later issue A might reply to B, as might also C and D. The discussion could go on as long as people had something to write about it. From this kind of continuing discussion children would sense that in the larger world out there questions are never answered, discussions never finished, that the continuum of human thought and ideas has no end to it.

Ken Macrorie has sent me some copies of an excellent journal of writing by high school and college students, *The Unduressed,* that he and some colleagues publish. The writing is extraordinarily vivid, personal, and powerful—particularly from the high school students. It shows us what can be done. The following words, quoted in *Up Taught* from John Dewey's *School and Society,* sum up very well what Macrorie, Moffett, I, and many others feel about what schools do to the language of children.

> Think of the absurdity of having to teach language as a thing by itself. If there is anything the child will do before he goes to school, it is to talk of the things that interest him. But when there are no vital interests appealed to in school, when language is used simply for the repetition of lessons, it is not surprising that one of the chief difficulties of school work has come to be instruction in the mother tongue. Since the language taught is unnatural, not growing out of the real desire to communicate vital impressions and convictions, the freedom of children in its use gradually disappears, until finally the high school teacher has to invent all kinds of devices to assist in getting any spontaneous and full use of speech. Moreover, when the language instinct is appealed to in a social way, there is a continual contact with

reality. The result is that the child always has something on his mind to talk about, he has something to say: he has a thought to express, and a thought *is not a thought unless it is one's own.* [Italics mine.] In the traditional method, the child must say something that he has merely learned. There is all the difference between having something to say and having to say something.

27

MARKING AND GRADING

In the kind of learning I have been talking about there is no place and no need for conventional testing and grading. In a class where children are doing things, and not getting ready to do them sometime in the distant future, what they do tells us what they have learned. Unfortunately, and probably for some time, most schools demand grades. How can we make this business, always harmful to children, somewhat less harmful?

In recent classes, at the Harvard Graduate School of Education and at the University of California at Berkeley, as a short-time visitor I was able to give a Pass (in the first case) or an A (in the second) to all students who signed up, regardless of what else they did or did not do—though I would rather have given no grades at all. But in all my previous teaching I had to give regular grades. That is, I had to say that some students were better than others. At first I thought this a good thing, believing, as many teachers do today, that grades, particularly bad grades, spurred students on to work harder. Later I came to feel that it was bad, but it was grade or don't teach, and for many reasons which seemed to me good at the time, I wanted to teach. In time I arrived at a rule that seemed to work—if you must grade, grade as seldom as possible, as privately as possible, and as easily as possible.

Specifically, if we have to submit a grade or report card once a term, or quarter, or semester, that should be the *only* mark we give the child in that period. How then do we get the grade? To my students in ninth-, tenth-, and eleventh-grade English, in a very grade-conscious school, I said that I would get their grade from a cross section of what I felt to be their best work. What sense does an average grade make in a course like English? Do we average a serious writer's best work against his worst? If I assigned a paper, and a student did badly on it, this only showed that this was the wrong paper for him, where he could not show what ability he had. The remedy was to try to give a wide enough variety of choices and opportunities for writing, reading, and talking so that everyone would have a fairly good chance of showing his best talents.

It is not just in English that it makes no sense to figure students' grades by taking an average of all their daily or weekly work. It makes no sense in any subject. Take the case of arithmetic. Here are two children, trying to learn, say, long division. One child gets it at the first crack. All his homework and class papers in long division are excellent. At the end of the marking period he gets an A. The other child has a hard struggle. His first papers are very bad. Only after many failures does he finally catch on. But he does, and at the end of the marking period he too does a perfect paper. In a class where daily grades are averaged in, his perfect final paper will be averaged against all the failures he made while he was learning, and he will be given a low or perhaps even a failing mark. This is idiotic, unfair, outrageous. The aim of the class is to learn long division, not to have a contest to see who can learn it in the fewest number of tries. Anyone who learns it, however long it takes, however many times he fails along the way, should get a perfect mark for that part of the course.

It is not grading alone that is stupid, but the whole idea of trying to have a class move along on a schedule, like a train. Children do not learn things at the same time, or equally easily and quickly. Nor is it any better or wiser to label some children "fast" and some "slow" and to put them in different groups, each with its own little "fast" or "slow" train schedule. We all know people who found some parts of math easy and others hard. Because one part is hard for A, or easy for B, does not mean that everything need be. A might find long division easier than B, but B—if we have not *made* him stupid by officially *labeling* him stupid—may later find fractions, or decimals, or algebra, or calculus, much easier than A. Even if we do insist on making up for children a list of things that they are (as James Herndon says) Spozed to learn in school, we should give them the freedom to learn those things in the order and way and rate that is most natural and easy for them.

We should also mark as *privately* as we can. Only the teacher and the student, not the other children, should know what marks anyone is getting. It is no one else's business. No big 100's or 60's or A's or E's on individual papers, no gold stars on the walls. If for official records we have to make a kind of pecking order of the children, we should at least make it as invisible as possible. If the children feel they are all in some kind of race, and if everyone knows who are winners and who are losers, the losers are going to try to protect what little is left of their pride and dignity by getting out of the race, by refusing to run. Not only that, but a lot of them are going to try to put a stop to the whole race—which is what much of our school troubles today are about.

We can at least make clear to the children how little grades mean to us. In my last fifth-grade class, I told the children that I did not believe in grades, that learning could not be measured and labeled with a number or letter or word, that I only gave them grades because if I didn't the school wouldn't let me teach them at all, and that the grades had nothing to do with what I thought about them as people. This was lame and feeble enough, I admit. It might have been better for the children in the long run if I had fought the school on this issue (though it didn't seem as important then as it does now), even at the risk of getting fired for it. But what I did say was better than nothing. It did something to make them feel that the class was not just one more place where they raced against each other to get points from me. I then said that any grades I gave were for themselves and their parents and were nobody else's business, and that I didn't want people saying, I got so and so, what did you get? At least in my presence, the children seemed to obey this request. Later my ninth-, tenth-, and eleventh-grade students did not.

We should grade, if we have to, as easily as possible. Particularly at the low end. Put a safety net under everybody. To my ninth-, tenth-, and eleventh-graders I made it clear that nobody in class would get lower than a C—, whatever they might do or not do. This at least freed them from the burden of failure. Free of it, they went on to do good work, very often better work than they had done before. The only student who perhaps did not "deserve" the C— I gave him told me years later that although he did very little work in my class, he found there an interest in both reading and writing that continued to grow even after he left the school.

There is absolutely no excuse for a teacher or a school failing a student. We are there for them, not they for us. We have the age, the experience, the knowledge, the money, the power. If a student spends a year in my class and learns *something,* then I have no right to fail him. I must find a way to give him *some* positive and legitimate credit for whatever he has learned. If at the end of a year he has truly learned *nothing,* if the experience has brought nothing new at all into his life, has not in any way helped him to grow out into the world, then *I* am the one who should be failed, not him.

People say angrily, what good does it do to promote a child from one grade to the next if he doesn't know what he is supposed to know? One answer is, as I showed in *How Children Fail,* that most of the children who fool their teachers and testers into thinking that they know what they are supposed to know, don't really know it, and have to be "taught" it or most of it all over again. A more important reason is that the child who is kept back against his will is hardly ever helped, and is almost always badly hurt, by the experience. Sometimes children who feel themselves unready to go ahead may ask or even agree freely to repeat a year. Sometimes

254 | WHAT DO I DO MONDAY?

—not always—this helps them to get more confidence, and to do better in their later schooling. But children who are kept back against their will are humiliated, made to feel stupid, labeled as stupid, and thus are even less able to learn the following year whatever it was that caused them trouble the year before. I have known a number of children who at one time or another had been kept back a year or more. All were poor students and afraid of school. Almost all of them *still* did not know the things they had been kept back to learn.

We hear all the time how terrible it is that thirteen- or four-teen-year-old children in the seventh or eighth grade do not know how to read. It is terrible, and all the more so because the fault is not theirs but the school's, for reasons made very clear in Denni-son's *The Lives of Children.* But would these children be more likely to learn to read if they were surrounded by six-year-olds? It is worth noting—and this experience has been duplicated by many others—that the only way in which Dennison could get twelve-year-old José to have reading lessons at all was to have them *alone, behind a locked door,* so that none of the other children, whose own insecurities would surely have caused them to make fun of him, could see his struggles and failures. I have often said to teachers working with older children who were unable or barely able to read that if they wanted to help, not only would the help probably have to be given in secret, but even the offer to help. The problem lies almost wholly in the anxiety, shame, and self-contempt and self-hatred of such children, and putting them in classes with much younger children can only make this much worse. The remedy is to get away from all grading and labeling, and make school a place where each child and every child is helped, in the way most helpful to him, to find what is the best way for him to learn what he needs and wants to know.

In any case, we are simply not honest when we say or claim to believe that in keeping a child back we are doing it to help him. We do it to punish. Being kept back is a severe and long-lasting punishment, and schools use it so that the threat of it will "make" children do the work. If we think otherwise we are just fooling ourselves. The children are not fooled.

Teachers quite often ask me something like this, "If I give Jimmy a better grade than he deserves, say an A or a B, won't it make it harder for him when he gets into his next class and can't live up to that standard?"

There are two worries here. The first might be put something like this: "If I give Jimmy a good mark this year, and next year he doesn't do nearly as well, won't everyone think I am running an easy class or am a poor teacher?" When I say this to groups of teachers, I hear enough nervous laughter to tell me that this is exactly what many of them are thinking. Indeed, most teachers, and with good reason, are afraid of what may be said about them if they give Jimmy a better mark than he got *last* year. Even in the small and relatively humane and kindly schools where I have taught, I have often been challenged for giving A's or B's to children whom everyone had come to think of as only worth C's or D's. Even in these schools, it was hardly ever taken as likely or even possible that the child might really have been doing better work. Many other teachers have told me similar stories. Many have even told me that they have been specifically *forbidden* to give A's to children in a low track, the reason being, "If they *could* get A's, they wouldn't be in the low track." This is really terrible. We say that we want to help children who are doing badly in school to do better, but we all too often assume that they are incapable of improving. In such circumstances teachers are only being realistic in thinking that giving bad marks to children is a way of protecting themselves.

In *Up Taught* Ken Macrorie writes:

> At almost every university where I have taught including those that employed me only part time, I have received in my faculty mail box a notice from a department head that went essentially like this:
> Everyone who taught at least one English course last fall should have received a report showing percentages of grades given on different levels and in multi-section courses as well as the per-

centages of the grades he gave. These figures might well make us wonder if we are not somewhat "softer" in our grading than we really should be. This is not to imply that we should establish a departmental curve requiring so many C's, D's, and E's to be given by each instructor. However, to suggest some kind of upper limit in softness, anyone who finds himself giving, with any regularity, more than 20% A's, less than 20% C's, and no D's in ordinary undergraduate classes should ask himself if his students are really *that* good. Anyone who fairly frequently goes beyond these limits in assigning grades may legitimately be regarded by students (and by colleagues) as a soft touch.

We should note in passing the thinly veiled threat in the phrase "and by colleagues." The message is that your colleagues are going to have a lot to say about tenure and promotion, so you'd better stay in line. And it is too often the case that in most schools or universities a teacher who tries to teach with some openness and humanity will get as much pressure and disapproval from his threatened colleagues as from the administration—often a good deal more.

Not long ago, when a college teacher showed me one of these ugly and threatening memos, this one from the college dean, a thought suddenly came to mind. I said, "You know, these people sending out letters saying that it is against college or department policy to give more than a certain amount of high grades are really saying a most surprising thing. They are saying that nobody in the college or department is a good enough teacher to be able to teach his students what he is being paid to teach them. Nobody is good enough to get all his students to do good work. Not only that, nobody is good enough even to make much difference in the quality of the students."

We have to be braver, more generous, more hopeful than that. And we must realize that this high-mark, low-mark game can be played in more than one way. So I say, "If someone makes and edged remark to the effect that it's pretty strange that Jimmy, who got an A in your course last year, is not even doing C work this year, don't fall back on the defensive. Take the offensive. Say that it is indeed strange, that he was doing very good work a year ago, and you wonder what might have happened to cause the change." Teachers hearing this often laugh with delighted surprise and relief. Later they say to me, "I never thought of that." For a long time I didn't think of it myself. We don't have to give the children low grades to protect our reputation for being good teachers. We may be able to do the same by giving high grades. We must expect criticism and opposition and not give up easily.

Teachers also fear what may happen to Jimmy next year if they grade him easily this year. To this I say, "Make no mistake about it, if you have to send children on to their next class with labels around their necks, the better labels you can give them, the better off they will be." Robert Rosenthal, in his excellent and important book, *Pygmalion in the Classroom* (Holt, Rinehart, & Winston), has shown clearly that when we expect children to do well in school they are more likely to do well than when we expect them to do badly. Here, as in so many other areas of human life, the behavior we get from other people is much closer to what we *expect* to get than what we think we want to get. If Jimmy comes into that next teacher's class with an A stuck on him, the teacher will be pleased. We all like A students; they give us no trouble. He will think, "Good, another A student; won't have to worry about him, anyway; why don't they send me more like that?" He will welcome Jimmy to his class, make him feel at home, give him every encouragement. It is certain that, given this kind of treatment, Jimmy will in fact do much better work than he was used to doing. But suppose that it still is not as good as this teacher would like. He will think, "Perhaps he is having a little trouble getting adjusted, perhaps something happened to him over the summer, I must be patient and encouraging." After all, A students are valuable resources, and must be treated carefully. If on the other hand Jimmy comes to this teacher with a D hanging around his neck, the teacher will think, "Oh hell, another dummy, why do I always get so many of them, I wonder what's wrong with this one, what kind of trouble he will give me, we'll probably have to spend most of our time hashing over that old stuff," etc. These feelings will not be lost on Jimmy. He will catch them in the first day, in the first hour he is in that class. No, all labels are libels, but good labels are much less bad than bad labels.

There is a side advantage to be gained, a fringe benefit, from grading as seldom as possible. It will free us from the dull, useless, and time-wasting drudgery of correcting papers. Teachers, particularly those with big classes, spend an enormous amount of time on this donkey work. If papers have to be corrected—I say elsewhere why English papers should *not* be—we should let the children correct their own. Give them an answer book or answer sheet. Most publishers of textbooks that have problems in them supply the answers. We can get copies, or make copies for the children. If the class is in arithmetic, we can get a calculating machine—electric ones now cost as little as sixty dollars—and teach them to run it. We should anyway; these machines are what the children will be using in the larger world—nobody out there is figuring with pencil and paper.

Or we might have the children make up, as a class project, their own answer sheets. This will force them to confront and think about the vital question, "How can we tell whether an answer is right?" They think you find out by asking the teacher. But who tells the teacher? Someone, somewhere, has to have some other ways of deciding whether an answer is right. What are these ways? If you use a machine, how can you tell whether the machine is running properly, or when it breaks down, or has made a mistake? How do people in the larger world tell? How does the supermarket know that its cash registers are working properly? Perhaps some children could save some supermarket slips and check up on the machines. Machines *do* make mistakes. How do we check them? How does the bank check its computers? Such questions might lead a class into looking at double-entry bookkeeping, which is a subject so important and interesting, and so connected with the larger world outside, that it ought not to be saved for a few students studying accounting. But we could write a whole chapter, or a whole book, on the ways in which we could tie together arithmetic with a study of the economic life of the community. Such a book certainly needs to be written.

Elsewhere, in "Making Children Hate Reading" in *The Underachieving School,* I have said why I think spelling tests, and indeed most of what we do about spelling, is foolish and harmful —as they say in Washington, counter-productive. Meanwhile, if we must give spelling tests, let the children correct them by looking up each word, as they spelled it, in the dictionary. If they can't find it, either they are using the dictionary wrongly or they can't spell the word. Let them find, first of all, whether they *are* looking in the right place in the dictionary. Obviously, if they can't do that, the dictionary isn't going to be of much help to them in spelling. If they are using the dictionary properly, and still can't find the word, that means they have spelled it wrong. What then? For most children, I would tell them the correct spelling. To a certain kind of child, I might say, "How many other ways can you think of to spell it that would sound right, that I could read and know what the word was saying? Write a few of them, pick the one that looks most likely, and see if you can find it." Or I might tell him to ask one of his friends. This would confront him with the interesting problem—how do I tell which of my friends are good spellers when I don't spell well myself?

I deeply believe that all this messing with spelling is foolish. If children read for pleasure, and to find out things they want to find out, and write in order to say what they want to say, they will before long spell better than most people do now. How we cling, for complicated and unhealthy reasons, to the notion that nothing can be any good for us unless it is unpleasant. And to the idea that everything the children learn, they must learn *from us;* if not, what are we for? We want to help, and what a helper needs first and most is someone who *needs* help. We may be afraid of the thought that some of these people may get along fine without our help, may do better without it, that the help may only be making them dependent on us.

One year a student came into one of my English classes— very bright, quiet, a bit shy. At the beginning of the year I told the class that spelling was not going to be part of our year's work, that I would not fuss about their spelling, and indeed that I would only indicate or correct misspelled words on their papers if they put S's in the corner of their papers. Only the good spellers ever put S's in the corner of their papers. By the time I had read a couple of this student's papers, I realized that I had a problem—in James Herndon's nice definition, something that wasn't supposed to happen. His frequency of error, as they say, was about twenty-five words per page. Sometimes, in one paragraph, he spelled a word two or three different ways. I began to get cold feet. I could hear a voice from the future asking me, "But why didn't you *do* something?" So, like all of us in these situations, I began to think about covering my tracks a bit. Also, I really wanted to help.

So, one day, in private, I said to this student, "I really meant what I said about not bugging you about spelling. But I can see you have something of a problem. As it happened, I have worked with kids who spelled badly, and I think I know some tricks that may work. I don't want you to feel that I am indifferent. So if you would like some help, don't hesitate to ask—I'll be glad to give it." He looked at me a while, then heaved a great sigh up from his shoes and said slowly, "I've been getting help for years." I said, "Say no more. I won't raise the subject again, if you don't." He didn't, and I didn't. He was in my class for two years, wrote a number of interesting papers, and was in other areas a brilliant student. By the end of the second year in my class his misspelled words per page were down to five or less. By now they may well be down to none.

On this matter of corrections. We have our ends and means confused, our cart in front of the horse. We often talk and act as if children learned something in school—say, fractions—so that they could do papers about it. On the contrary, they do the papers *only* to learn something about fractions. There is *no other reason* for the papers. So why not say, here is the chapter on adding fractions, read it, ask about anything in it you don't understand, work out some of the examples in the text and then compare them with the text, and when you think you understand the chapter, do a few of the problems at the end. Then check them with your answer sheet. If you got them right, you are ready for the next chapter. If not, try them again, see if you can catch your own mistake. If you can't, ask a friend, or come and ask me—that's what I'm for—and I'll try to help you find where you got off the trail.

Many people say, "But won't the children cheat?" This shows how much we, like the children, have slipped into the habit of thinking of school as a contest, a battle of wits between teachers and children, waged according to certain rules. There is no contest—or there shouldn't be. If the children know that we are not trying to judge or catch or trap or humiliate or defeat them, they will quickly stop trying to think of ways to escape or outwit us. Then we can begin—many of us for the first time—to do our real job, which is not proving that children are not learning, but helping them learn.

Another pet myth of schools is that the more problems on long division, or fractions or whatever, a child does, the better he will understand them. This whole notion of learning through drill rests on a very simple and fundamental misconception, that understandings, what we might call mental skills (though I don't like the word skills, for reasons I have said before), are like physical skills, that learning to know a certain thing is like learning to make a certain movement. They are not the same. Drill makes sense when we are training nerves and muscles, whether in playing scales on an instrument, or shooting baskets, or throwing a pot on a wheel, or knitting, or learning a dance step, or practicing football plays. These carefully and sometimes painfully learned patterns of action, if repeated often enough, become more natural, unconscious, instinctive—though as musicians, athletes, dancers know, they must be relearned and relearned. But the mind is not a muscle, and ways of training that work well for nerves and muscles, when applied to the mind work very badly or not at all. The child who has shown with a few long-division problems that he can do long division should not be given more to do, but encouraged to move ahead as quickly as possible into further kinds of arithmetic and mathematics where he can use *and* extend what he has already learned. If we try to keep him doing what he already knows how to do, he is likely to grow bored and careless.

Sometimes parents say to me, "My child comes home from school every night with enormous amounts of homework. I look at it, and see that most of it is just repetitive busywork. What can I do about it?" First, find out if possible why the teacher does this. Many teachers give a lot of homework because they feel, and fear, and with good reason, that if they don't the parents will make a lot of trouble for them. If this is the problem, perhaps you can say, or get together with other parents to say, "Look, we don't want our children spending hours every evening on homework, we like their company, there are other things for them to do at home, and it is making them hate school." This may be all that is needed. After all, the teacher has to correct all that homework. But another teacher may be a worshipper of homework. Perhaps, like many parents, he believes that only homework will keep children out of trouble and away from the TV set. (It doesn't say much for the morality or intelligence of so many parents that they expect the schools to use homework to solve their TV problems for them. In fact, the transfer, *by the parents,* of so much of their own authority and responsibility to the schools is in most ways a cowardly and contemptible business—I can't make my boy cut his hair, but *you* can, by threatening to destroy his whole future.) Or the teacher may believe in drill as the only way to fix understanding. Or he may believe, as many do, that the school should make life dull and unpleasant for children, on the principle that whatever they dislike is good for them, and that anyway that is what the rest of their lives will be like. (These things have been said to me many times.) In none of these cases is argument very likely to change the teacher's mind. In that case, I say to parents, if you can't get a new teacher or a new school, tell your child to do enough of the problems to convince himself and you that he knows how to do them, and then do the rest yourself. And they look at me in amazement and delight. Such a simple and obvious solution!

For years parents have been pumped full of propaganda that parents and schools should stand shoulder to shoulder, and work together. "Work together against the children," it would be more honest to say. James Herndon—I think this will be in his next book—tells of the lower-income father of a boy who long had trouble in school, saying of the schools in amazement and rage, as many other parents might say if they only thought enough, "For years they've been making me hate my kid!" This rule about parents and teachers always working together is a bad and silly one. The only good rule is that people, whether parents or teachers, who trust and respect and value children should support them against other people, whether parents or teachers, who do not. Where, as is still so often and tragically the case, schools are petty, tyrannical, and absurd, parents should back their children against them, help them in every way they can to survive, and even to resist. It works the other way, as well. Teachers in many parts of the country are used to hearing parents say that the only way to deal with their children is to beat them, hard and often. More than once a parent has told me that his child was untrustworthy, no good, and that I had to watch him every second and keep the screws clamped on tight. To this I say, "What you think about your child, and how you treat him, is your own business. I happen to think that all children are worthy of and need trust and respect, and that's the way I'm going to deal with your child." It took me a long time to get used to the fact that very often, when I told parents that their kids were bright and capable and that I liked them, I would find myself in an argument. No, it is children that are important, not some mythical ideal of cooperation between home and school.

To sum up, whatever concessions we may have to make to testing, marking, and grading in the short run, in the long run our duty is to oppose them. To some groups of teachers, after they had shown by raised hands that on the whole they thought grades did more harm than good, I used to ask two more questions. First, "How many of you give grades?" Almost all did. Second, "How many of you have said publicly, or even to the parents of the children you teach, or to the school you work in, that you think on the whole grades hurt more than they help?" Almost no hands were raised. Now we can hardly call ourselves professional while we act like this. I don't happen to agree with or like most of the positions that the medical profession takes on public policy, but one thing is certain, and that is that when the public appears to be taking steps or getting ready to take steps that doctors disapprove of, they make their feelings known. It is time for teachers to be just as vocal, and not just about salaries and working conditions, either, but about the whole nature of their work and relations with children. If public pressure makes us do things we think are harmful, or at least not helpful, the very least we can do is say to the public that we think they are wrong, and that we are doing these things under protest. Many teachers in California, for example, have complained about all the tests that the state legislature is forcing them to give their pupils. I say, "I agree with you that this is bad. But where did the idea come from in the first place that learning could be measured with numbers? Did a legislator think it up? No, so-called educators developed these ideas, and sold them to the public and their legislators, and if we think this is all a lot of harmful nonsense, it's our duty to do all we can to unsell it."

In the article, "Why We Need a New Schooling," which I wrote for *Look* magazine (January 13, 1970), I said that any tests that were not a personal matter between the learner and someone helping him learn, but were given instead to grade and label students for someone else's purposes (employers, colleges, evaluators of schools, administrators, anxious parents, etc.), were illegitimate and harmful. I then said that students should organize to refuse to take such tests, and that *teachers should organize to refuse to give them.* The students will probably lead the way in this. We may not have long to wait before they begin. When they do, we should give them all the support and cooperation we can. They are not trying to destroy our authority, but to restore it. Only when we stop being judges, graders, labelers, can we begin to be true teachers, educators, helpers of growth and learning.

Hearing my comparison with doctors, teachers may feel, "Doctors can afford to be braver than we are; they are richer." I don't say that this is not an important difference. But a more important difference is this. A doctor, like a lawyer, is a professional because he can say to his patient, or client, "If you don't like my medicine, or law, you don't have to take it. Go somewhere else." It is because his relation with his patient is based on mutual consent that the doctor can afford to be professional, that is, to say and do what *he* thinks right. Precisely the opposite is true of us. It is because our relationship with the public, the parents of the children we teach, is *not* voluntary, *not* based on mutual consent, that we are not allowed to be professional. Because the parents, whether they like it or not, have to send their children to our classes, because for most of them there is no other option, they are bound to try to make us say and do in those classes whatever they want, whether *we* like it or not. Only when all parents, not just rich ones, have a truly free choice in education, when they can take their children out of a school they don't like, and have a choice of many others to send them to, or the possibility of starting their own, or of educating their children outside of school altogether—only then will we teachers begin to stop being what most of us still are and if we are honest know we are, which is jailers and baby-sitters, cops without uniforms, and begin to be professionals, freely exercising an important, valued, and honored skill and art.

28

TROUBLED CHILDREN
AND OTHERS

When we, parent or teacher, try in school or any other setting to cut down the amount of direction, coercion, threat, and punishment in our work with children, to work with them instead on a basis of greater freedom and mutual respect, and to give them more of the management of their own lives and learning, we are almost sure to run into some problems. We will have to cope with some of the consequences of the children's not having been treated this way before, the bad aftereffects of their previous lives both in and out of school. This often comes as a shock to many well-meaning people, particularly in schools that are trying to become more free, open, non-coercive. They think, "If we just start being nice to children, they will in turn be nice to us." It is not as easy as that. Many of the children will begin to express, in words and often in violent and destructive behavior, a lot of bottled-up anger and resentment that they never before were able, or at least felt able, to express. Everyone says in city schools, "If you don't crack down on the kids from the first day, they take advantage of you, etc." But it is just as great and difficult a problem with richer sub-urban kids.

Some of what I have already written in this book deals with the problem. But this is just a start. For one thing, it would take a book and more to say even what we now think we know about the problem. For another, we don't know very much. Only as we work with more children in more open situations will we learn better how in these situations we can help them get over the damage of their earlier lives.

Of the books that deal with this problem, *How to Live with Your Special Child,* by George von Hilsheimer, is indispensable. Please add it to your list. Don't expect to agree with every word of it; I don't myself. But we must know and think about what it says in order to move ahead. I will quote here from it—enough, I hope, to make you want to read it. Please don't take these few quotes for the whole. Many of them may seem theoretical, but the book is full of the most specific, day-to-day, practical suggestions, which may be useful to a great many people, people who might not agree about many things and who might not like other parts of the book.

The first few pages are a good introduction both to the book and to the man. Von Hilsheimer is a paradoxical man, a mixture of things that many people think can't be mixed. He is a behaviorist (far more than I am, I think) who is also a humanist. He is a conservative, in the truest and deepest sense of the word, not the nutty way it is used today to describe many people who are in love with cruelty, destruction, and death; but he is also, as all such true conservatives must be, a radical. He has great faith in people and no illusions about them. But let his words speak for themselves.

> This handbook is written for people who work with people. It is written to help guide those children whose actions are in themselves unproductively dangerous, unpleasant, uncomfortable, or merely unwanted. . . . [It] is based on the conviction that unwanted behavior can readily be changed, and that this is worth doing. It is for teachers who have the compassion to see that ready relief from an embarrassing behavior is worth weeks of talk. [It] describes techniques aimed at enlarging self-control. *It is not a program for detailed control of others.* [Italics mine.]
> My biases and goals are toward waking people up, increasing their awareness, loosening their roots, dissolving their armor, disinhibiting, decongesting, enlarging the field of their being, in short,

making people more alive. . . . There are more appropriate human means of self-control than by irrational automatic inhibition. The evidence is overwhelming that as people are freed from barriers to feeling and action, their controls become more refined and their abilities enhanced.

In the context of his book it is clear enough, but I should perhaps explain here what he means by "irrational automatic inhibition." An example of this might be, if you smack a child every time he reaches toward or touches the stove, after a while he will not touch the stove. What he is saying is that even when this way works, which is by no means always, it is not the best way.

These procedures have grown out of ten years of experiment and demonstration in programs initiated and operated by *Humanitas*. . . . directed to a wide range of human beings in North America—migrant farmers and their children, farm families, urban slum dwellers (both U.S. Negro and Canadian Anglo), Indian families in reservations or in cities, middle class families, wealthy families, families in church, school, and in remedial, rehabilitative, correctional and therapeutic institutions.

In short, the things he recommends have been tried out, often in very difficult situations, often when nothing else seemed to work, and they work. Later in the book is a section called "Children in Trouble." If everyone who works with children, in any capacity, could read just these few pages, we would have many fewer problems than we do. He says, in part:

Some children are in trouble.

Some children in trouble repeat actions that get them into trouble.

Most children in trouble live in neighborhoods and homes and go to schools where many children do not get into trouble.

Some kinds of trouble that children are in: wearing unusual clothes, talking very strangely, being dirty and behaving queerly, but not really harming people or property (this is mostly trouble from adult's reactions to them which is very constant and very hostile); doing poorly in school; leaving school; quitting work; running away from home; breaking laws; using drugs or alcohol; sexual misadventure; physically damaging themselves; trying to kill themselves (some manage and are no longer in trouble); none of these, but being very unhappy.

Most children in any of these kinds of trouble are in more than one or soon will be.

Most children in trouble say that they are very unhappy.

Most children in trouble have very ordinary ideas about what is right and what is wrong.

Most children in trouble don't like themselves or anyone else.

Most children in trouble are bored and do not see anything to do; they don't know how to do much anyway.

Most children in trouble see little reason to be any other way.

Von Hilsheimer, being a very old-fashioned kind of person, has a very strong bias in favor of competence, energy, the will and ability to find work worth doing and doing it.

[They need] to know some adults who have jobs *other than the children themselves* [italics mine], but who are interested in the children;

to know some adults who have many skills and yet who are strong enough not to need to appear perfect, controlled, and as if they didn't need to grow more themselves;

to know some adults who behave toward children with the same *gravity, respect and attention and lack of impertinence* [italics mine] that they would grant a friend in trouble;

to know some adults who will give them attention most strongly when they are doing worthwhile things and who are obviously not interested in them simply because they are bad;

to know some adults who will tell them "no" fairly, consistently and really mean it;

to know some adults who understand that haircuts, fingernails, clothing and cleanliness are trivial and so teach children that knowledge, self-control and ability are important;

to know some adults who are strong enough *not to need to make children need them* [italics mine]; who can force children to make decisions for themselves and can help them live with and overcome bad decisions and so learn to make good ones.

The first chapter in the book is called "The Forgotten Flesh." No chapter in the book deals with matters that are more important or about which most people who deal with troubled children are more ignorant.

. . . It is almost certain that a troubling child will have a disabling or uncomfortable medical disorder. His characteristic style of response to the people around him will almost certainly be built around those disorders. . . . it is still uncharacteristic for a child to be sent to a behavior specialist or a care center having enjoyed fundamental medical examination. . . . Simply removing disabilities will not teach a child to read. . . . Often, though, it really does seem as though treating the disorder has taught a child to read, calculate, and cooperate. Curing the disorder . . . permits already learned skills to surface. It may enable the child to see and to organize the seeing. . . .

Nearly every slum child, most hyperactive and delinquent kids, and many inadequate, weak, unreactive tuned-out kids habitually do not eat enough proteins—particularly in the morning—and eat too many sweets and carbohydrates. . . . Any child who persists in troubling or inadequate behavior when a majority of his peers have improved ought to be examined for hypoglycemia. . . . Nearly every child sent to us has been found to suffer a deficiency of B vitamins. . . . Hyperactivity and other troubling behavior or inadequacies are always symptoms demanding an inspection both of the B vitamins in the child's ordinary diet, and of his metabolic ability to process the foods. . . . Any child who seems suddenly to lose energy in mid-morning or mid-afternoon is likely a victim of poor diet, of a diet unadjusted to his individual ability to process foods, or of hypoglycemia.

If the teacher will note behavior, pulse and respiration rates, perceptual and attention span abilities both before and after eating she will be able to point to any large difference in these functions that surely signal allergic reactions. . . .

It has always amazed me that hospitals and residential treatment centers . . . can't take the trouble to replace the spongy garbage called bread, the instant potatoes and other overprocessed, depleted "foods" that are the standard diet.

Elsewhere I have suggested how the measurement of such things as heartbeat, blood pressure, respiration rate, and exploring the ways in which these things vary under different conditions of exertion, fatigue, stress, and so on, might be a very constructive and interesting part of the children's work in a class, tying into their work with numbers, opening into some study of physiology, and giving them great self-awareness and self-control. What von Hilsheimer says here about institutional diet seems to me to apply equally to any of the school "hot lunches" I have ever eaten or heard about. They are mostly starch and junk, the kind of food you would expect to get in the cheapest roadside stands, not worth the money and trouble to cook and serve them. I hope these lunches and lunch programs were not typical—thin, overcooked hamburgers on spongy buns, macaroni, etc., but I have serious doubts. They may hold off hunger until the children can get home to the icebox, or to the store for candy or pop, but that's about all they do. "Hot lunches" seem to be a big issue with parents in many cities. What they ought to be plugging for, hot or cold, is really nutritious food.

It is important that teachers be aware that meals with their children are a very important part of the teaching structure. Most bratty kids have only known meals that were unpleasant—chaotic, poorly prepared and served, noisy, the characteristic time for criticism, punishment, and argument. It is important that the adults surrounding the child make the meal relaxed, attractive and pleasant . . . that the programs just before and after meals be pleasant, relaxing, and enjoyable.

With this in mind, what can we say of the conditions under which most children eat school meals—crowded like cattle into a large bare cafeteria, bad food shoved at them, as often as not adults prowling around telling them in threatening tones to sit still, be quiet, hurry up. Children I know in one school (suburban, by the way, and generally felt to be the best school in town) are regularly told that they have to eat their meal quickly, no dawdling, usually no talking, though after they have finished they have to wait in silence in the cafeteria for ten minutes or more because under the school schedule there is no place else for them to go.

> Years of work with disturbing and failing youngsters have convinced us that, far from being unable to cope with abstraction, they are practically incapable of dealing with the world around them and their own internal feelings in a concrete and specific way.

This is a point of great importance, and one of the central ideas in the book. It is also very close to what I mean when I say that people are in trouble if their verbal or symbolic models of reality are badly out of adjustment, out of touch with their non-verbal, non-abstract mental model of reality, the sum of their true hopes, fears, expectations, and feelings. Thus a man might say, thinking he ought to, that Negroes deserve a fair break when in fact his stomach knots and his blood pressure rises ten points with fear or anger or disgust whenever he sees one. He is quite literally "out of touch" with his own feelings.

> In our society it is easier and socially more acceptable to express anger, hostility, rejection, aloofness, and criticism than affection, warmth, desire, approval or satisfaction. . . . We have been impressed by the almost total inability of troubling adolescents to express *or accept* [italics mine] positive emotions. . . . Children need to be touched. . . . In the families of most failing and difficult children, touching is limited to bare essentials, and to punishment erratically and unjustly exploded out. Animals deprived of touching and contact with other animals are in many ways less healthy, smaller, less capable. Animals held and fondled by human experimenters are more competent than those which are not.
> Nearly every troubling child suffers constantly from the tension of his muscles. If you go around a room of delinquent teens gently rubbing neck and shoulder muscles you will be astonished at the amount of pain, the fear of contact, the ejaculations of "Hey, what are you trying to do to me—Ouch!"
> . . . An alert teacher will notice that troubled children cannot

breathe. Their breathing—and that of many if not most Americans—is thoroughly artificial. It is shallow, locked up into the chest with practically no abdominal movement and no chest movement at all. Observe a baby . . . [My note: to see it done right, that is.]

This is going to be hard to do anything about, at least in many places. In most schools children, except the very young, are strictly and explicitly forbidden to touch each other. "Keep your hands to yourself!" is a common school command. Almost all high schools specifically forbid what they call "public displays of affection." Nor is it any safer, or in many cases even legal, for a teacher to touch the children. Women might conventionally be allowed to touch girls, but on the whole not boys; men teachers take a considerable risk if they touch either. How are we to cure ourselves of this sickness, the fear of touching, and how do we keep children from catching the sickness?

A very important part of this book, which cannot well be quoted or summarized, is about the bodily reeducation, the training in relaxation and self-awareness, of these terribly strung-up children. It calls to mind the scene in *The Lives of Children* where Dennison stops a near-hysterical Vicente and for a second has him breathe so that he can feel his own diaphragm pushing against Dennison's hand. Again, it may be hard for many schools or teachers to do much about this, since many Americans make into a virtue their hatred and contempt and fear and ill-treatment of their own bodies, and would lash out in rage against attempts to have young people learn to be aware of and respect their physical being. But in spite of the difficulty we must make the effort.

Von Hilsheimer has many good suggestions to make about the classroom, its organization, and its work. Here his book is a good companion to those of Hawkins, Kohl, and others.

A simple way of enriching the [classroom structure] is to break the age segregation. Kids teaching kids is the most effective social and teaching model now reported in the literature. . . . An ideal elementary classroom has at least two teachers, and often involves as many as ten at one time (by teachers of course I mean volunteers, aides and "real" teachers—all used to advance . . . learning and not just for janitorial, nursing and secretarial tasks).

So far, of course, a great many of our school systems have done all they could to discourage or forbid outright the use of outside resource people in the classroom. This is a most serious and needless mistake.

The number of students can be more than thirty or so. The room should be large and ideally has an easily accessible half-second-story for reading and solitary quiet study or withdrawal for sleep or sloth.

The Children's Community Workshop School in New York City, Santa Fe Community School, both independent public schools, and others have such hideaways. The one in New York is a little cave, only about three feet high, built at the top of an old hallway, overlooking the main classroom, and reached only by a ladder. The one in Santa Fe is built like a little house across one corner of the classroom. Children can go inside and play on the ground floor, or they can go upstairs into a little balcony. And a few years ago some people at Redlands College in California built and for a year or more worked and taught in a two-level classroom—which I did not have the good luck to see. There is a lot of wasted space up in the air in our classrooms—what in the context of our cities' architects call "air rights." We need to make better use of that space.

The main room is organized with formal foci—messy corners, neat book corners, production corners and display corners. A less than ideal classroom can . . . still be organized into foci of activities, emotional styles . . . I have worked with two other teachers in an absolutely bare room, 40 x 50 feet, with 100 illiterate, preschool children of migrant farmers and have been satisfied that our accomplishment was more than if we had separated into three classes.

Privacy and safety are critical for learning of all kinds. It is certain that the highly aroused, frightened child who is the typical failure or troublemaker needs more rather than less privacy, more rather than less safety and insulation. [My note: again, see Dennison on José.] It is essential that structures be created in the classroom, if they are but large cardboard cartons and paper block walls, that enable children to build safety and privacy into the structure of their social life at school.

Children like nooks and hiding places. One of the nicest bits of Al Fiering's film of the Fayerweather Street School in Cambridge, *Children Are People,* is of two little girls, about six years old if that, snuggled into a corner made of two pieces of cardboard, reading together. They were going slowly, with plenty of time for reflection and private talk and jokes. Thinking of that scene, I can't help feeling, no corner, no reading.

Von Hilsheimer talks of "enriching structures." People are always talking to me about "structured" and "unstructured situations. To this I say that there is no such thing as an "unstructured" human situation; all situations have a structure; children live every second of their lives surrounded by structures, little ones, big ones, little ones inside of big ones. The question to ask is, what kind of structures? And here von Hilsheimer makes a point that I would like to see written in letters a foot high on the walls of every school.

> . . . Unfortunately, most people think the word "structure" is limited to something like the military hierarchy and the pseudo-structures of the lecture room and textbook. *It is as if biologists thought that a crystal or even a block of homogeneous and undifferentiated matter had more structure than a living cell.* [Italics mine.] . . . The richer the selection of artifacts, gadgets, objects, spaces and relationships, the busier, more purposive and satisfactory the behavior of the pupils is going to be.

The converse is just as true. Every day I read—today in *Time* magazine—of more and more violence and vandalism in our schools. The school people respond, much of the time, by bringing in more and more of various kinds of police. We might do better to find out and change the things that make children hate the schools. As von Hilsheimer says, "dropouts commit more crimes while they are in school than after dropping out, and there are more crimes by kids on school days than on weekdays and holidays." There is a message for us here. Is it really so hard to read?

It is, of course, important that the schoolroom be attractive to the pupil. This seldom means the nice orderly displays that so delight a certain type of pedagogue. Children love bright, vivid, dynamically ordered relationships and structures. A classroom that does not reflect this electricity is a classroom that *actively harms children.* [Italics mine.] The schoolroom may be in a gloomy and ancient building, but have vitality built into it by a good teacher working with her children.

Some of the best schools I have seen in England were in gloomy and ancient buildings, but made colorful, alive, and human by all kinds of displays of the painting, ceramics, and other sculpture, both of the children themselves and of mature artists. I very seldom find this here. Visiting schools, I look to see whether the halls and walls are decorated with art work. In the hundreds of schools I have seen, most if them in communities of more than average wealth, I have yet to see as many as ten so decorated. In most school buildings, new or old, the walls and locker fronts are bare. It is hard to understand or forgive this. Society may make schools do some things they don't want to do, and lack of money may prevent them from doing other things they would like to do. But nobody but the people in the schools themselves makes them so cold and ugly. Do the learning places of our children really have to be designed to fit the convenience and whims of our school custodians?

In the next chapter I discuss more specifically some further ways to make the classroom more flexible, colorful, interesting.

. . . It is very clear that inappropriate demands on the child can create substantial difficulties. If the reader doubts this, try the simple experiment of signing your name while picking up your writing-hand-side foot and moving it in a counter-clockwise motion. [My note: I tried it—wow!] Children forced to perform beyond their developed capacity experience the same sense of impossibility and frustration. Imagine carrying out such tasks all day long! Kids are made to.

A good teacher has to remember that skills almost impossible to teach at one age are easily taught at another. [My note: this opposes the fashionable view that the earlier you can teach anything, the better.] No child is without skills. The effective teacher will focus on those skills to find the level of development at which the child now works. By complicating and enlarging the existing skills the good teacher avoids both premature pressure on the child and the trap of infantilizing the child and boring him by asking him to do too little.

Unfortunately, much of the time we manage the miracle of doing both these things at the same time; our demands on children are all too often both inappropriate and boring.

Every organism is born with a posture of growth and expansion toward the future. It is critical that the child's optimistic posture of growth toward the future be cherished and sustained. This posture is destroyed both by demands beyond his competence, and by abandoning the child to less than appropriate demands. The important principle is that the child ought to be the source of data and guidance.

Here he underlines the points that in their books are so well made by Frances Hawkins and George Dennison, and that I try to make clear in mine. The child wants to grow, to step forward, to move out into the world. But he has to move from where he is. If we can't or won't reach him where he is, we can't encourage or help him make those next steps. Instead, we freeze him into immobility, into strategies of faking what he doesn't really know.

The teacher has got to keep in mind that this kid is failing at tasks remarkably simpler than tasks he has already accomplished. Adding two and two is hardly as sophisticated as hitting a baseball. It is infinitely easier to learn to read and write than to listen and speak. If the child is failing it is because failing works for him. [My note: by protecting him against what looks to him like worse pains and dangers.]

The failing child has been *taught to fail*. [Italics mine.] It is up to you to create a learning excitement that recaptures skills he had when he learned to bring food to his mouth, to walk and to talk. The jobs he has now are much simpler.

The proper job of a child is to play and play and play. There is no play that does not teach, and no experience out of which a child cannot learn. With remedial problems the critical awareness the teacher needs to keep is that these kids have been insulated from their perceptions and skills and need to have situations provided in which the play can be enriched with artifacts or natural forms. [My note: Mrs. Hawkins again.] If the child thinks that the play is a Learning Experience you might just as well go back to *Dick and Jane*.

I note in passing that this is the trouble with the "games" used by many of the high-powered curriculum reformers in their highly directed courses of study. The children know that these "games" are not games, but gimmicks. They play them, because they are a lot more interesting than sitting in a seat and listening to a teacher talk, which is what they would have to do if they didn't play them. But they don't play with anything like the energy, vivacity, or intelligence they bring to their true play, the games they think up and play for their own reasons.

We have to invent ways of breaking up the pupil's failure experience, and his "what-does-teacher-want-now" set. So we've got to get him to write and talk about things he doesn't usually have in school, things that are funny or interesting because they are of immediate use to him. All such materials are full of data and skills that will be of use twenty years from now.

Write about—ghosts, family fights, the thing you like best in the world, who should die, your enemies, the things and people you love most, pirates, killers, dangerous beasts, cars, being married, the thing you would most like to blow up . . . etc.

The important principles here are that children spontaneously talk about love, hate, violence, death, strong things, nasty things, forbidden things.

These and many other suggestions are all part of a splendid chapter called "The Creative Use of Creativity." Is it possible, then, to make *uncreative* use of creativity? Yes; we do it all the time.

Witches at Hallowe'en; turkeys at Thanksgiving; wreaths, etc., at Christmas; hearts at Valentine's Day; round they go on the bulletin boards of our classrooms, year after year, regular as the earth around the sun.

. . . [to teach reading] use comic books or anything else the pupil will respond to. Start with simple, well-written fun comics— Casper, Tom & Jerry, Woody Woodpecker, etc. But quickly move on to the full range of comics including things you may think are garbage. We want these kids to read. If they read they will expand their reading. [My note: as is made clear in Daniel Fader's *Hooked on Books*.] You might be amazed at the vocabulary counts in Marvel or other comics.

. . . Do not censor [the student's] material. If you can't stand certain words think first of teaching other children. If you think you will want to stick it out then very matter of factly tell your children that these words frighten you and would they please lay off. Don't give them power over you by moralizing, or reacting blindly and irrationally. You are the professional. Would you like it if your doctor retched when he looked down your strep laden throat?

. . . Ask the children to write, talk into a tape, or discuss: How you would organize the best school in the world. [My note: Robert Coles has had some eloquent answers from children about this.] What would a class be like? Suppose a Man From Mars came to visit: the MFM says his people don't live in families. How might they live? The MFM says no one ever fights in his world? How must they raise their children? The MFM says there are no schools on Mars. How do children learn? The MFM says there are no races, no games with scores, and no one ever wants to be bigger, faster, better or have more than someone else. How must they raise their children? Why isn't it like that here? Do animals have races? Would you like that way of being? [and many more] . . . The teacher should not "grade," approve or disapprove, but merely support production by indicating that she hears and understands, questioning for clarity or further penetration of the idea, and rephrasing both for understanding and for its own sake.

Later there is a superb chapter called "A Thousand and One Lesson Plans." Still later von Hilsheimer makes an interesting point about programmed instruction, something I have never much liked.

> Another advantage of programmed instruction, particularly by machine, is that it enables the special teacher to break the conditioned transaction [my note: like conditioned reflex] that troubled kids have in which learning has something to do with the fight against authority.

This is important, because the children, and there are many of them, who first adopt a strategy of deliberate failure to protect themselves against the demands of adults, demands they would be willing to try to meet if they thought they could, later almost always begin to see this strategy as a way of attacking and hurting adults. "You're so smart, you want to teach me to read, you're going to work some kind of a miracle, eh, teach this dumb kid nobody else could teach? Well, go right ahead, smart guy; I'll show you how smart you are." But there is no kick in doing this to a machine. The machine doesn't care whether we learn what is in it or not, or even whether we operate it the right way or not. If we do one thing, we get one result; if we do another, we get another result; the choice is up to us. For children locked into hostility and defiance, ready to do themselves any kind of injury if only to spite those who are trying to help them, this may be essential. You can learn to work a machine without having to feel that you are selling out to it.

> Charles Slack has been having Puerto Rican janitors (preferably with little or no English) bring teaching machines into cells with young criminals. The janitor gets it across that the machine is supposed to teach the kids. He also gets it across that since it is the machine's job to *teach,* if the kid makes a mistake the machine will give him a dime for wasting his time.
>
> Nearly everyone rubs their eyes at this point. The machine gives the student a dime if the student make a mistake because the machine has not done its job and taught him. These young criminals do not work on mistakes or on making dimes. No one has to con these kids into the advantages of knowing. They do quite well for themselves if the social consequences and structures

of the *teaching* process are changed. Many of these hoods work for hours at a time on the machines and graduate from jail to college.

There may be another reason why machines, technical aids, high-powered teaching "methods" of a kind I ordinarily don't like, may be useful with such kids. Over the years they have come to see learning as an entirely external and passive process. It's like going to a doctor to get a shot. The teacher comes and tries to inject you with some learning. But something is wrong with you; the shots never take, the learning never sticks; you're immune. In this despairing frame of mind they need something almost magical, a sense of new, untried, and very powerful medicine, so powerful that even they will not be able to resist it, but instead may learn something. Only this kind of hope will lure them into taking the necessary active part in the learning itself.

I was once a consultant to a program to teach adult illiterates to read, using Caleb Gattegno's *Words in Color,* a good method for this kind of situation. In one class a very intelligent and energetic man, a refugee from Appalachia, who was doing very well, stopped in the middle of his work to say to the class, "That stuff they used to give us in school was horse and buggy stuff. This here is *jet* stuff!" Of course, the powers were in him; as von Hilsheimer says, it was a matter of finding a way to let them surface, of making available to him the very considerable learning skills that he had—and all of us have. That is what this book can help us do.

29

NEW SPACES FOR
LEARNING

As I was writing about ways to enrich the structure of the learning environment, a friend sent me a most interesting news clipping from the West Coast. In the November 6, 1969 issue of the *Lake Oswego* (Oregon) *Review,* there is a story entitled "Autonomous Learning Laboratory for Pedagogs; 'It' For Students," which says, in part:

> That slice of space behind the gymnasium (at Riverdale School) is today the "autonomous learning laboratory" to the pedagogue; the "experience center" to Riverdale staff; and just plain "It" to students. "It" is a place where youngsters can do their thing: Make a statue; develop a film; listen to records; plug in TV shows; read a magazine; see newborn mice; make a tape recording; take things apart; put them together; think; muse; ponder; build. The creation of Tony Hille, resource teacher, "it" has become the most popular bit of square footage at [the] school.
>
> Hille . . . recalled the aspects of his grade school years which fascinated him and then designed "it." He remembered:
>
> Climbing; so it has balconies that go around and about, in and out.
>
> Retreats; to get away from everything and everybody. Hence the box thing that seems to hang in mid-air. Soundproofed with egg cartons it's a perfect hideaway. . . .

282

Building; hence the long work bench and an array of tools that would satisfy the pro as well as the amateur. . . . Hille devotes an entire wall to storing a fantastic collection of bits and pieces.
Animals; the bright green iguana lives at peace with a couple of boa constrictors. Turtles, rats, mice, frogs, and baby mice dwell in separate cages.
Youngsters explore the unseen with the microscopes; use the teaching machine, film strips.
. . . In the background ready to assist when necessary are the resource teacher and a couple of aides. Otherwise, it's up to the kids to learn and with ears, eyes, nose and hands.

Along with the story are some wonderful pictures I wish I could reproduce here. One shows the balcony and the egg-crate hideaway, another a lot of the old non-school furniture with which the room is both divided and furnished. The children look to be from ten years old down to about six. One boy, perhaps seven or eight, is lying on his back on a sofa with feet up in the air, reading a magazine that looks rather like *Popular Science*. At the end of the sofa is a rack with copies of the *Scientific American*. Were they put there for the picture? Maybe. From experience I know that many kids like looking at the *Scientific American,* even if they can't understand a word in it. There are often good stories about animals and animal experiments, the photographs are good and the drawings even better. Also, there are many ads of exciting looking technical equipment. A child reading it feels, as he should, plugged into the world of the adults, the continuum of human experience.

Some other very interesting materials have been developed by Gerard Pottebaum and an organization called The Tree House (833 Stoneybrook Drive; Kettering, Ohio 45429). The basic materials, which he calls the Learning Environment, are a set of free-standing vertical panels, rather like the panels in a folding Japanese screen, except that they are not hinged together but can stand separately. These panels are light enough so that they can be easily moved about the classroom. With them come a number of large sheets of paper to be mounted in or on them, and it is what is printed on these sheets, or can be put on them, that gives the environment its many characters.

Here are some quotes from a descriptive bulletin:

Making Space Speak

> The Tree House Learning Environment provides educators with an opportunity in either the traditional classroom or in the new schools without walls, to use space as a medium of communication.
>
> The appropriateness of special enclosures as a teaching medium can be readily appreciated by observing the way children play. Give a child a large box and soon he will be inside it. [My note: any large appliance store always has a supply of these large cartons behind the store; you can have what you can take away.] Should a friend be near, he will invite him inside too.
>
> Children playing in a yard where there is lawn furniture will soon use the furniture to create a special, spacially arranged world. A bench will mark off the wall of a house, the hose will serve as the highway to the shopping center indicated by the patio table. In this activity, the children are arranging space—not simply the furniture and equipment—in order to create a world in which they can relate to each other. The furniture marks off spaces in which their imaginations can make present an adult world that they can control and adjust to through play.

It may well be that one of the things that poor kids really need, and don't get much from their environment, is this kind of space, to move in, adjust, make use of. This might be a reason why they are, as the schools would put it, more "restless," why they have a greater need to move about in school than other children who have plenty of space to move about in outside of the school. But of course in most schools we don't meet this need, either because we don't recognize or acknowledge it, or because we don't know how to meet it. But there is much we could do.

> Another example, familiar especially to parents, is the child's use of blankets or sheets to create enclosures. A blanket spread over two chairs and the coffee table forms a space where the

child can enclose himself with weapons and ammunition if he wants the space to be a fortress, with dishes and a little food should he want the space to be a kitchen, or with stuffed animals should he be in a jungle. Such an enclosure provides an opportunity for special conversations between a child and the parent who spends time with him there. Frequently, they talk on about things that no other environment releases . . .

When my sister and I were little, and much excited by overnight journeys in Pullman cars, we used to visit our grandmother in the summer. There were no other children of our age around, and not much visible to do. Like all little children, we made our own play. A favorite game was to take some of the kind of folding wood and canvas chairs often called director's chairs, tip them forward onto the ground, and cover their backs with a towel or blanket. This enclosed space became a lower berth in a Pullman car, and for hours, huddled under these chairs, we would go on imaginary trips and invent games and dramas built around them.

In a classroom, background noises of pages turning, conversations, someone writing on the blackboard, create an environment of children at work. These noises can help to encourage children to join in—to work, too. The hum of sounds help to muffle distracting noises. In a moment of silence, for instance, during a test, the dropped pencil can disrupt the entire class. Should there be a background of sounds, such a noise goes unnoticed.

This is one of the first things that I, and most visitors, noticed and were struck by in the classrooms in Leicestershire. They were not silent, there was quite a hum of talk and activity, but they seemed quieter, and certainly much more busy, than the silent classrooms we were used to. Dead silence can be very distracting. In time it can lead to dreaming, or perhaps to philosophizing, to deep thought. But at first, as I found when I went to a Quaker meeting and sat with many other people in a silent room, it makes us restless and anxious; we wonder what is going to happen, we listen to the silence, we wait for something to interrupt it, we think of ways to interrupt it.

The Learning Environment is not designed to eliminate sounds. But it does provide control over another kind of distraction more disrupting than excessive noise: motion.

Teachers with experience in schools without walls have found the motion and movement which accompany dramatizations, exercises, movies and television are distracting. The power of movement to distract can be seen again in a visit to a noisy factory or office of typists. Someone, or a group, walking through such a place, draws the attention of everyone there, regardless of how quietly one moves.

The Learning Environment does eliminate distractions of movement [my note: by eliminating the distractions, not the movement] in both the traditional classroom and the large school-room without walls. . . . as when a portion of the class is involved in art activities, watching television, or when the teacher is making a presentation to a small group of students. . . .

In its most elementary application, the Learning Environment helps the teacher to change the shape of the classroom as one would change a piece of modeling clay. Such changes create different moods . . .

By varying the arrangement of space in the classroom, the teacher lends variety and interest to the experience children have in the classroom space which as it stands is basically static and uninviting. . . .

Roy Ilsley, head of the Battling Brook Primary School in Leicestershire, told me last time I visited them that I had come just too late to see their jungle. Jungle? Apparently the children in one class had made it over into a tropical jungle. With cardboard, paper, cloth, and anything else they could find or make, they created trees, vines, all the dark greenery of the jungle, and filled it with what seemed the proper kinds of birds and animals. The project lasted a long time; there were always things to perfect and add. Naturally, in doing this they were strongly moved to learn all they could about real jungles and the people and animals who live there. Then, after many months, and just before my visit, they grew tired of their jungle, took it all down, and went on to other things.

. . . Part of the human nature of school children is their need to move about, to go places. Every teacher knows the honor he can bestow on a child to have him deliver something to another class-room, or to the office. Even getting out of one's desk to erase the blackboard is a treat. [My note: we have to wonder about the quality of life and learning in a classroom in which this *is* a treat.] The child's need to move about, to be active, is not diffi-cult to accommodate.

In the traditional classroom, the Learning Environment creates more opportunities for the children *to have some place to go.* [Italics mine.] It provides a sense of separation from the class-room without actually leaving the room. Without the Learning Environment, this experience of separation is not available. The Environment creates a real place to visit. The self-contained class-room is especially in need of such flexibility. . . . in the open-space school . . . another problem presents itself as it does in the self-contained classroom: Lack of privacy.

. . . providing for . . . privacy, intimacy, and movement, the Learning Environment enables the teacher to heighten the chil-dren's consciousness of the relationship between their course of study and their experience. . . .

Inside the Learning Environment, the teacher (and/or stu-dents) can introduce what are called changes of exposure. These exposures vary from scenes of our galaxy system, to panels of water, to schematic designs of how the eye sees or how the ear hears. They are printed on large panels which are attached to and cover the panels of the basic unit. (The basic unit depicts darkness and light, or night and day, by alternating black and yellow/gold panels.)

The intensity of focus provided by these exposures was best demonstrated when a group of primary-grade children entered the Environment for an exposure to water. Completely sur-rounded by panels full of waves, and sounds of the sea, the children began to "splash" about, making gestures of swimming, jumping over the edge as if at a pool, laughing, and calling for life preservers.

From out of this basic exposure, the teacher was able to move into any of several directions—a study of sea life, or sea fables and other related literature, of water as a natural resource, or transportation by sea, river, and canal. The teacher can [use] slides shown on white rear-screen projection surfaces which are mounted between the space arrangers [room-dividers]. The rear-screen surfaces enable the teacher to keep the equipment outside the Environment. . . . As the teacher goes into various subject areas based on the group's experience, the children can create their own art work of visual variations in the basic exposure . . . surround themselves with their own expressions of their expanding awareness of their human experiences.

This opens up possibilities we can hardly imagine. Not only can we use photographs or slides taken by others of the sea, jungle, desert, mountains, a host of environments, but we can use slides taken by us and/or the children themselves of their own neighborhoods, town, city. How much better to talk about life in a city surrounded by pictures of the city; to talk about trains surrounded by pictures of railroad stations or freight yards or engines and cars. And there are almost endless artistic possibilities, too. A friend of mine, a very gifted photographer named John Pearson of Berkeley, California, showed me one evening in his house a fascinating exhibit of slides he had taken. He had two projectors, focused on the same screen. In front of the lenses of the projectors was a piece of cardboard, just wide enough so that as it covered one lens it uncovered the other. By sliding the cardboard slowly from one side to the other he was able to fade out one slide as the other slide came in, to have one image change almost magically into the other. The possibilities here, of contrasting one kind of shape or color or pattern or set of ideas against another, are infinite. To this some might say that such equipment is expensive. No more so, and in fact less so, than much of the stuff that sits unused for most of the year in many an Audio-Visual closet. This, like other needed equipment, could be purchased jointly by a number of schools, or even a number of individual teachers working in different schools, and then shared around.

With these back-lighted panels we can do interesting things in mathematics. Years ago Bill Hull showed me what he called a Shadow Box—a box with a light source inside it, one side made of translucent material against which shadows could be projected, and a way of putting objects inside the box and turning them by knobs on the outside. Thus you could put a geometrical shape, of cardboard or wire, two-dimensional or three, into the box, turn it this way and that, and make a variety of shadows. One game was to put a solid shape inside, close the box, and then give another person, who could use the knobs to turn the object any way he wanted, thus making different shadows, the job of guessing the shape of the object inside the box. Or you could give him an object to put inside, and then give him the task of finding a way to make a shadow of a certain shape. Or with how many different kinds of objects could you make a given shadow? Games like this could be played with a rear-projection screen as well as a shadow box. This, of course, is nibbling, to use Mrs. Hawkins' phrase, at what mathematicians call Projective Geometry. And from a very interesting book called *Towards a Visual Culture,* by Caleb Gattegno (published by Outerbridge and Dienstfrey), about the possible uses of television in education, we may find many other ideas that we could adapt to this medium. There is a rich field here to explore.

Aside from [being] a special medium of communication, the Learning Environment provides a list of other specific functions, covering a variety of situations, and accommodating gatherings of adults as well as children:

—In both the self-contained classroom and the school without walls, there never seems to be enough wall space. The surface of the space-arrangers can serve to exhibit art work, student papers, visual aids. The canvas panels are ideal to use with felt figures. Such figures can be used in telling a story: geometric shapes of different colors can be used in games to enrich the students' ability to use mathematical concepts; felt-backed letters of different textures can be applied to the canvas surfaces by children learning letter forms.

—The space-arrangers can enclose a portion of a class who may be watching a movie, television, or a slide presentation.

—The Learning Environment can be used as a set for dramatizations held in the classroom, the open-space school, or in the assembly hall.

—The boxes used as seats can be stacked in various shapes and forms, used to hold banners, or function as modular display arrangements.

—In schools where weekend classes are held in religion, language, art or other subjects, the space-arrangers, tables, and box seats can be used instead of the desks containing the belongings of other children who use the [class] during the week. . . . When not in use, the space-arrangers, tables, and seats can be stored in a closet. . . . Teaching with the Environment . . . allows the teacher to leave undisturbed the material hanging on the walls of the room. The space-arrangers provide the weekend teacher with an abundance of clear wall space for material appropriate to the subject being taught.

What we are talking about here is a "regular" school whose facilities are used by special schools on evenings or weekends. I am just as interested in what might be called the reverse of this situation, in which a weekday school with no building of its own rents or borrows space from buildings ordinarily used only on weekends, like church schools. This is important, because a great many open, non-coercive schools, when they begin and for some time after, don't have enough money to have their own building. Dennison's First Street School had to do this; so for a while did the Fayerweather Street School in Cambridge; the Little School of Seattle has for years been working in space rented from a church. This sort of arrangement makes problems. The borrowers or renters of the space are very limited in what they can put on the walls and in general do to and with the environment. The Teaching Environment described here, or adaptations of it, could help solve many of these problems. It might even make it possible for two or even three different classes to use the same room, or two or more schools to use the same space. Our communities are full of unused or under-used space. If two or even more schools—new schools, community schools, independent public schools—could share this space, using it at different times, an important part of their costs could be greatly reduced. In most school systems, split or double sessions are felt to be a kind of educational disaster or disgrace, like walking around with a big hole in the seat of one's pants. With the right kind of equipment, split or multiple sessons might be a way of getting more and better education for our money.

These space-arrangers leave us with the problem of noise. What we desperately need here, both in schools and in all parts of our ever more crowded and noise-ridden society, is a new invention —development, rather, since the inventing seems to have been done. This is a lightweight and effective sound barrier. Up till now to shut out sound you had to have mass, bulk, weight—which from the point of view of building meant money. Good sound insulation and isolation were expensive. But a recent issue of the *Scientific American* had an article describing a new and effective way of damping vibrations—which is what sound is—by using a kind of sandwich of thin sheets of metal with a gummy or semi-liquid plastic in between. I don't know that anyone is trying to use such materials as sound barriers, but this is an engineering problem we could surely solve if we put enough thought and money into it. It is certainly one of the most urgent needs of the times. If we can solve this problem, many new enrichments of life will be possible, both in and out of our schools.

[From a letter from Mr. Pottebaum]
We're still plugging away at developing the learning environment, and have found a way of developing large graphics that now enable us to really put a small group of children in the branches of trees, let them get an ant's view of mapletree seeds, a spider's view of being in a web, etc. etc. The kids are finding these exposures "real cool" and "tough." [My note: as who wouldn't?]

All these ideas of ways to divide space are just a beginning. We can use furniture, free-standing shelves and cabinets, pieces of cardboard tri-wall (from Educational Development Center; 55 Chapel Street; Newton, Massachusetts); cardboard boxes; hanging paper; old curtains or bedspreads or even rugs; long strips of cloth, perhaps toweling, perhaps dyed in different colors; hanging sculptures of paper or wood or foil or metal or other materials; string stretched between posts or furniture, or between ceiling and floor, to make walls or barriers, or even strung to make compound shapes using perhaps different colors. In other words, not only can we have sculpture in the classroom, but the classroom can itself *be* a kind of ever-changing sculpture. But here we have enough possibilities for what children—and more and more adults, most of whom don't know where they got the expression—would call a Whole Nother Book.

30

SOME BEGINNINGS

There will be a sequel to this book, with more ideas about Math, Writing, History, Geography, Science, Social Studies, Art, Foreign Languages, Music, Drama, Sports, School Organization, School Design and Equipment, and other things. There may well be more than one sequel. Every day people are finding better ways to help children in their growing and learning, ways that I will want to make as well known as I can.

Meanwhile, let me take a few final pages for the very important subject of how to begin. People very often talk to me, or write to me, saying in effect, I am just one person (student, teacher, parent), I would like to see and help bring about in my own school or community some of the changes you talk about, but how do I start?

When we want to bring about change there are, in general, certain things we must try to do. The first is to get the word out, tell as many people as we can about the kinds of changes we want to make and our reasons for wanting to make them. In our case, we have to educate people about education. As we educate, we must also find our friends and allies, the people who agree with at least much of what we say and want. There are always more of them than we think, if we could only find out who and where they are.

293

Part of being a good tactician of change is having better ways to find our allies. Once we find them, we have to get together with them, see what strength and talents we have, and think how best to use them in our own tactical situation—school, community, or whatever.

One appendix of this book lists what I call Other Sources of Information about New Education. The best single source of information about the kind of schools I am talking about—free, open, non-coercive, libertarian, radical, pick what name you like best— is the New Schools Exchange. They publish, every year or so, a directory of such schools. They also publish a newsletter, which has information about further new schools as they start, letters and short articles from people working in new schools, and a kind of classified ad section, both for teachers looking for new schools and new schools looking for teachers. From these sources you can learn whether there are any schools near you that are doing or trying to do some of the things I talk about in this book. If there are, this can be very helpful in many ways, which I will talk about shortly.

This Magazine Is About Schools, a quarterly published in Toronto, is a little weighted toward Canadian schools and educational problems, but there is much good writing and information by Americans and news of American schools in it. Another good source is the bi-monthly magazine *Change in Higher Education,* though, as its title indicates, it is about colleges and universities. Still, even if you are interested in bringing about change at the elementary or secondary school level, any free colleges or universities near you will be a source of ideas and of allies. The once-a-month education issue of the *Saturday Review* always has good material in it. *Colloquy* often speaks of new ideas in religious or church education. The monthly *Grade Teacher* has a very good regular column by Herbert Kohl, with many practical short-run suggestions about ways of getting started.

Kohl has also written a new book, *The Open Classroom,* (New York Review/Vintage paperback). It suggests, in the most clear, vivid, and practical ways, how teachers can cope with and resist the demands of the rigid schools, free themselves and their students from the trap of fear, compulsion, and rebellion in which they are caught, and find ways for real learning and exploration. One important point he makes is that change-minded teachers, in a school, school district, metropolitan area, or state, must find, meet, and keep in touch with one another for mutual advice, encouragement, and support. This is essential, if only for the sake of morale; many such teachers have told me that what discourages them most of all is being isolated, having no one to talk to.

The Whole Earth Catalog, a fascinating but hard-to-describe publication, has among other things interesting information about schools, books on education, ways of building schools, and books and materials to use in them. They plan to publish soon a special catalog entirely about education, to be named *Big Rock Candy Mountain.* Nat Hentoff's column in the *Village Voice,* a weekly newspaper in New York, often discusses new education and educational problems. The Ortega Park Teacher's Laboratory is a source of ideas, material, and information in the San Francisco Bay area; Boston has its Educational Development Center; 55 Chapel Street, Newton, Massachusetts. The Teacher Drop-Out Center has much the same kind of information as the New Schools Exchange, but since one may have some information that the other does not, it is worth being in touch with both of them.

I have said that we have to educate people about education. As we do this, we must above all educate ourselves. As we know more about new ways of teaching and learning, we will be more sure about what we want and why we want it, and better able to talk to others, answer questions, deal with objections, consider alternatives and consequences. In the Appendix is my own list of recommended books and articles. They are well and clearly written, interesting, and to the point. No two of them say exactly the same thing, and all of them have in many and different ways stimulated and helped my own thinking. The list is long; naturally no one will read everything on it in a month, or a year. But I do feel that anyone who wants to bring about fundamental educational change ought eventually to read most of the books on this list. Some of the books on the list, above all, Dennison's, I have already talked about in some detail, and urgently recommended. Of the others, I would recommend, to start with, those by Richardson, Herndon, Goodman, Fader, Illich, and Fromm. Those interested in the points that Illich makes in his articles should read Taylor's book, which is less about education than the background of world and social crisis and change against which it takes place.

Some of these books are in low-cost paperback, including *How Children Fail;* Herndon's *The Way It Spozed to Be;* Kohl's *Thirty-six Children;* Fader's *Hooked on Books;* and most of the books of Erich Fromm. You might get copies of each of these, to lend. Also, in whatever stores in your community sell paperback books, you might try to get the owners or managers to stock these books. Goodman's books, though slightly more expensive, are so well known that bookstores might stock them as well—if they don't already. I have reprinted and am selling from my office at 100 copies for a dollar the article "Why We Need a New Schooling" that I wrote for *Look* magazine. This would perhaps be the easiest and least expensive way of putting some of these ideas before large numbers of people. If you decide to distribute some of them, it might be useful to put your own address on each copy, so that anyone in the community who was in favor of these ideas or wanted to learn more about them could get in touch with you.

As for the more expensive books, you might check to see which are now in your library, and ask them to get those they do not now have. If there is a teacher's library at the school or schools, try also to get these books in there. If neither of these can be done, you might get together with your allies, as you find them, and buy some of these books for a library of your own, or donate some copies to the local library, or perhaps do both. You could also ask your local bookstores to stock some of them. In addition, you might get together a very informal organization called, say, an Educational Study Group. Such a group could buy and distribute literature, have its own educational lending library, of books and perhaps other kinds of materials, hold small meetings to discuss educational ideas, inform itself about educational needs, doings, and changes in and near the community, and have discussions with teachers, administrators, school board members, and students. As you become larger, you could hold public meetings, bringing in films and/or speakers from outside the community. Or you could urge already existing local organizations, like the PTA, to have such films and speakers.

There is much that students can do to make their schools better, to get more wholeness into their learning. Some have already taken first steps. In many schools, students have put on programs, from a day to a week, in which they have planned courses and brought in speakers and resource persons from outside the school. Some of the courses that they have started in these programs have later become part of the regular school curriculum. There should be more of this. In general, students should demand and plan for a much larger share in determining their own education. I have often urged that in any school or school system the students set up what we might call a Committee on Educational Policy, not in any way connected with Student Government or any other existing school organizations. In this committee students would think and talk about their schooling, what they get, what they lack, what they need, and what they would like to change. In time, if they could arouse enough student support for certain changes, they could write them into a proposal, and begin to take steps to get them adopted by the school. In some cases, faculty and administration might give support. Where they did not, the students would have to try to get support from parents, citizens, and school board members. If board opposition was strong enough, I see no reason why students would not try to find adults friendly to their proposals who might be willing to run for the board, and back them at the next board election. All this will take much work and organization. But there are many reasons why students ought to move in this direction. One is that, without some such action, many schools simply will not begin to make the kinds of changes that are needed. Another is that, in doing this kind of thinking, planning, and working, the students will be getting much more true learning and education than they could ever get in any classroom. Most important of all, they will be showing and convincing at least a great many older people that they are serious, informed, determined, and that they should be given the kinds of social and political responsibilities that until now we have denied them.

But the most valuable of all resources, in learning and in helping others to learn about this new education, is one of the schools themselves. Reading about the kind of schools and learning that I have been talking about is no substitute for seeing the thing done. When I first heard about the public elementary schools in Leicestershire County in Great Britain, I wholly believed in what they were doing. But I was absolutely bowled over when I actually saw them doing it. Here were children in large classes managing their own work for long stretches of time without the teacher intervening, or in some cases being there at all. Here was a lunchroom full of five- to seven-year-olds getting all their food from the kitchen and serving themselves at their tables. Here was a school assembly, the children coming in, not in lines, seating themselves with groups of friends, as they chose, later leaving the room at the end of the assembly, not in lines, and all of this without any orders or threats from teachers, spoken or otherwise. I could hardly believe my eyes. Children *were* sensible people, and if you treated them as if they *could* act sensibly, after a while—if you start later, it may take longer—they believed it and *did* act sensibly. But it took me some time to grasp that what I thought I saw happening was in fact happening; and still more time to begin to learn how it was happening, how these schools and teachers did what they did. For make no mistake about it—starting and running this kind of school, or class, is not easy, and we have a great deal to learn from the experience good and bad of those who have done it and are doing it.

There is much heated and not very helpful argument among teachers and teachers-to-be about whether they should work in public schools or start independent and free schools of their own. This is one of those decisions that depends on the tactical situation. If a public school will allow a teacher to do a good many things that he thinks are important and helpful to children, and not require that he do too many things that are harmful, it is obviously a good place to work. It may even be a good place to work if he only thinks that there is a fairly good chance of getting it to move in the right direction. It is movement that is important. But if a school seems not only bad but unwilling to change, immovable, a teacher who works there will probably not only be wasting his time, but in spite of his good intentions will, as much as anyone else in the school, be doing more harm than good to his students. It would probably be better to get out and find a school, or join others in making one, in which he can do at least a good part of what he thinks ought to be done.

Some people argue that since most free schools have to charge tuition, this leaves poor kids in the lurch. True, but only partly. Free schools are important agents of change, both as a training device and as a model. When they work well, other people in the community understand what they are doing and want them for their own children. This can put pressure on the public schools to start some such schools of their own, which they have done and are doing in quite a few places. Or it may rouse public support for the voucher plan, in which parents are given money directly for their children's education, to spend where they wish. Or it may bring closer a time when independent schools with no tuition and non-selective policies, no weeding out of children, at the door or later, will be considered "public" and supported from tax funds on the basis of the number of students attending. In Denmark any ten parents can start and get tax support for a school—why not here?

Some say, this is all very well, but since most children are in public schools, reformers have to work within that system. Such people seem to me to make a stronger commitment to the system than to the children. They also tie their own hands and greatly limit their change-making power.

Of course, any schools that look as if we might be able, without too much delay, to change them so that children may truly learn and grow there are all worth working with. But there are many other schools and school systems so topheavy or bureaucratic or power hungry and fear ridden that the best thing we can do for the children in them will probably be to make available something better. I have met some fine teachers who have told me that for as long as twenty years or more they have been working in this or that school or system to bring about some of the kinds of changes I am urging, and with no success at all. I can admire their courage but not their tactical judgment. Not only have they wasted their time, skill, and devotion; they have given them to an institution that has made bad use of them.

There is no necessary reason why a chance to attend independent schools based on freedom and choice in learning should be limited to a few middle-class children. I have already suggested a way in which such schools might be supported without charging tuition, or in which poor people might be enabled to afford them. There is still another possibility. Young people themselves might be able to raise much of the money to support the kind of schools they want and need. George Dennison, and others active in this movement for new education, are organizing what will be called the New Nation Fund. The idea is that young people (and sympathetic adults) on their birthday (or any time they feel like it) will send a gift to the Fund, which in turn will contribute money to the support of free schools. Some might say that not enough money could be raised this way to support more than a handful of schools. Possibly, though even this would keep some very important model schools alive. But I read some years ago that what was called the "Teen-Age Market" spent something on the order of fifteen billion dollars a year. This is very nearly half as much as the cost of our entire educational system. Very recently I read that in 1969 total sales in the record industry, which sells mostly to young people, were over two billion dollars. I am not assuming that young people, in order to get the kinds of schools they want, are going to stop buying everything else. But they have more economic power than they think. And we can almost certainly find ways to provide education at far less cost per pupil than most conventional schools.

There is one thing I plan to try to do to help this learning. Of all the things that the director (i.e. superintendent) of the Leicestershire County Schools did to help bring about these educational changes, perhaps the most important, even essential, was to form a staff of advisors. These advisors were just that. They were not supervisors or inspectors, telling schools and teachers what to do and checking up to make sure they did it. They had no power over the schools and teachers; they could not even come into a school building unless invited. Their job was to think of ways to help, and to help in every way they could, the people in the schools who wanted to make or were trying to make changes in their ways of dealing with and working with children.

Most of us who know those schools believe that if schools and school systems here are to make these same changes, they will need the advice and support of a similar group of advisors, people who can bring to them the ideas and experience of others who have done and are doing the same work. I, and a group of my friends and colleagues—Associates as we will call ourselves—have now formed such a group. Some of us operate out of my office in Boston; others are based in other parts of the country. We plan to make ourselves available for short periods of time or long ones—anything from a single meeting or day of meetings to several weeks—to groups of people, whether parents, teachers, schools, school systems, or any combination of these, who want our help in making these educational changes. We will do a variety of things, speak at meetings large or small, show slides or films, visit classes and work with teachers, hold seminars or workshops, demonstrate the use of certain materials, advise on other materials, and in general be useful in whatever way we can. I have made up, and on request will send from my office, a list of these Associates, with information about their interests, concerns, and experience. Those interested may decide on which Associate they want to work with, get in touch with him, and work out questions of place, time, fee, and so on.

So much for ways to begin. Please don't feel limited by them. They are beginnings, not endings. As I said at the very start of this book, I am trying above all else to suggest some directions in which people can find or make ideas of their own. When you do, pass the word along to me and to the other sources of information I have mentioned. Let us know about any experiences, *successful or not,* from which we can all learn things that will help us do this work better. Whatever you do, as you do it keep some kind of record of it, if only in a rough journal. Part of the trouble of our times is that so many people feel that their lives and the institutions around them have somehow slipped out of their control, or even the possibility of their control. We all need to be reminded and reassured that what we think of as ordinary people *can* shape their lives and the society around them.

People say to me things like, "It's all very well for you to talk about making changes, but you're a famous author, etc., and I'm just an average housewife, student, teacher, etc." But when I began to try to put some of my journals and letters together into what became the book *How Children Fail,* I was not a famous author, or a famous anything; I was a fifth-grade teacher fired from a job and not sure where the next one was coming from. Much of the most important work in this field has been done by people who seemed not to have, and would have said they did not have, any special gifts or advantages or qualifications whatever. Other people say that we can't do anything because there are not enough of us. We don't know how many of us there are. There are probably more than we think. In almost every community there are surely many people who are deeply dissatisfied with conventional schooling and what it does to their own and indeed all children, and who want something very different. Even if these people are only 10 percent or 5 percent of the community, that is enough to start making important changes in the schools, or, that failing, to start schools or learning centers of their own, and by so doing, show what can and needs to be done.

Every day's headlines show more clearly that the old ways, the "tried and true" ways, are simply and quite spectacularly not working. No point in arguing about who's to blame. The time has come to do something very different. The way to begin is—to begin.

Appendix 1

TRIANGULAR NUMBERS

Here is what I thought as I worked out the proof that no triangular numbers are prime.

First I began writing them out, in a column, as at the right. As I went along, to check my arithmetic, I added each two successive triangular numbers to see if the result was a square. I did this up to about 121 or 144; then it got to be too much work. I got a check from 105 + 120 = 225, which I recognize as the square of 15, so I knew I had made no mistakes. Then 190 + 210 gave me 400, so I knew I was still all right.

As I worked these out and wrote them down, I noticed that there were always two odds and then two evens. I wondered about that for a second, and then saw that when you are adding first an odd, then an even, an odd, an even, and so on, your answers are going to come out pairs of odds, then pairs of evens, then pairs of odds, and so on. (You can check this out for yourself.)

All this time I was looking for primes. I felt a faint "Aha!' when I saw 153, but soon saw that since the digits added up to 9, divisible by 3, the

1
3
6
10
15
21
28
36
45
55
66
78
91
105
120
136
153
171
190
210
231
253

whole number was divisible by 3. So that wouldn't work. The same was true of 171 and again 231. I wondered whether 3 was a factor of all the odd triangular numbers, but then saw that it was not a factor of 91, so gave that up. Then I saw 253 and felt more hope.

This might be a good place to say, by the way, that the scientist or mathematician or thinker very rarely goes out collecting information or evidence just to see what turns up, but not caring what turns up. This is not what his "objectivity"—such as he has—consists of. He goes out there looking for something, as in this case I was looking for a prime number, and hoping I would find it. The scientist is not indifferent. His objectivity consists of this, that when the evidence begins to show him that his hunch was no good, that what he was looking for is not there, he thinks, "So be it," and starts looking for or thinking about something else. He does not lie to himself or others about what the evidence is telling him.

As I said in the previous chapter, when you are checking a number to see whether it is prime, the only things you need try to divide it by are themselves prime—which saves a lot of trouble. Three did not work—the digits did not add up to a product of 3. Five was out by inspection. Seven missed by 1. But as soon as I began thinking about the 11 I saw that it would work. My heart sank a little. Actually, I probably should have been glad. In general, I would suppose that it was harder to prove that a thing was not prime than that it was.

At this point I decided to try the hypothesis, hunch, or guess that triangular numbers were *not* prime, and to see if I could see and prove why not. I felt that the answer must lie in the

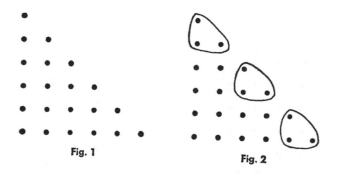

Fig. 1   Fig. 2

triangle itself, as a shape, so I drew a 6-line triangle of dots (Fig. 1). Then I began to look at it. I had that 3 still in the back of my mind, so I began seeing the dots as groups of 3's (Fig. 2). If you lift a bunch of 3-groups off your triangle, do you get anything, can you put them on top of something else to make a rectangle? If you can, you have your proof, since a rectangular number is by definition composite, factorable, not prime.

After thinking about this a bit my eye fell on the triangle at the end of my drawing (Fig. 3). I thought, perhaps I can lift it off, turn it upside down, and put it up on top. Perhaps I can get a rectangle. But I had one dot left over, sticking out (Fig. 4). I thought that's no good. I then thought, well, what happens if we have an odd number of rows of dots in our triangle? I drew a five-row triangle (Fig. 5). Right away I could see that we were in business. The little three-dot triangle at the lower right could turn upside down and fit very neatly in the space on top, giving us the rectangle we were looking for (Fig. 6).

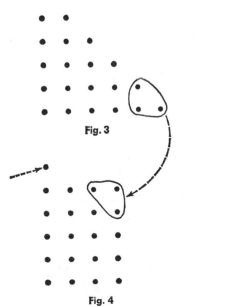

Fig. 3

Fig. 4

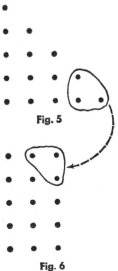

Fig. 5

Fig. 6

You may wonder why I use the word "we" as I describe my thinking. I wonder about it myself. It comes so naturally that there must be a good reason for it. I think it is that I feel two parts of my mind or self are working in partnership. One is the conscious and directing and deciding part, the part that chose to try to work out this proof instead of doing something else. The other is the subconscious or less conscious idea-producing or problem-solving part, the (as they say) creative part. The conscious part is (sometimes) like the hard-pushing president of a company; the other part, like a sometimes brilliant but temperamental and erratic scientist out in the laboratory. The president may invite or even urge that scientist out there to go to work, but he can't make him; neither can he fire him; neither can he get some other scientist—that's the only one he's got. All he can do is be nice to him and hope.

Back to the proof. Something about my dot triangle and drawing dissatisfied me. I wanted the pattern to stand out more vividly, to say more clearly to me whatever it had to say. So I drew a five-row triangle, this time using a grid of squares, as in Fig. 7.

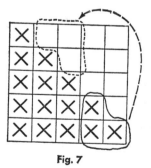

Fig. 7

Yes, no doubt about it, that little triangle in the lower right did fit up there on top, as I had thought. So then, will it work for 7? Here I did a dumb thing. The righthand edge of my five-square was close to the edge of the paper I was working on—as it happens, the back of a discarded letter. So I thought I would add my two extra rows on the left side, and drew Fig. 8. After looking at it a second, I said, "Dumbbell!" Then I drew Fig. 9. Sure enough, the shaded triangle fitted neatly into the dotted space, giving me my rectangle.

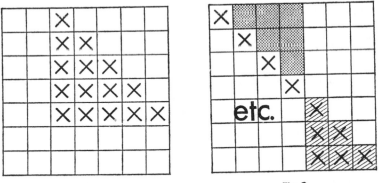

Fig. 8   **Fig. 9**

After looking at it a few seconds more, I saw that it gave me the materials for a general formula for the number of dots in any odd-row triangle. In the case of my 7-triangle, my rectangle was 7 squares long and 4, or one-half of $(7 + 1)$, squares wide. So for a triangle of N rows, the number would be $\dfrac{(N + 1) \times N}{2}$. Then I checked this against my 5-triangle, also the 9, 11, and 13, writing down numbers as at the right.

15	5×3
21	
28	7×4
36	
45	9×5
55	
66	11×6
78	
91	13×7
105	
120	15×8

By the time I came to the 9×5 I could see how the pattern was shaping up, and wrote the next factors rather quickly. In my haste I wrote 12×7 opposite the 91. When I began checking the factors to see if they worked, and came to that 12×7, I had an instant's panic, and thought, "What's this? It doesn't fit." Then I saw my mistake, corrected it, and saw that the formula worked.

Then I thought, we seem to have this proved for odd-triangles, but what can we do about the even? I looked at those numbers for a while, and then I saw it. What gets added to the 15, or 5×3, in order to make the next triangular number, is a 6. But 6 is a product of 3, so (5×3) + a product of 3 must itself be divisible by 3. In the same way, we add 8, a product of 4, to 28, also a product of 4, to get 36, which must therefore be divisible by 4. And so on down the line: to each of our odd triangles, in order to get the next or even triangle, we add a number which is a product of one of the factors of the odd triangle. This means that that factor—3 in the first example above, 4 in the second—is a factor of the even triangles, which proves that it is not prime.

So I sat back feeling pleased. But in a while I began to think of something that Wertheimer had said, in his most interesting book *Productive Thinking*. He described some proofs as being ugly and some beautiful. This proof seemed ugly—a little twisted and roundabout and cumbersome. There must be a more direct line to it. What I could have done then, but did not do, was to make an algebraic expression of my rather clumsy way of stating the number of dots in the even triangles. Having done so, I could have simplified it and eventually arrived at something neater. But I didn't do that. Instead I went back to my diagrams of triangles, feeling that the answer would be there if I only looked for it in the right place. So I drew Fig. 10. Note that this time I only drew the x's along the edge of the triangle, since that was where the action was, so to

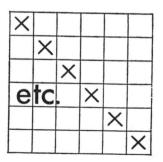

Fig. 10

speak. Since nothing happened to all the x's in the lower lefthand part of the figure, I didn't need to put them in. And this is an important part of mathematics, simplifying a problem and making the looked-for patterns more visible by leaving everything out that is not needed.

Looking at this diagram I thought, since we didn't get anywhere trying to cut a three-dot or three-x triangle off the lower righthand corner and putting it somewhere else, suppose we cut off a bigger triangle and see what we can do with that. I then shaded in the six-x triangle, as in Fig. 11. What could we do with that? In a second, I saw. We could fit it into the space marked off with dots, at the top of Fig. 12. This gave us our rectangle, and the proof that the even triangle was not prime. I quickly checked it with a 4-triangle, saw that it was okay, and the job was done.

Then I thought, what sort of formula do we get for the number of an even-triangle? Looking at Fig. 12, I saw that one side of the rectangle was half of 6, or 6/2 long; the other side was one larger than 6. Checking against the 4, I saw that the same was true there, which gives the formula $\frac{N \times (N + 1)}{2}$. Both this and the formula for the odd rows, $\frac{(N + 1) \times N}{2}$, were on my scrap of paper. I hadn't considered before the fact that they looked slightly different. But now, even as I wrote this part of the chapter,

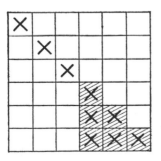

Fig. 11

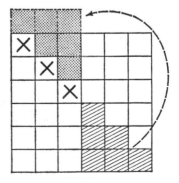

Fig. 12

I thought, it doesn't make any sense that there should be one formula for odd-triangles and another for even-triangles. They ought to be the same. So I looked a bit more closely at both formulas and soon saw that in fact they were the same. Which I should have seen sooner.

So there is the proof—at least, *a* proof—that triangular numbers are not prime. And there is the end of one small journey of mathematical exploration. What I hope I have made more clear is that mathematics is not, at bottom, a matter of mysterious and complicated formulas and ideas, but simply a way of thinking, of using your mind to look at the world a certain way and to solve certain kinds of problems in it. And also, that it can give much pleasure.

BOOKS AND ARTICLES

EDUCATION AND SOCIETY

AGEE, JAMES. *Let Us Now Praise Famous Men.* Ballantine paperback.
AXLINE, VIRGINIA. *Dibs: In Search of Self.* Ballantine paperback, 1967.
————. *Play Therapy.* Ballantine paperback, 1969.
BERG, IVAN. *Education and Jobs: The Great Training Robbery.* Frederick A. Praeger, 1970.
COLE, LAWRENCE. *Street Kids.* Grossman Publishers, 1970.
COLES, ROBERT. *Children of Crisis.* Delta paperback, 1968.
————. *Uprooted Children.* University of Pittsburgh Press, 1970.
COOK, ANN, and HERBERT MACK. *The Excitement of Learning.* Queens College, Institute for Community Studies, 1969.
DENNISON, GEORGE. *The Lives of Children.* Random House, 1969.
FADER, DANIEL, and ELTON B. MCNEILL. *Hooked on Books.* Berkeley paperback, 1968.
FRIEDENBERG, EDGAR. *Coming of Age in America.* Vintage paperback, 1963.
————. "The Hidden Costs of Opportunity," *Atlantic Monthly* (February 1969).
————. *The Vanishing Adolescent.* Dell paperback, 1959.
————. "What the Schools Do," *This Magazine Is About Schools* (Autumn, 1969).

313

GATTEGNO, CALEB. *Toward a Visual Culture.* Outerbridge & Dienstfrey, 1969.

————. *What We Owe Children.* Outerbridge & Dienstfrey, 1970.

GOODMAN, PAUL. *Compulsory Miseducation.* Vintage paperback, 1962.

————. *Growing Up Absurd.* Vintage paperback, 1956.

————. *The New Reformation.* Random House, 1970.

GORDON, JULIA. *My Country School Diary.* Dell paperback, 1970.

HAWKINS, FRANCES. *The Logic of Action, from a Teacher's Notebook.* University of Colorado, Center for Environmental Studies.

HENTOFF, NAT. *Our Children Are Dying.* Viking paperback, 1967.

HERNDON, JAMES. *The Way It Spozed to Be.* Simon & Schuster, 1968. Bantam paperback.

HOLT, JOHN. *How Children Fail.* Pitman Publishing. Dell paperback, 1970.

————. *How Children Learn.* Pitman Publishing, hardcover and paperback, 1967.

————. *The Underachieving School.* Pitman Publishing, 1969.

————. "Letter from Berkeley," *New York Times Magazine* (February 22, 1970).

————. "To the Rescue," *The New York Review of Books* (October 8, 1969).

————. "Why We Need New Schooling," *Look* (January 13, 1970).

————, and others. Ronald and Beatrice Gross (eds.). *Radical School Reform.* Simon & Schuster, 1970.

————, and others. *Summerhill: For and Against.* Hart Publishing, 1970.

ILLICH, IVAN. *Celebration of Awareness: A Call for Institutional Revolution.* Doubleday, 1970.

————. "Commencement at the University of Puerto Rico," *The New York Review of Books* (October 8, 1969).

————. "Outwitting the 'Developed' Countries," *The New York Review of Books* (November 6, 1969).

————. "Why We Must Abolish Schooling," *The New York Review of Books* (July 2, 1970).

JEROME, JUDSON. *Culture Out of Anarchy.* Herder and Herder, 1970.

JOSEPH, STEPHEN (ed.). *The Me Nobody Knows.* Avon paperback, 1969.

KOCH, KENNETH. *Wishes, Lies and Dreams.* Chelsea House Publishers, 1970.

KOHL, HERBERT. *The Open Classroom.* The New York Review of Books, 1969.

————. "Teaching the Unteachable." The New York Review of Books pamphlet, 1967.

————. *Thirty-six Children.* New American Library, 1958. Signet paperback.

KOZOL, JONATHAN. *Death at an Early Age.* Houghton Mifflin, 1968. Penguin paperback.

LEDERMAN, JANET. *Anger and the Rocking Chair.* McGraw-Hill, 1969.

LEONARD, GEORGE. *Education and Ecstasy.* Delacorte Press, 1968.

MACRORIE, KENNETH. *Up Taught.* Hayden Book Co., 1970.

MARIN, PETER. "The Open Truth and Fiery Vehemence of Youth," *The Center Magazine* (January 1969). Book in preparation.

NEILL, A. S. *Summerhill.* Hart Publishing. Hardcover and paperback, 1960.

————. *Talking of Summerhill.* London: Victor Gollancz, 1967.

O'GORMAN, NED. *The Storefront.* Harper & Row, 1970.

POSTMAN, NEIL, and C. WEINGARTNER. *Teaching as a Subversive Activity.* Delacorte Press, 1969.

RATHBONE, CHARLES. *Open Education: Selected Readings.* Citation Press, paper, 1970.

RICHARDSON, ELWYN. *In the Early World.* Pantheon Books, 1970.

Schoolboys of Barbiana. *Letter to a Teacher.* Random House, 1970.

SILBERMAN, CHARLES. *Crisis in the Classroom.* Random House, 1970.

TAYLOR, EDMOND. *Richer by Asia.* Houghton Mifflin, 1964.

VON HILSHEIMER, GEORGE. *How to Live with Your Special Child.* Acropolis Books, 1970.

HUMAN PSYCHOLOGY AND DEVELOPMENT

FROMM, ERICH. *The Art of Loving.* Bantam paperback, 1956.

————. *Escape from Freedom.* Avon paperback, 1941.

————. *Man for Himself.* Fawcett Premier paperback, 1947.

————. *The Sane Society.* Avon paperback, 1955.

GREEN, HANNAH. *I Never Promised You a Rose Garden.* Signet paperback, 1964.

GRIER, WILLIAM, and PRICE M. COBBS. *Black Rage.* Basic Books, 1968. Bantam paperback.

LAING, R. D. *The Divided Self.* Penguin paperback, 1965.

————. *The Politics of Experience.* Ballantine paperback, 1967.

————, and A. ESTERSON. *Sanity, Madness and the Family.* Pelican Books paperback, 1965.

————. *Self and Others.* Pantheon Books, 1970.

MASLOW, ABRAHAM. *Motivation and Personality.* Revised edition. Harper & Row, 1970.

————. "The Need to Know and Fear of Knowing," *Journal of General Psychology* (1963).

————. "Some Educational Implications of the Humanistic Psychologies," *Harvard Educational Review* (Fall 1968).

————. *Toward a Psychology of Being.* Insight (Van Nostrand) paperback, 1968.

MAY, ROLLO. *Love and Will.* W. W. Norton, 1969.

————. *Man's Search for Himself.* Signet paperback, 1967.

O'BRIEN, BARBARA. *Operators and Things.* Ace paperback, 1958.

ROGERS, CARL. *On Becoming a Person.* Houghton Mifflin, 1961.

ROSENTHAL, ROBERT, and LENORE JACOBSON. *Pygmalion in the Classroom.* Holt, Rinehart & Winston, 1968.

VAN DER BERG, J. H. *The Changing Nature of Man.* W. W. Norton, 1961. Delta paperback, 1964.

FILMS

BLOEDOW, JERRY. *Sometimes I Even Like Me.* One hour on Lewis-Wadhams School, 40 East 43rd Street, New York, N.Y. Rent $60.

FELT, HENRY. *Battling Brook Primary School (Four Days in September)*

————. *Medbourne Primary School (Four Days in May)*

————. *Westfield Infant School (Two Days in May).* All available from E. D. C., 55 Chapel Street, Newton, Mass.

FIERING, AL. *Children as People.* 16 mm./black and white. 35 minutes. Fayerweather Street School, John Holt narrator. Polymorph Films, 331 Newbury Street, Boston, Mass. Rent $30; purchase $235.

GHETTO KIDS. *The Jungle.* Churchill Films, 622 North Robertson Street, Los Angeles, Calif.

LEITMAN, ALAN. *They Can Do It.* 16 mm./black and white. 35 minutes. E. D. C., 55 Chapel Street, Newton, Mass. Rent $10; purchase $125.

National Film Board of Canada. *Summerhill.* 30 minutes. Contemporary Films, McGraw-Hill.

WEBER, LILLIAN. *Infants School.* 30 minutes. E. D. C., 55 Chapel Street, Newton, Mass.

WISEMAN, FRED. *The Cool World.* 16 mm./35 mm. OSTI, 264 Third Street, Cambridge, Mass. Rent $100.

———. *High School.* Same as above.
———. *Law and Order.* Same as above.

OTHER SOURCES OF INFORMATION
ABOUT NEW EDUCATION

About Education, 219 Broad Street, Philadelphia, Pa.
Anarchy Magazine, Freedom Press, 84a White Chapel High St., London, England.
Big Rock Candy Mountain, Portola Institute, Inc., 1115 Merrill St., Menlow Park, Calif. 94025.
CIDOC (Center for Intercultural Documentation), Box 479, Cuernavaca, Mexico.
Change, 59 East 54th Street, New York, N.Y. 10022.
Colloquy, United Church Press, 391 Steel Way, Lancaster, Pa.
Grade Teacher, 23 Leroy Avenue, Darien, Conn. 06820.
Humanitas, Box 606, Orange City, Fla. 32763.
Herbert Kohl, Special consultant to public schools, 178 Tamalpais, Berkeley, Calif.
Manas, P.O. Box 4173, Woodside, Calif. 94062.
New England Free Press, 691 Tremont Street, Boston, Mass. 02118.
The New Republic, 1244 19th Street, NW, Washington, D.C. 20036.
The New Schools Exchange, 2840 Hidden Valley Lane, Santa Barbara, Calif. 93103.
The New York Review of Books, 250 West 57th Street, New York, N.Y. 10019.
Ortega Park Teacher's Lab, P.O. Box 4173, Woodside, Calif. 94062.
Dan Pinck, Pinck-Leodas Associates, 2000 Massachusetts Avenue, Cambridge, Mass.
Project Follow Through, E. D. C., 55 Chapel Street, Newton, Mass.
Psychology Today, P.O. Box 60407, Terminal Annex, Los Angeles, Calif. 90060.
"Radicals in the Professions," Newsletter of Radical Education Project, P.O. Box 625, Ann Arbor, Mich.
Charles Rathbone, Bibliography of British Primary Education readings, Oberlin College, Oberlin, Ohio.
The Saturday Review, 380 Madison Avenue, New York, N.Y. 10017. Monthly education issue.

Schools for the Future, Specialized seminars. 821 Broadway, New York, N.Y.

The Summerhill Society, 6063 Hargis Street, Los Angeles, Calif. 90035; and 339 Lafayette Street, New York, N.Y. 10012.

Teacher Drop-Out Center, School of Education, University of Massachusetts, Amherst, Mass. 01002.

"Teachers and Writers Collaboration," Newsletter, Pratt Center for Community Development, 244 Vanderbilt Avenue, Brooklyn, N.Y. 11205.

This Magazine Is About Schools, P.O. Box 876, Terminal A, Toronto, Canada.

The Village Voice, Nat Hentoff's Column, 61 Christopher Street, New York, N.Y.

Vocations for Social Change, Canyon, Calif. 94516.

The Whole Earth Catalogue, Portola Institute, 1115 Merrill St., Menlow Park, Calif. 94025.